D1218633

American Women in World War 1
They Also Served

— *American Women in World War 1* —
They Also Served

Lettie Gavin

—————

University Press of Colorado

Copyright 1997 by the University Press of Colorado

Published by the University Press of Colorado
P.O. Box 849
Niwot, Colorado 80544
(303) 530-5337

The University Press of Colorado is a cooperative publishing enterprise, supported, in part, by Adams State College, Colorado State University, Fort Lewis College, Mesa State College, Metropolitan State College of Denver, University of Colorado, University of Northern Colorado, University of Southern Colorado, and Western State College of Colorado.

Library of Congress Cataloging-in-Publication Data
Gavin, Lettie, 1922–
    American women in World War I / Lettie Gavin.
      p.   cm.
    Includes index.
    ISBN 0-87081-432-X
    1. World War, 1914–1918—Women—United States. 2. Women—United States—History—20th century. I. Title.
    D639.W7G38   1997
    940.4'0082—dc20
                                96-38466
                                CIP

This book was designed and typeset in Nadianne and Times by Rhonda Miller.
The paper used in this publication meets the minimum requirements of the American National Standard for Information Sciences—Permanence of Paper for Printed Library Materials. ANSI Z39.48–1948

10 9 8 7 6 5 4 3 2 1

Contents

Acknowledgments

Thanks to those wonderful American women of 1917–1918, who proudly stepped forward during the emergency to offer their time, talent, energy, and devotion to help the United States win the "war to end all wars." To one of them, in particular, Merle Egan Anderson, Hello Girl of the Army Signal Corps, who fought the U.S. Army for sixty years—and won, won veteran's status and honorable discharge for herself and her sister telephone operators.

Thanks to Tom, who encouraged me and shared his vast understanding of the Great War. Ron, who supported me in every way. Julie, who asked, "Where are the therapists?" (Thus was born Chapter 5.) Dr. Gordonn A. Logan, who extended the life I used to write this book. Leila Charbonneau, who understands The Chicago Manual of Style and put her tidy stamp on the text. Helene M. Sillia, historian, Women's Overseas Service League. Linda L. Hewitt, Captain, USMC(R), who chronicled the Women Marines in World War I. Richard J. Sommers, archivist-historian, U.S. Army Military Institute, Carlisle, PA. Florence W. Lehman, archivist, Reed College, Portland, OR. Kathleen Jacklin, archivist, Cornell University, Ithaca, NY. Mary Karabaich, American Red Cross, Seattle, WA. Barbara Schroeder, World War II veteran, who provided solid information in several World War I areas. Henry I. Shaw and Mike Miller, US Marine Corps History and Museums Division, Washington, D.C. Merlin Berglin, Pope County Historical Society, Glenwood, MN. Rick Caldwell, librarian, Museum of History and Industry, Seattle, WA. Susan Miller and Judith Johnson, The Salvation Army, National Archives. Frances Dingman, The Salvation Army, Western Territory Headquarters. Carol J. Dage, Liberty Memorial Museum, Kansas City, MO. Stephen E. Novak, Medical Archives, New York Hospital–Cornell Medical Center. Agnes F. Hoover, Naval Historical Center, Washington, D.C. Charlotte Palmer Seeley and Michael Knapp, National Archives, Washington, D.C.

And special thanks to the families of the women in the Great War, who have generously shared their private and precious memories. Louise S. Fritz, daughter of Nell G. Storey, Army Nurse Corps. Gloria Rand and Beth Petrie, daughters of Minnie Arthur, U.S. Marine Corps. Louise Ferguson, daughter of Marie

S.A. LeBlanc, Hello Girl, Army Signal Corps. Joseph A. King and his sisters, devoted children of Margaret Mary Fitzgerald, U.S. Navy Yeoman (F). Shannon Applegate, grand-niece of Eva and Evea Applegate, Reconstruction Aides. Jeannine Davis Mayes, daughter of Cordelia DuPuis, Hello Girl, Army Signal Corps. Mr. and Mrs. Charles E. Dingley, cousins of Nellie Dingley, Army Nurse Corps. Jacquie Kelly and Tam Moore, children of Harriet Forest Moore, Reconstruction Aide.

And a special dedication to Army Maj. Marie T. Rossi, who took her rightful place among her male fellow Americans and served as a helicopter pilot throughout the Persian Gulf War. She died in 1991 when her airship crashed the day after that war ended.

Introduction

While the Great War of 1914–1918 put an end to the "old order" in Europe, it also contributed immensely to the world progress of what we now call the Women's Movement. In the early twentieth century, a woman's place was considered to be in the home, the school, the church. This philosophy was to change drastically during the course of the war, as women took over from their absent men in hundreds of new and challenging occupations, many of which had previously been considered inappropriate.

The war, in fact, marked the beginning of a new era in the history of women, both in the United States and in Europe. Many believed that those four years of war liberated women from old molds and stereotypes, provided new opportunities for them, and made them economically independent. Women working diligently and efficiently laid the foundation for higher wages, better jobs, improved working conditions, and a more competitive status in the labor market.

Great Britain was perhaps the first nation to feel the manpower pinch, as it sent thousands of men to France in August 1914 to battle German aggression. Each man who marched away left behind a job in a factory, a schoolroom, a bank, in the postal service, or on a farm. Those jobs were filled by women. When it became clear that many of these men would never come home, the old notion of a "woman's place" had to be reconsidered. "The scarcity of men makes the employment of women a necessity," U.S. author Harry Franklin Porter wrote in a national magazine. Women simply had to take over every job they could possibly manage.

In England, women clerks numbered more than 100,000 by 1916, and thousands of women had enlisted in Queen Mary's Women's Auxiliary Army Corps (WAAC), taking over for men who were fighting in France. WAACs and Volunteer Aid Detachment (VAD) women worked as nursing assistants, cooks, motor drivers, farmers, prison guards, and munitions workers, among other war-related duties. Still, the British government called for more: "Wanted, 30,000 women a week to replace men for the armies," Mabel Potter Daggett reported in her 1918 book Women Wanted. At length, every British female who could perform a service was wearing some sort of uniform. "Who works, fights," said Lloyd George, the British prime minister, in a speech to Parliament.

It was the same in each of the other warring countries. In the first year of the war, Germany had half a million women in the munitions industry alone, and nearly all the bank clerks were women. France had 400,000 "munitionettes," and in the Bank of France in Paris there were 700 women clerks. "In the ultimate analysis," said German diplomat Count Johann Heinrich von Bernstorff, "it is the nation with the best women that's going to win the war."

Yet, in spite of these examples in Europe, the United States did not seem prepared to utilize its womanpower upon entering the war in April 1917. The exception was the U.S. Navy. Josephus Daniels, the wise and foresighted secretary of the Navy, was one of the few officials in Washington, DC, who recognized the remedy for the government's obvious manpower shortage. "Enroll women in the naval service as yeomen and we will have the best clerical assistance the country can provide," he said. More than 11,000 females joined the Navy before the war ended some nineteen months later. Women likewise swamped Marine Corps recruiting stations when enrollment was opened to females in August 1918, and some 350 signed up before hostilities ceased in November.

The U.S. Army, on the other hand, never did officially sanction the enlistment of women, even though Army officials overseas repeatedly asked for such personnel. Gen. John J. Pershing, the U.S. commander-in-chief in France, observed the service of British and French women and asked the War Department to send over U.S. women with clerical skills so that the men in these jobs could be sent to the Front. Similar requests came in from other field commanders overseas. Two of these—the Central Records Office and the Central Post Office—even "borrowed" hundreds of British WAACs for duty at their headquarters in Bourges, France, when no U.S. women were sent over.

A handful of U.S. women enlisted for duty overseas as French-speaking telephone operators with the Army Signal Corps, and a small group of female physical and occupational therapists and dietitians went to France as Army Medical Department "reconstruction aides."

Several thousand U.S. women, of course, did serve as Army and Navy nurses. They had no rank or benefits, but they were accorded full veteran's status when the war ended. Women doctors, on the other hand, were never accepted by the Army, although doctors were badly needed, especially during the heavy fighting as the war ground to a close in 1918. Hundreds of women doctors were ready for service, but they had to find their own way to France. And they did.

"We were not called to the colors," said one, Dr. Esther Pohl Lovejoy, "but we decided to go anyway." More thousands of American women went overseas under the auspices of the YMCA, the YWCA, the American Red Cross, the Salvation Army, and other private social service organizations. Thousands more worked at home—some compensated, some as volunteers—in a vast variety of war service occupations. The work of these devoted women is widely believed to have inspired a new respect for all women, especially the women of the United States and their place in society.

"One thing that emerges from this war . . . is the conviction that women must be admitted to a complete partnership in the government of nations," said Lloyd George in a public address. Women's wartime service raised to prominence the issue of women's suffrage, long sought in the United States and abroad. U.S. president Woodrow Wilson observed, "Unless we enfranchise women, we shall have fought to safeguard a democracy which, to that extent, we have never bothered to create." The U.S. Congress finally approved the controversial Nineteenth Amendment in June 1919, giving female citizens the right to vote. One suffrage leader, Harriot Stanton Blatch, commented joyously, "American women have begun to go over the top. They are going up the scaling-ladder and out into All Man's Land."

Esther V. Hasson, first superintendent of the Navy Nurse Corps, wrote in 1919, "Sometimes I think we will need a special race of women created just for the work, as there are so many conflicting demands to be considered." Many believe the Great War produced that special race of women. Now, nearly eighty years later, their voices call out for their story to be told, related here, by the women themselves.

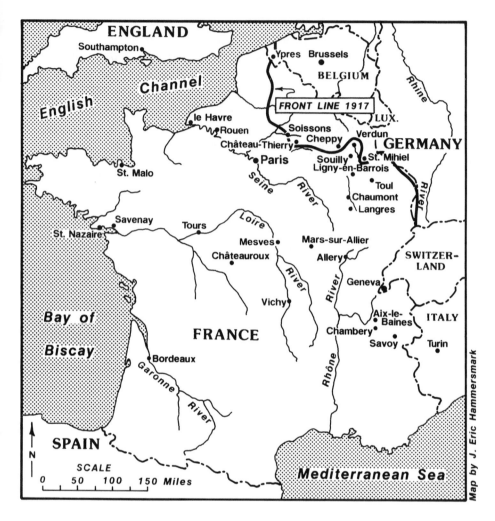

France in 1917

— *American Women in World War 1* —
They Also Served

=1=
The First Women of the Navy

"Is there any regulation which specifies that a Navy yeoman be a man?" With that question to his counsel, U.S. secretary of the Navy Josephus Daniels made military history. And he also solved the tremendous manpower shortage that plagued the Navy in the spring of 1917 as the United States prepared to enter the war in Europe. Navy shore stations, where activities were increasing dramatically, urgently needed help. Every bureau and naval establishment called for more stenographers, draftsmen, and other clerical help. The Navy was awash in its own paperwork, but every man was needed at sea on the hundreds of naval vessels then readying for action in the Great War.

Secretary of the Navy Josephus Daniels waves to the crowd before a speech at the League Island Navy Yard, Philadelphia, PA, in 1917. Daniels is generally credited with being the first U.S. official to approve enlistment of women in the armed forces. Some 11,000 female yeomen joined the Navy before the end of the war in 1918. (Philadelphia Press Photo, Naval Historical Center, Washington Navy Yard, Washington, DC)

Faced with the need for drastic action, Daniels shrewdly questioned counsel about gender regulations. He was advised that the law did not specifically indicate that Navy yeomen (clerks) must be male. The secretary then shocked Navy colleagues by his order: "Enroll women in the naval service as yeomen and we will have the best clerical assistance the country can provide."[1]

When the Navy's call went out in early 1917 for female yeomen, popularly christened "yeomanettes," many newspapers published bitterly critical letters from readers. Even the Navy's own board of legal advisors reacted violently. "W-o-m-e-n in the Navy, fantastic, ridiculous," they cried. "Petticoats in the Navy! Damn'd outrage! Helluva mess! Back to sea f'r me!"[2]

It would seem no one was completely pleased with the order; the concept of women in the military was unheard of. Men were firmly in charge—women's suffrage was not yet law—and apparently intended to stay that way. But Secretary Daniels's order came from the top, and as such, it was carried out without delay. In addition, Daniels believed that "a woman who works as well as a man ought to receive the same pay." That order, too, caused great consternation among Navy stalwarts, but they obeyed, as they always did. Accordingly, in March 1917, commandants of all naval districts permitted women to enlist in the Naval Reserve Force in such essential noncombat ratings as yeomen, radio electricians, pharmacists, chemists, draftsmen, accountants, and telephone operators.

Within a month—by the time the United States entered the Great War on April 6, 1917—200 eager young women had become Navy yeomen, the very first officially recognized military enlisted women in the country's history. Among them was Helen Dunbar McCrery of Seattle, WA. "They needed girls who had stenographic skills; I was good at it," she recalled many years later. "I could take dictation pretty fast. It was the Gregg method of shorthand, but I invented some of my own. They gave us uniforms just as fast as they could get them made. Oh, I had the neatest suit you ever saw. We had white shirts, and they were the devil because you always had a ring around the neck. We had to have two of them, because you had to wash one every night."[3] The numbers of female yeomen increased rapidly over the next few months, reaching a peak strength of more than 11,000 in 1918 and providing a huge pool of talent from which the Navy could draw.

Today, when women work in many traditionally masculine professions, it may be difficult to appreciate the courage and independence of the women who volunteered for Navy service in 1917. These women were born and raised in the Victorian era, when "ladies" were expected to walk a traditional, narrow social path indeed. But knowing their country needed them for broader service, and perhaps inspired by their counterparts in Europe, U.S. women stepped forward to serve. They were, in fact, eager to participate in the national effort. And they served so well that serious consideration was given to commissioning some of them as Navy officers. The war ended, however, before such promotions were realized.

There were few requirements for the first female yeomen. A woman had to be between eighteen and thirty-five years of age, of good character and neat appearance. The Navy preferred high school graduates with business or office experience but did not require a college education. A prospective yeomanette simply presented herself at a recruiting station, was interviewed for qualifications, and filled out application forms. After she passed the perfunctory physical exam, she was sworn in and signed up for a four-year hitch. The entire process often took less than a day.

The new yeomanettes, unlike their male counterparts, received no formal recruit training before starting their duties. They simply began work immediately in Navy offices all over the country. Their training, if any, would come later. Young Sarah Ellen Story was assigned to the Navy's Appraisers Stores Department in Boston, MA. Later she recalled, "I was put in the Fuel Office, headed by an old timer, Lt. Healy. He said to me, 'Do you know anything about filing?' And when I said yes, he took the entire contents of the file and dumped it on a big desk and said, 'See if you can put these where we can find them.' The bookkeepers had not found a system then, either. This was in late 1918 and I wonder how we won the war."[4]

A young Virginia recruit, Estelle Kemper, recalled that she enlisted and reported for duty that same afternoon. "By nightfall, I felt like an old hand. After dinner I phoned my family in Richmond. My father answered the phone and I told him proudly that I had joined the Navy. Never immune to my bombshells, he gulped and said quickly, 'I'll call your mother.' When I repeated my announcement to her, she was stunned into silence for a moment, then asked weakly, 'Oh, Sister, can you ever get out?' The poor dear probably saw me in bell-bottomed trousers, swabbing decks, keeping close to the rail, for I was not born to the sea!"[5]

Because their work was mainly clerical, some Navy women had to learn those skills, and many took additional schooling at night to study naval terminology, routine, and procedure. In many instances, their training also included military drill. For thirty minutes one day a week, some recruits practiced marching in straight columns and executing simple formations. Some carried rifles to emphasize their military readiness. The Navy was quick to realize the positive publicity generated by these women in uniform, and the female yeomen often were paraded in support of war bond drives, rallies, recruiting campaigns, troop send-offs, and other official occasions.

At first, many of these Navy women had no uniforms. They wore civilian clothes, with armbands indicating their ratings. Secretary Daniels later took credit for the dark blue tailored uniform that eventually evolved: "Some people thought they ought to wear something like pants. Some had different ideas. The length of the skirt, that was a serious problem. Should we have a long skirt that would sweep the decks? Or something that revealed more leg? Never in my life have I attempted anything, great or small, without the wise counsel of the women. We decided on [skirts] about eight inches from the ground."[6]

Additional instructions came later, inspired no doubt by each woman's inclination to dress distinctively. The orders came down: "No fur neckpieces, muffs, spats or other adornment shall be worn with the uniform, nor shall any part of the uniform be worn without the uniform complete."[7] The insignia of the female yeomen, two crossed quills, was the same as that of the enlisted male yeoman of the regular Navy, and the badge was worn on the left sleeve of the uniform blouse.

A Boston newspaper observed the female enlistees and commented:

> Pity the Navy's poor "yeogirls." They have to have two wardrobes in these days of the high cost of clothes. One [wardrobe] is a thing of strictly tailored garments, made according to Navy specifications and varying not so much as a hair's breadth. Government uniforms and their accompaniments have to be of good materials. One cannot scrimp in the amount of material used, or save on its cost. An average, serviceable yeowoman's suit [Norfolk jacket and skirt] costs $35 today. The winter outer garment, which has been specified as the full-length naval cape, lined throughout, is modestly priced at $45.[8]

Then there were summer and winter hats, boots with military heels, leather gloves (although regulations specified white cotton), and tailored blouses. "It costs Uncle Sam's yeowomen $150 annually for just the bare essentials of uniform dress. This amount can be stretched to $200 easily with the addition of the white uniforms for summer, the white hats and shoes, and the extra skirts of white and serge."

As U.S. women flocked to join the colors, Secretary Daniels had other puzzlements: what to call the new female enlistees. The popular term was "yeomanette." But, said Daniels, "I never did like this 'ette' business. I always thought if a woman does a job, she ought to have the name of the job."[9] The women enlistees were therefore known as yeomen, but a parenthetical "F" for "female" was added to distinguish them from their male counterparts when sea duty was assigned.[10]

True to Daniels's word, the female yeomen earned the same pay as their male counterparts: $28.75 per month (starting), less twenty cents for hospitalization. They drew subsistence pay of $1.25 per day, which was later raised to $1.50. The women also received a uniform allowance, medical care, and war risk insurance.[11] Discipline, too, was the same for the women as for the male sailors. Yeomen (F) learned to obey orders and follow routine without question. Punishment, however, did not extend to time in the brig; usually it involved loss of liberty or pay.

As U.S. participation in the war increased, more and more women joined the Navy, coming from every state in the union, and from Alaska, Hawaii, and Puerto Rico. They came from every walk of life and every socioeconomic background, though most came from middle-class families. Like American men, these women traded the shelter of comfortable homes for spare, crowded living quarters, for the strict discipline and regulation of their lives, and for the long, lonely separation from families and friends—all new experiences for the protected women of that day. Many worked in hastily constructed barren, drafty buildings, and thousands toiled from early morning until far into the night under tremendous pressure in order to accomplish the necessary work of shipping vast numbers of men and supplies out to sea. They served in the bureaus in Washington, at Navy yards, in all naval districts, and at many shore stations.

Although Yeomen (F) were not permitted to go to sea, a few were sent overseas. Five Navy women went to France, for example, to work with nurses in the hospitals of the Navy Bureau of Medicine and Surgery. One worked in the Office of Naval Intelligence in Puerto Rico, and a handful were scattered in such far-off places as Guam, Hawaii, and the Panama Canal Zone.[12]

The Navy women often worked ten hours a day, six days a week. Although they were widely considered "the weaker sex," they asked for, and expected, no preferential treatment. They worked hard at a variety of jobs, many of them admittedly tedious. "Humdrum" is an adjective that crops up often in the memories of many of those first Navy women. Yeoman (F) Nell Weston Halstead of Chicago recalled being assigned to the file room of the Bureau of Engineering, typing endless excerpts from incoming and outgoing letters. Looking back on her service, she expressed surprise that she "didn't jump down the captain's throat . . . just to relieve the monotony. One day it got my goat so completely that I boldly sailed into the captain's office—he was an oldtimer in the Navy, with basso voice and glowering eye—and I told him we didn't like our jobs and we wanted to go to France. Imagine it! Well, he just looked at me and said, 'What the hell could a girl do on a battleship? Get back to your job.' And needless to say, back I went."[13]

But not all Yeomen (F) toiled at routine jobs. One woman directed priority orders sent to railroad officials to move the Navy's supplies. Another supervised manufacturers who produced clothing for 250,000 sailors. Yeomen (F) rapidly became the Navy's switchboard operators. Other women were commissary stewards, librarians, fingerprint experts, torpedo assemblers, telegraphers, and camouflage designers.

For many of them, the Navy experience changed their lives. Helen McCrery embarked on her career as a Yeoman (F) in the spring of 1917, just days before the United States entered the European war. Her orders arrived from Seattle, WA, dated April 3, 1917, sending her to duty at the Thirteenth Naval District, Navy Yard, Puget Sound, WA, where she would be in charge of forty young women on the Bremerton base. Thus began one of Helen McCrery's "busiest and happiest experiences." She recalled:

> Three weeks after I enlisted, I became chief yeoman to Rear Admiral Robert E. Coontz, commandant of the Navy Yard. He was the kindest, nicest man I ever knew. He always wanted me to march right behind him in our parades, because, he said, 'I want people to see that we have girls in the Navy.' We marched in all the parades. We took great pride in our marching. We broke our necks never to lose a step. But the thing was, the men marched with a 30-inch stride. That was too long for us and I protested. I showed them my short step and they decided, 'Well, I guess the fellows had better shorten their stride.'[14]

Gertrude Madden, believed to be the youngest of the Bremerton Yeomen (F), also had fond memories of Admiral Coontz. "Knowing that he often went to his office on Sundays," she recalled, "I called him to get permission to go to a picnic 'out of uniform' that day. He said, 'Going out of uniform is permitted only when going hunting or fishing. Will there be boys there?' I answered in the affirmative. He replied, 'Well, then, you'll be fishing, won't you?' "[15]

As U.S. women flocked to enlist, seventeen-year-old Frances Treherne watched with envy as the new Navy women "strutted proudly" around New York in their smart uniforms. "I was so impressed. I set right out for Washington to enlist, but I was too young. On my eighteenth birthday, though, I was sworn in." That was in September 1918. Miss Treherne was appalled, however, when her uniform was issued. "We stood in line to get those snappy uniforms, and an old 'chief' kept us in line with a stick. He kept prodding us along with his stick, and I thought, 'Don't you dare touch ME.' When I picked up my uniform, I was just sick. It was such poor material, just trashy, and the color was horrible. Someone had been profiteering. You see, cheating the government was going on then, too. Eventually we were issued good uniforms, and I was always proud to wear mine."[16]

One of the Navy's first enlisted women, Lou MacPherson Guthrie, was a rural schoolteacher from North Carolina working with the Bureau of War Risk Insurance in Washington, DC, in the spring of 1917. She clearly remembered the "wildly exciting day when the American Navy called for 100 women war workers to enlist and do accounting work at the Navy Yard. This would release sailors to man the warships."[17] Lou and three of her friends passed enlistment examinations with high marks and were assigned to the Navy Yard. For a time, Miss MacPherson worked the graveyard shift, midnight to 8 A.M., at the Navy Yard. "We liked it, even though we had to get off the street car at midnight in the worst section of the city and walk down the wharf. Here wharf rats nearly as big as opossums scuttled across our path in the moonlight. But it was quite safe. There was very little crime recorded in the city then. We felt no timidity about walking alone at midnight on poorly lighted streets."

In time, of course, many more young women enlisted in the Navy, and the unique glamour of the uniform seemed to evaporate. Lou MacPherson recalled, "The work was becoming routine; the boys were overseas. We felt stalemated in Washington." The declaration of the Armistice on November 11, 1918, provided a great deal of excitement for Lou and her friends. "It was so thrilling! The war was over! All the offices closed and we literally danced in the streets with any passersby who came along. Next day, it was hard to get back to our humdrum duties."

Ann Dunn was one Yeoman (F) who stayed on at her Navy job even after the war ended. Following her enlistment in 1918, Miss Dunn was assigned "keeper of the logs," and held forth in a locked room on the third floor of the Navy Building in Washington, DC. In that room were 14,000 volumes filled with stories of heroism, conquests, and daily combat with the sea, all written by men of the Navy, dating back to 1861.

From Navy ships all over the world, commanders each month sent their log books to Washington to be filed by the devoted Yeoman (F). If a monsoon happened in the China Sea, or a sailor developed measles in the North Atlantic, no time was lost in getting a terse but complete report of the incident to Miss Dunn. To her, the most gripping story in her files was told in the log of the *USS Mount Vernon*, a World War I transport that fell victim to a German U-boat attack off the French coast in September 1918. Thirty-five men were killed when the torpedo smashed into the Mount Vernon's boiler room, and the vessel seemed doomed. But every survivor rushed immediately to his post. Guns of the Mount Vernon barked. Engineers braved death to fire up the boilers. And the ship limped back to Brest.

Throughout her tenure as keeper of the logs, Miss Dunn zealously guarded her records and remained on the alert for souvenir hunters and espionage agents. "There must be a million dollars' worth of autographs on those pages," she said. "And those autograph hunters will stop at nothing to get some rare signature."[18]

Among the first young women on the West Coast to enlist when the Navy called for recruits in 1917 was Florence Whetsel of Medford, OR. Florence was a telephone operator and an expert at switchboard repair, so she was enlisted with an electrician's rating. She was one of thirteen of Medford's twenty local operators and three of the five long-distance operators who joined the Navy en masse, causing serious disruption of the town's telephone exchange. Then, as luck would have it, the female detachment was called to duty before the town's male enlistees were summoned, and all the young women marched off to service while the young men stood on the sidelines with the tearful parents.[19]

Florence Whetsel wound up at the Navy Yard at Bremerton, WA, drawing charts of submarine activities in the war zone and filling out license permits for small boats in the Puget Sound area. Years later, she remembered the funny moments. The young women were taught the manual of arms (although they never fired a gun of any kind) and were sent to various cities for recruiting parades. In Yakima, WA, startled residents saw the Yeoman (F) contingent come marching down the main street carrying light rifles—while the enlisted men followed carrying the luggage.

One of Florence Whetsel's favorite memories was of a red-faced, tobacco-chewing, sea-dog chief petty officer who was placed in charge of her office. He could handle the toughest crew of men, but a room full of women left him almost speechless. To avoid using the wrong words, he compromised on a jaunty query, "How's tricks?," a question he asked over and over. He proved to be one of their most considerate, helpful superiors.

These memories brought smiles to the Navy women, but there were sad times, too. Yeomen (F) were sometimes notified of the illness or death of parents or the wounding or death of a husband, brother, or sweetheart on duty in the war zones. One of the most tragic cases was that of Yeoman (F) Alice Regina Costello, who, in the space of six months, received death notices for three of her brothers. She gave no outward sign of her deep sorrow; instead, she carried on in accordance with the highest naval tradition.[20]

An outstanding 1917 Navy enlistee was Joy Bright. Later Joy Bright Hancock, she served throughout the First World War and subsequently worked as a civilian employee of the Navy Bureau of Aeronautics, becoming one of the first women to be commissioned an officer in the Women Accepted for

Volunteer Emergency Service, the WAVES of the Second World War. Hancock was the WAVE representative in the Bureau of Aeronautics in World War II and, from 1946 to 1953, served as assistant chief of naval personnel for women.[21]

Joy Bright remembered her early days as a Navy yeoman, when she was assigned to sell Liberty Bonds in theaters, going up and down the aisles during intermission to make sales. "We also participated in Liberty Bond parades on Broad Street in Philadelphia," she recalled.

> Our training for this activity was acquired at the Navy Yard twice a week, when Marines taught us the rudiments of drill. But we learned hardly more than "forward march," "halt," and the necessity of maintaining straight lines and keeping in step.
>
> No instructions were ever given to the effect that we were not to break step for any obstacle that might be in the way. But sometimes there was sharp provocation for changing direction, as, for example, the time when we marched behind beautiful, high-spirited horses that had not been housebroken. After a particularly shabby parade performance, our instructor gave us explicit directions: "You don't kick it, you don't jump over it, you step in it."
>
> After a year, I was a seasoned yeoman. At that time, when there was yet no designation on the rolls signifying sex, I received orders to duty aboard a combat ship. My commanding officer had never approved of women being attached to the Navy in a military capacity, so when I presented these orders to him, he was blunt, "Carry them out." Upon reporting to the Fourth Naval District in Philadelphia, I was told in no uncertain terms that the Navy had no intention of ordering women to sea for duty on combat ships. My orders being so endorsed, I returned to my job in the construction superintendent's office.[22]

Another recruit, Agnes Carlson, was assigned to the naval base at New London, CT. Because no housing was provided for the women recruits, she looked around town for a place to live and found a room with breakfast for $7 a week.

> Our work consisted mostly of typing copies of naval orders for food; a pile of papers more than a foot high appeared at the front desk each morning. Each yeoman was ordered to take five of the originals to her desk and make five copies. Some orders covered a sheet, some two sheets, some were merely a couple of lines. Our superior, suspicious of our prettiest yeoman, who trotted up the aisle for replenishment more often than any of the rest of us, found that this attractive young lady was going through the pile and

picking out the two-liners. Very shortly, this errant yeoman got trimmed down to size in a voice for all to hear.

Miss Carlson also recalled that "Not everyone approved of women in the Navy. But I was proud when my younger brother—too young to enlist himself—got into a fist fight with an older civilian who made some derogatory remarks about the girls who were serving as Yeomanettes."[23]

Young Virginia recruit Estelle Kemper had just graduated from college in the spring of 1918 when she rushed to Washington, DC, to enlist in the Navy. She later wrote, "The process of joining up (if a girl) was simple and speedy: first an interview by a chief clerk and then a physical exam at the Naval Hospital, an oath of allegiance and, presto, one was a "Yeoman (F)," signed up for four years!" Because the Navy had been a thoroughly male organization and had made not provisions for women, the procedure for male recruits was followed when it came time to administer routine physicals. As Miss Kemper recalled, "I joined a long line of stripped females, holding bath towels around their middles, shivering in spite of the hot summer day. Male recruits may not mind being herded together in the 'altogether,' but those poor stripped feminine patriots were a sorry sight, as they cringed in that open hallway, waiting to be scrutinized by a strange doctor in a Navy uniform." The doctor who finally appeared did not inspire confidence. "As I remember it, there was only one weary, over-aged M.D. responsible for examining that long line of girls, and he was not one bit interested in anything but getting through his work and going home to supper. He weighed us, measured us, listened to our hearts, and passed us along at furious speed."[24]

Although patriotism inspired most young U.S. women to join the Navy in 1917, there were other compelling reasons. Jean Cook, a teenager in Connecticut, enlisted as her means of coping with grief. "When America joined the war, my boy friend enlisted and was sent right overseas," she said. "He and two friends—they were all machine gunners—were killed when a German shell scored a direct hit on their dugout. I wanted to get even with the German Kaiser, so I enlisted in the Navy. It was my first time away from home."[25]

Margaret Mary Fitzgerald was just eighteen when she saw a poster calling on women to join the war effort in 1918: "American Navy—We Need YOU." She marched straight into the recruiting office and signed up before she even discussed her decision with her parents. "I wasn't a sneaky child, but I didn't even tell my mother about enlisting," she recalled. "We had just returned from the Philippines, where my father had been stationed with the Army Quartermaster Corps. And I had this idea that I could join up and maybe be stationed with my father who was being transferred to New York." As it turned out, Miss

Fitzgerald was sent to the U.S. naval hospital at Bremerton, WA, and was stationed there until the war ended fourteen months later. In the process, she became, at nineteen, the youngest woman chief petty officer in the history of the Navy, serving as an aide to the commander of the Puget Sound Naval Hospital.

At Bremerton, there were good and bad times for Miss Fitzgerald. The worst was watching many of her friends die in the 1918 Spanish influenza epidemic.[26] As the epidemic swept the country and around the world, the Yeomen (F) at every post volunteered to care for thousands of afflicted military and civilians. Some doctors objected to such volunteer help because the Navy women were not trained as nurses, but the yeomanettes argued that they were certainly capable of handing a pill and a glass of water to the patients. Sadly, some of those volunteers were stricken and died, and others suffered permanent impairment to their health. The epidemic killed 548,000 U.S. citizens that year, nearly twice the number killed in combat overseas. It has never been determined just how many Navy women were lost to the flu, but fifty-one reportedly died while on active service between 1917 and 1920, twenty of these in 1918 before the Armistice.[27]

A Yeoman (F) secretary working at the State Pier and Experimental Station in New London, CT, had vivid memories of that dark time. "It was a particularly virulent type of flu," Olive Stark O'Sullivan wrote seventy years later. "And the deaths were very many. A person would be absent one day and the next day you heard he was dead. I roomed across town from the pier and it seemed I could never go to and fro without seeing a flag-draped coffin en route to the railroad station. And at the station, it seemed that coffins were always stacked up waiting for a train."[28]

The sight of a particular coffin inspired a column by The Commentator in the New London Day newspaper. It was published November 12, 1918, the day after the Armistice ended the war. "I have just seen the strangest little cortege I ever saw in my life," it began, "the military funeral procession of a woman. We are rather used, we New Londoners, to the sight of a flag-covered coffin passing through the streets in a ship-gray truck, with sailors marching beside it and behind. But when standing at the head and foot of the coffin are girls, and marching soberly beside the truck are girls, girls in the uniform of the American Navy—it all seems strange and unusual, and somehow very, very sad."

From the West Coast, young Margaret Mary Fitzgerald wrote home to her mother from her post in Washington state. "The influenza is raging pretty bad here. . . . 46 [Navy personnel] have died at our hospital within the last two weeks and one of our doctors died this morning. The movies, barber shops, churches, etc., are all closed in town. The movies just shut down last night as the epidemic appeared amongst people outside the Navy." But it was the happier memories that stayed with this one-time shortstop for the Yeoman (F) baseball team at Bremerton Navy Yard. "It was such an honor to be one of the first women in the Navy," she told interviewers shortly before her death at age eighty-five. "It was a beautiful part of my life."[29]

Frieda Mae Greene was a twenty-two-year-old salesclerk in a five-and-dime store in Portsmouth, OH, in 1918 when she heard that the Navy was enlisting women. The next day she signed up and then phoned home. "My mother was furious," she recalled. "She told me, 'Frieda, you come home right now.' " Later, mother and daughter appeared at the recruiter's office, where her mother insisted that Frieda be released from service, explaining that Frieda hadn't told her father yet. "The recruiter told us to go home and ask my father. And that night, father said to my mother, 'Why not let her go?' It was a wonderful opportunity for me. I'd had a limited education but the Navy gave me credit for two years of high school and gave me the chance at a good job. I felt I was helping with the war effort, too."

The Navy dispatched Frieda Greene to the Norfolk Navy Yard in Virginia, where she was measured for a uniform and assigned a desk to check dock receipts in the freight office. "I thought the pay was great," she said. "I got $41 a month plus a $2 a day subsistence allowance to pay for housing in town because the Navy had no quarters on base for women." A few months later, still waiting for her uniform, the young clerk heard the announcement of the Armistice. But like many of her fellow yeomanettes, she stayed with the Navy until all the women were discharged the following year.

Much later, well into her nineties, Frieda Greene Hardin could still wear her First World War uniform and always took an active part in veterans' affairs and activities. She was applauded roundly each time she appeared at various public events over the years, trim and attractive in her Navy blues and snappy straw hat, her Great War Victory Medal pinned to her blouse.[30]

Undoubtedly one of the most talented of the thousands of Yeomen (F) was Daisy Pratt Erd of Chicago, who enlisted in Boston, MA, in April 1917. On May 4, she was made chief yeoman in charge of the women employees at the Boston Navy Yard and soon had more than 200 young women under her supervision. A visiting Boston newspaper writer reported on Mrs. Erd's efforts to benefit her charges. "The lunch room, recently opened [by her] for the women yeomen, was crowded. . . . Many of the girls get their breakfast here. . . . For lunch today there was beef chop suey; breaded veal cutlets and mashed potatoes; these both cost fifteen cents. Then tea or coffee is five cents, and the dessert, two kinds of pie or ice cream, is five cents. The lunch room is run absolutely at cost."

Mrs. Erd had complete charge of the female yeomen. "I give all examinations myself and know all the girls personally," she said. Asked what percentage of applicants she accepted, Mrs. Erd gave a startling reply. "About one in 25." She then elaborated. "Most applicants can't spell. I give that examination first. If the applicant fails to pass the spelling, I don't examine her any further."

Her extensive work was such that Congressman James A. Gallivan of the Twelfth District, Massachusetts, wrote Secretary Daniels asking him to commission Mrs. Erd an officer in the Navy. Daniels responded that her service "justifies my belief in the capacity of women to do important work and to relieve the men who must go to sea." But, he pointed out, "I have no authority to make a woman an ensign and I have given orders that no men shall be made ensigns who do not pass the examinations necessary to qualify them for important duty at sea." Representative Gallivan sent Daniels's letter to Mrs. Erd as "a pleasant souvenir for you to look upon after this war is over."

Chief Yeoman Erd was also a composer of some talent and, after joining the Navy, wrote words and music for a tune, "Uncle Sam's Ships." Thousands of copies of the song were sold, and all the proceeds went into the Naval Reserve fund for Navy welfare work. She later wrote "We'll Carry the Star Spangled Banner Thru the Trenches," again with royalties donated to the Navy Relief Society. She also composed "The Admiral Wood One-Step," dedicated to Rear Admiral Spencer S. Wood, commandant of the First Naval District, Boston. After the Armistice in November 1918, she turned out yet another song, "Welcome Home," to greet the returning troops of the American Expeditionary Forces, "soldiers who have been doing their bit on the other side."

After the war, Mrs. Erd joined other Boston veterans to form the first women's post of the American Legion. She was elected commander of this post, whose charter membership included 200 Yeomen (F). She also planned to establish a permanent industrial union at Legion headquarters to obtain work for all Yeomen (F) who were discharged from the service at the end of the war. Another of her peacetime campaigns was for a $100 Massachusetts state bonus for women who had served in the war. She explained to a state meeting that "the girls did men's jobs and are entitled to the same consideration by the state as were soldiers and sailors. Many of the women gave up better positions to enter the Naval service and make it possible for just so many more men to go to sea. We did a man's job, and why shouldn't we be treated like the men are treated in the matter of bonuses? We represent as fine a lot of young women as ever lived."

One of her greatest treasures from her Navy days was a gold medal engraved with "Boston Navy Yard, FOR MERIT, War Service," presented March 18, 1918, by Capt. W. R. Rush, USN, commandant of the navy yard. The medal, along with some of her papers, was presented to the Naval Historical Center in Washington, DC, in October 1973, but no further record of her activities after the 1920s is now available.[31]

Another early enlistee was Bernice Duncan Smith, a young Los Angeles office worker. Riding to work on the streetcar in the spring of 1917, she read in her newspaper that the Navy was opening enlistment to women. She rushed to the nearest recruiting office and presented her newspaper, demanding to sign up. The recruiters retreated to their commander's office. "Captain, there's a girl here who wants to join the Navy," they announced. "We don't take women," the officer told her. Brandishing her newspaper, Bernice Smith said boldly, "This newspaper says they are enlisting women in Washington, D.C., and if they are doing it, so can you. Sir, if I were a man, I would join the Navy. This is the first time in history that my family hasn't been represented in an American war, and you've just got to take me." A few days later, Bernice, at the age of twenty, became one of the first California women to enlist. She worked at the recruiting office until she was rated a chief petty officer and transferred to the U.S. submarine base (for the *USS Alert*) at San Pedro, CA.

Miss Smith was discharged in February 1920. She tried to re-enlist during World War II but was rejected by the Navy and the Marine Corps as "too old." The Army, however, accepted her, and she served at military postal facilities in Michigan and California. Later, carrying on the family tradition, her son was a Marine in the Second World War, and two of her grandsons served in Vietnam, one in the Army and the other in the Navy, like his grandmother.[32]

Four days before the United States entered the Great War, nineteen-year-old Gertrude "Trudie" French was sworn into service at the Boston Navy Yard. "I was very impressed and thrilled as I placed my hand on the Bible and repeated the Oath of Allegiance," she recalled. But her simple patriotic act set off a considerable disturbance at home. "My mother just could not believe what I was telling her. She broke into tears and insisted I just could not do that. . . . I finally succeeded in calming her down when I explained that I would not serve aboard ship or overseas. My father was not happy, either, with what I had done, but he didn't object so strenuously."[33]

The young enlistee was assigned to the recruiting office in Boston—her mother needn't have worried. There was plenty of hard work for the Yeomen (F) but plenty of social life, too. Sports were a big part of Yeoman (F) life. The women had a rowing team, a track relay team, and a basketball team, with Trudie French as captain. The Boston Globe printed an animated photograph of that team in February 1918, showing the Navy women wearing heavy blue serge bloomers, the regulation Navy jumper and black neckerchief, long black stockings, and high white tennis shoes.

Trudie French wound up her service career as a happy Navy bride. In the spring of 1919, Miss French and six other Navy women volunteered for duty at the U.S. Naval Training Station, Great Lakes, IL, traveling overnight by Pullman sleeper car, a thrilling new experience for the young Yeomen (F). "A group of Navy men had gathered at the gates to Great Lakes to look over the new lady sailors," Trudie recalled. "Little did I know then that in that group was my future husband, F. Harvey Howalt, a radioman who had served on the *USS Pennsylvania* and the *USS Connecticut* in the Atlantic fleet."[34]

When the war ended in November 1918, approximately 11,274 women had served in the Navy. One of them, Agnes Carlson, on duty at the naval base in New London, CT, recalled that Armistice Day began as a joyous occasion. "But it suddenly turned to tragedy. We were all given the day off and excitedly piled into an open truck, commandeered by a fellow sailor. We careened all over town, singing and yelling, standing up in the truck until we rounded a corner at the top of a hill. There we all leaned to one side and the side broke out, throwing most of us to the ground. My drill partner fell under the wheels and was killed,"[35] one of those who died on active service during the war years, most from influenza and its complications during the epidemic of 1918–1919.

Some of the First World War Navy women served as chief petty officers, but none was ever commissioned. All who served received honorable discharges and full veterans' benefits and were entitled to wear the World War I Victory Medal. Upon discharge, the Yeomen (F) were included in provisions for military preference in obtaining civil service ratings, and some of them enjoyed long and distinguished careers in federal service. Indeed, twenty years later, in November 1943, some 112 former Yeomen (F) were still serving in the Navy Bureau of Supplies and Accounts.[36]

As they returned to civilian life, those first Navy women carried with them a grateful "Well done" from secretary of the Navy Josephus Daniels. Later calling them "the elect of their sex," he told the Navy veterans, "You more than came up to my expectations. I feel it is one of the greatest honors of my life to have been associated with you in the days of emergency and war."[37]

What began as a daring experiment by Daniels and his officers had ended in overwhelming success. And the enthusiasm and capable participation of the country's female population on all fronts was duly noted in Washington. Many believe that the roles these women played in the wartime military and civilian arenas were a moving force behind the 1919 passage of the Nineteenth Amendment, which granted women the right to vote.

The Yeomen (F) of World War I were pioneers. As the first enlisted women in any branch of the U.S. military, they did release deskbound men for combat, as proclaimed by their widely publicized slogan, "Free a Man to Fight." But more importantly, their dedicated service opened a variety of occupational opportunities to women and introduced the idea of equal pay for equal work. Simply stated, the Yeomen (F) blazed the trail for more complete involvement of women in this country's life, and they paved the way for the women's liberation movement that followed many years later.

The last of the Yeomen (F) was released from service in July 1919, prompting the following burst of poetry from Yeoman (F) E. Lyle McLeod, one of the Navy's first enlisted women:[38]

Doggerel From a Sea Dog

No More

I ain't a yeomanette, no more
I'm just a plain civilian as before.
Wish I could ship another cruise;
Hate to doff my Navy blues;
Can't walk in these French-heeled shoes, no more.

Nothin' is the same, no more!
I just go to town and not "ashore."
No longer is my dinner "chow."
I must punch a time clock now;
No wonder smiles adorn my brow—no more.

I'll not get a "forty-eight" no more.
Josephus won't control my fate no more.
All the Navy slang I learn
For my good English I must spurn
To my salty ways I'll turn—no more.

When a gob goes marching by, no more
Dare I look him in the eyes on shore,
For no longer will he see
Just a "sister gob" in me
Bound by fellowship are we—no more.

No! I ain't a yeomanette no more
And though I hate the very thought of war,
If Uncle Sam should ever say,
"I need ten thousand girls today,"
Would he get 'em?
Well, I'll say! And more.

Notes

1. Lou MacPherson Guthrie, "I Was a Yeomanette," U.S. Naval Institute Proceedings (Dec. 1984): 60–64. Unless otherwise noted, all successive quotes appearing in this chapter are from Guthrie's article.

2. Eunice C. Dessez, The First Enlisted Women, 1917–1918 (Philadelphia: Dorrance, 1955), 50.

3. Author interview with Helen Dunbar McCrery Burns, November 1987, and material from Mrs. Burns's scrapbook, loaned by her nephew, Charles Southern, Sequim, WA.

4. Letter from Sarah Story Oxner to Lettie Gavin, April 1, 1989.

5. Mrs. Henry F. Butler, I Was a Yeoman (F), Naval Historical Foundation Publication, ser. 2, no. 7 (Jan. 1, 1967), 3.

6. Excerpt from an address by Ambassador Josephus Daniels at the thirteenth annual reunion of The National Yeomen F in Chicago, September 27, 1939; The Note Book, newsletter published by The National Yeomen F, vol. 4, no. 8 (Sept. 30, 1939): 2.

7. Dessez, 50.

8. Daisy M. Pratt Erd file, newspaper clipping (unidentified, but probably the Boston Globe), included in archival material donated to the Naval Historical Center, Washington, DC.

9. The Note Book, 2.

10. Lt. Donna J. Fournier, USNR, "Forgotten Enlisted Women of World War I," The Retired Officer Magazine (October 1984): 31.

11. Dessez, 17.

12. Fournier, 31.

13. Nell Weston Halstead, "Then and Now, Women in White," American Legion Magazine (October 1937): 34–35.

14. Author interview with Helen Dunbar McCrery Burns, Port Townsend, WA, 1988.

15. Letter from Gertrude McGowan Madden to Lettie Gavin, 1989.

16. Author telephone interview with Frances Treherne Johnson, Bremerton, WA, October 1988.

17. Guthrie, 60.

18. Unidentified magazine clipping entitled "Woman Guards Navy Logs."

19. Willis Werner, "The Fact-o-graph," San Diego Sun, June 30, 1938, included in archival material donated to the Naval Historical Center, Washington, DC.

20. Dessez, 26.

21. Capt. Joy Bright Hancock, USN (Ret.), Lady in the Navy (Annapolis, MD: Naval Institute Press, 1972), ix.

22. Ibid., 25.

23. Letter from Agnes Carlson Lukens to Lettie Gavin, June 29, 1987.

24. Butler, 2–3.

25. Author telephone interview with Jean M.W. Cook, Guilford, CT, 1987.

26. Family records of Margaret Mary Fitzgerald King, loaned by her son, Joseph King, Walnut Creek, CA, 1988.

27. Dessez, 63.

28. Letter from Olive Stark O'Sullivan to Lettie Gavin, 1989.

29. King family records.

30. Author interviews and correspondence with Frieda Greene Hardin, Stockton, California, 1987–1988.

31. Erd archival material.

32. Author interviews with Bernice Duncan Smith Tongate, Retsil, WA, 1987–1988.

33. Gertrude S. French Howalt, "My Experience as a Yeoman (F), USNRF WWI 1917–20," unpublished memoir, 1978–1979, 2.

34. Howalt memoir.

35. Letter from Agnes Carlson Lukens to Lettie Gavin, June 29, 1987.

36. Dessez, 23.

37. The Note Book, 2.

38. This poem appears in Helen Dunbar McCrery Burns's scrapbook, loaned by Charles Southern, Sequim, WA.

The first Pacific Coast women to join the Navy were sworn in by Lt. W. R. Cushman at the Los Angeles recruiting office in 1917. Wearing borrowed "middy blouses" for the photograph are, left to right, Amy F.M. Norberg, Merlee Adams, and Bernice Duncan Smith. "My family had no sons to send, so I went," Bernice Smith Tongate recalled many years later. (National Archives photo no. 165–WW–598–B–6)

Yeomen (F) were promptly put to work at vital noncombat jobs such as typing, filing, telephone duty, caring for documents, and other secretarial and clerical work. Some of the first recruits are shown at their desks in the huge Navy Department filing section, Washington, DC. They often described their work as "tedious." (Naval Historical Center, Washington Navy Yard, Washington, DC)

Rear Admiral Victor Blue, center, inspects a contingent of Yeomen (F) on the Washington Monument grounds, Washington, DC, in 1918. The smartly uniformed Navy women often participated in War Bond parades, recruiting drives, and other official ceremonies in the nation's capital and throughout the country. (Naval History Photo no. 53165, Naval Historical Center, Washington Navy Yard, Washington, DC)

The hand that rocked the cradle for so many generations now grasped the butt of a rifle. The Yeomen (F) were taught the manual of arms, but most never fired a gun. This determined group was receiving training at the Naval Training Center, San Francisco, CA. (National Archives photo no. 165-WW-598-B-1)

The object of the Yeoman (F) uniform was not necessarily to fit the girl, but rather to cover the female form from neck to (almost) ankle. This group of proud Navy women, pictured at the U.S. Naval Station, New Orleans, LA, wore their summer whites, with straw hats for shade, but they apparently had not received orders directing conformity in shoes and stockings. (Naval History Photo no. 53167, Naval Historical Center, Washington Navy Yard, Washington, DC)

Recreation was an important phase of Navy life for the Yeomen (F). Teams of women often participated in softball games, whaleboat rowing races, drill teams, and other sports competitions. One ninety-eight-pound Yeoman (F), Margaret Mary Fitzgerald, was an aide to the commander of the Puget Sound Naval Hospital and also played shortstop on the Yeoman–Navy Nurse baseball team. She is pictured here, fourth from right, wearing a cap. (Courtesy of Joseph King, Walnut Creek, CA)

One of the most talented of the Yeomen (F) was Daisy Pratt Erd, left, who joined the Navy in 1917 and became a chief yeoman at the Boston Navy Yard. She wrote several patriotic songs that were sold to benefit Navy welfare work. Joy Bright, below, is pictured as a Yeoman (F) First Class in February 1918. As Joy Bright Hancock, she served as a WAVE officer in the Bureau of Aeronautics in World War II. (Lettie Gavin collection, Naval History Photos no. 94771 and no. 94945, Naval Historical Center, Washington Navy Yard, Washington, DC)

Navy women of the First World War were not permitted to serve at sea. The closest these 1918 Yeomen (F) came to sea duty was a ride on a Navy tug from their station at the Puget Sound Navy Yard at Bremerton, WA, to Seattle, where they often spent their leave time. (Lettie Gavin collection, donated by the late Gertrude McGowan Madden, top right)

= 2 =
Women Marines

Although the United States Navy enlisted some 11,000 women to help in the war effort of 1917–1918, the Marine Corps was not so quick to utilize the additional assistance offered by the country's female citizens. Thus, it was not until August 1918, just four months before the end of the war, that the Corps opened its ranks to women.

That summer, the heavy fighting and mounting casualties overseas began to sap the strength of the Corps and aggravate an already acute shortage of trained clerical personnel. As fast as men could be spared from Marine Corps offices in the United States, they were sent to join Marine units in France. But more office workers were needed, and the Marine Corps at last looked into the possibility of allowing female enlistees. Marine Corps commandant Maj. Gen. George Barnett solicited the opinions of the major Marine departments about using female clerical help. The estimate came back that about 40 percent of the work could be performed equally well by women. Marine officers believed, however, that it would require a larger number of women to do the work of the men—a ratio of about three to two.

In August 1918, General Barnett addressed Navy secretary Josephus Daniels, asking authority "to enroll women in the Marine Corps Reserve for clerical duty at Headquarters Marine Corps and at other Corps offices in the United States where their services might be utilized to replace men who may be qualified for active field service." Secretary Daniels, already pleased that his Navy women were performing excellent service, must have replied with satisfaction, approving the Marine plan to enroll women.[1]

The wonder is that it took the Marine leadership so long to discover what the Navy had learned more than a year before: that substantial help was available from U.S. women. Another explanation may be that the Marine Corps finally observed the change in the national attitude toward women at this time and hoped to utilize the obvious public relations value in recruiting females. U.S. women were writing a bright new chapter in the history of the Navy, and they were serving in uniform overseas with the Army Signal Corps, the Army Medical Department, and the French Army, plus the Red Cross, the YMCA, the Salvation Army, and various other social service groups.

Recruiting commenced immediately, although not with complete enthusiasm on the part of Marine Corps regulars. Sgt. George W. Kase, a stalwart and salty Marine Corps recruiter, expressed his doubts. "Women in the military service, other than the medical branches, are a deterrent to the progress and efficiency of anything military," he declared. Despite his misgivings, however, he did his duty, complying with the August 1918 authorization "to enroll 24 females in the Reserve for active duty as clerks in the several Marine Corps facilities in the Philadelphia area, retaining two for our office."[2]

"Free a Man to Fight" became the Marines' slogan as the Corps began recruiting women. It was a slogan similar to one used successfully by the British in 1917: "Release a Man for Sea Service." The idea appealed to U.S. women as well. Local newspapers printed the announcement, and on August 13, thousands of women flooded into recruiting offices across the country. Their enthusiasm was overwhelming. In New York City alone, 2,000 hopeful applicants lined up at the 23rd Street recruiting office in response to a newspaper article announcing that the Marine Corps was looking for "intelligent young women."

Sergeant Kase in Philadelphia also had "an influx of applicants." But he wrote later—still determined in his point of view—that "our two female Marines were promoted to corporal in due time, on a conventional rather than meritorious basis." Kase obviously remained unconvinced of the worth of females in the military.[3]

The first female Marine is thought to have been Opha Mae Johnson, who was working as a civil service employee at Headquarters Marine Corps. She joined up on August 13 and was assigned as a clerk in the Office of the Quartermaster. By the end of the war, Mrs. Johnson had attained the rank of sergeant.

Recruiters were told to enroll only women between the ages of eighteen and forty, although an applicant slightly under eighteen who was a desirable candidate in every other aspect could be signed on with the consent of her parents. Recruits had to be of excellent character and neat appearance, with experience as stenographers, bookkeepers, accountants, and typists, and with training in handling correspondence and general office work. Each was asked to submit character references and letters of recommendation. The competition was so intense that the Marines enrolled only 305 women during the four months before the war ended.

Florence Elaine Gertler was among the many hundreds who crowded around the New York recruiting office. She remembered that

> male noncommissioned officers went up and down the line asking questions
> about experience, family responsibilities and so on, and by the process of

elimination got the line down to a few hundred. Applicants were interviewed by one officer and finally were given a stenographic test. The officer who conducted the shorthand test dictated so fast that one after another, the girls left the room. Those who remained were taken, one by one, into the colonel's office and told to read back their notes. If the colonel was satisfied with our reading, we were required to type our notes and were timed for speed and accuracy. More and more applicants dropped by the wayside until only five of us were left.[4]

Within a week, all five were sworn in, and Miss Gertler reported for duty as a secretary to the assistant adjutant and inspector, Capt. Francis C. Cushing. She later learned that the testing officer called those five his "100 percent girls" because of the unusually high speed and accuracy requirements placed on them that first day of recruiting.

Every applicant also was required to submit to a thorough physical examination before her final acceptance. That seemingly simple task, however, presented problems, since enlistment requirements established by naval medical regulations were designed for men. Accordingly, Marine headquarters issued a circular on August 14 giving detailed instructions to the medical examiners, advising each "to use such tact and courtesy as will avoid offending in any way the sensibilities of the applicant." Examiners were admonished nonetheless not "to deviate from a proper fulfillment of the requirements. The applicant should be previously instructed to arrange her clothing in a way that will insure ease, facility and thoroughness in the examination. . . . Corsets should invariably be removed."[5]

The Corps was determined to accept nothing but the best, most highly trained women possible, but they discovered that only a few were able to meet the rigid requirements. There was no time for training, and the female recruits, like their Navy sisters the year before, were expected to step in and be on their own in a matter of days—in some cases within a matter of hours—after their arrival at their duty posts.

Minnie Arthur, age twenty-one, a former student at the Indianapolis Conservatory of Music, was "all fired up to get into the war." She read the news account that women were wanted in the Marines and hurried to telephone the recruiter. A male voice told her he already had 400 applications and could accept only one. "But come in anyway," he added. She did, and she was thrilled when she happened to be that one. It also turned out that she became the only woman Marine enlisted in the state of Indiana.[6]

Elizabeth Shoemaker, working as a stenographer in New York City, arrived early at a busy Marine Corps recruiting office, only to find a long line of hopeful young women winding around the block and down the street. She took her place at the end of the line and slowly inched forward up the stairs to the rooms where interviews and examinations were being conducted. One by one the women were told to step aside. "You had to be 100 percent perfect, mentally and physically," she recalled. Even though she had been working as a speed stenographer, Miss Shoemaker failed the typing test that day and was turned down. "I was terribly disappointed," she said later. "But the next day I did my hair differently and dressed differently, and I went back to the recruiting office. I was afraid I would be recognized, and I was. The amazed colonel said to me, 'Weren't you here yesterday?' When I admitted that I had been there before, he got up, leaned over the desk and shook my hand. He said, 'That's the spirit that will lick the Germans. I'll allow you to take the test again.' " This time Miss Shoemaker passed and proudly became a Marine reservist.[7]

These women had a variety of reasons for joining the Marine Corps, but each was moved by a strong patriotic desire to serve her country in time of war. Theresa Lake, a Texas statistician, signed up because her sweetheart had been killed overseas. Pvt. Lillian Patterson saw her service as support for her husband at the Front in France, and Pvt. Mary English enlisted to join her brother in the service. Pvt. Mary Sharkey said she believed that the opportunity to be a member of "such an elite branch of the service" was the opportunity to serve in the most meaningful way possible.

The Macias family of Jersey City, NJ, was well represented by not one, but two recruits: sisters Edith and Sarah were sworn in together on September 5, 1918. Their parents "nearly fainted" when told of the double enlistment of their only daughters but proudly hung two blue silk service stars in their window the next day. Other parents were anxious and fearful as their adored and sheltered daughters set off on a worrisome new adventure in a chaotic world at war. As Cpl. Pearl Chandley recalled, "When I was leaving home to go some seven hundred miles away, a neighborhood friend admonished my father and said he was being very foolish to allow a girl so young to go so far from home alone. My father's reply was, 'If my daughter wanted to break my heart, she could do it right here under my nose.' "[8]

All female recruits were enrolled as privates in the Marine Corps Reserve for a period of four years. The pay was the same as for enlisted men of corresponding rank: private, $15 per month; private first class, $18; corporal, $21; and sergeant, $30. An additional $83.40 per month was paid out for subsistence and quarters, because there were no barracks available for the women Marines. Her first paycheck was a delightful surprise for Pvt. Ingrid Jonassen.

"I never expected to be paid for my services," she said later. "I thought we would receive only room and board."[9]

But pay had to be earned, and the women recruits were advised in strong terms that they were expected to abide by the same rules and regulations as the men; presumably they would receive the same discipline. Any woman who failed to maintain the high standards expected of a Marine would be "summarily disenrolled," according to Col. Albert S. McLemore, who was in charge of Marine Corps recruiting. Disenrollment was probably the ultimate discipline for a woman Marine, and there is no record that it was ever used in 1918. Though punishment was not as rigid for the women reservists as for the men, still it was Marine discipline, consisting of confinement to quarters (although there were no quarters at the time for women Marines), loss of rating, or assignment to KP, which for the women usually consisted of a Saturday afternoon washing office windows, sweeping floors, or cleaning bathrooms at Headquarters Marine Corps.

We must realize, however, that most infractions on the part of the women were the result of ignorance rather than mischievous or malignant intent. Pvt. Elizabeth Shoemaker met disaster on her first visit home in her new uniform. "I was having such a good time that I wanted to stay longer than my short furlough," she recalled. "So I wired my colonel that I wouldn't be back for three more days. Worst of all, I sent him my regards." When Miss Shoemaker returned to duty, she was given a deck court-martial and emerged badly shaken. "But when I came out of the colonel's office, there was a crowd of enlisted men waiting to congratulate me. . . . They told me, 'Now you are a real Marine.' But because of my court-martial, I never became a sergeant; I remained a corporal."[10]

Conduct, on duty and off, was a serious matter. Colonel McLemore felt constrained to advise the enlistees as he administered the oath that he wanted it "distinctly understood that there was to be no flirtatious philandering with the enlisted men at headquarters on the part of the female reservists."

The women soon learned, too, that if they expected equal privileges, they would have to assume equal responsibilities. Corporal Shoemaker remembered

> a typical hard-boiled sergeant at Marine Corps Headquarters who ordered us to sweep the floor and wash the windows in our offices. Two pretty girls, from wealthy families, rushed to the colonel's office and refused to undertake such labor. He was very angry with them, reminded them that they had [freely] enlisted, and advised them that they couldn't change their minds about their duties. He ordered them to wash those windows and they did it.

It was wonderful discipline for young girls and we came to love the Marine Corps better than anything in life.

Although they were somewhat tardy in enrolling women, the Marine Corps was not to be outdone by the Navy women's snappy uniforms. The female Marine recruits were issued a smartly tailored version of the men's forest green wool uniforms (tan khaki for summer). The women did not have a "dress blue" uniform such as the men wore on special occasions. Accessories for the women included a specially designed shirt, regulation necktie and overcoat, high-topped brown shoes for winter, and oxfords for spring and summer—the first low shoes most of them had ever worn. Matching overseas caps on which they proudly wore the globe-and-anchor insignia of the Corps were the preferred headgear. During inclement weather, however, the women were permitted to wear the broad-brimmed campaign hats that made such excellent umbrellas.

Uniforms were supplied promptly to the women who were assigned to Washington, DC, where local tailors and quartermaster's supplies were immediately available. Women recruited in other cities were not uniformed so promptly. Some waited months for a uniform, and others never received a uniform at all.

The Marine Corps was believed to have been more strict than the Navy concerning dress regulations, even though both branches of the service forbade any frills and fancy additions to the basic uniform. "The Navy Department girls were quite a bit more feminized," one woman Marine recalled. "For instance, while the Navy girls wore lace collars and jewelry, the Marine girls, even on the hottest Washington summer day, were not allowed to turn down their collars or remove their neckties."[11] The women of both services probably adhered fairly strictly to the uniform dress code. It just may have been easier to add a string of beads, a brooch, or a bracelet to the white Navy blouse than to the sharply tailored shirt of the Marine uniform.

Raincoats, purses, and gloves were not issued to the female Marines, and the wearing of Sam Browne belts, rifle insignia, spats, and nonregulation shoes and the use of swagger sticks were not permitted. "Female reservists must be made to understand that the wearing of the uniform by them confers no priviledge [sic] to deviate from the uniform as prescribed in regulations," thundered General Barnett.[12]

Even though the uniform regulations were strict, "the women used their ingenuity and were put to relatively little inconvenience," said Pvt. Mary Sharkey. "The coat or blouse had a large pocket on each side which extended across the front. These commodious cavities were handy, but putting too many things in them created bulges, which was strictly against regulations. To avoid this, I kept a comb and brush in my desk, tucked my handkerchief inside a sleeve, and carried a small change purse so as to appear trim and neat. There was no need for a wallet."[13]

Strict regulations were also applied to the natural high spirits of the young women Marines. General Barnett roared again at his troops of both sexes: "Enlisted men and women on duty at these headquarters have been observed skylarking together on the streets, and not infrequently have been noticed walking arm in arm. . . . Such practices must cease and . . . they must at all times conduct themselves in a dignified and soldierly manner."[14]

As to a name for the new Marines, their only official title has always been Marine Reserve (F). But of course, many nicknames cropped up in 1918. One female Marine heard the title "Lady Hell Cats" used by an enthusiastic Marine in Quantico as her group marched by. "Skirt Marines" was another sobriquet, and the most popular and most widely used was "Marinette," which the women hated. Officially, the Corps disapproved of such titles and posted notices forbidding their use. Nevertheless, many still referred to the Reservists (F) as Marinettes.

Women Marines were enlisted mainly for clerical duties. But in addition to their routine office work, they were often drilled and trained in the simpler drill movements so that they could parade and take part in various events, especially in the nation's capital. The Corps admittedly realized a great deal of popular support and publicity from such appearances by the Marine Reserve (F) units.

"At first the male drill instructors were indignant to have been selected to teach drill to women," said Pfc. Edith Macias. "As a result they showed us no mercy and taught us the same way as they did male recruits." Another female recruit recalled that her drill instructor went along the line ordering them into the correct positions with commands such as "Stick out your chest" and "Suck in that gut." "They were perfectionists, even stinkers," said Pfc. Florence Gertler, "but they were good."

To the surprise of veteran Marines, most of the female recruits were fascinated with drill, and they marched with a great deal of energy and enthusiasm. A few other women Marines—a minority—never quite got the hang of marching to command. "We all loved it," said one female noncom, "but we couldn't do it. . . . We had several drill instructors and they all tore their hair and went crazy. Some even pleaded with us and tried to bribe us to do better."[15] One of the recruits recalled later that her biggest thrill during the war was the day the female contingent was parading in uniform on Pennsylvania Avenue in Washington, DC, around the Treasury Building, when "twenty across, we made a perfect quarter-turn to go on up Sixteenth Street Northwest."[16]

Cpl. Pearl Chandley recalled that she was among the twenty-five women Marines chosen as bodyguards for President Woodrow Wilson during one parade. They were positioned with the president, his wife, and members of the cabinet in a stand erected just inside the White House fence. "Directly across on Pennsylvania Avenue, were chairs and wheel-chairs for the uniformed and much decorated men Marines [veterans of the fighting overseas]. I believe this was called the Victory Parade. I knew that I'd be hungry standing so long on such a hot day, as all the returned Marines and all the tanks and equipment passed by, so I put a chocolate bar in the pocket of my uniform skirt. It melted—they were not wrapped then as they are now. Luckily my jacket covered the stain."[17]

Although their stenographic chores were hardly exciting, many of the young women were thrilled to be in direct contact with those who were fighting and dying "over there." As Pvt. Lela Leibrand, of the female reservists, wrote in 1918:

> There's romance in the work [at headquarters]—real, live human romance. We keep in closer touch with you [soldiers] than you dream. If you are transferred, we know where from and where to. If you are hurt, we know when, where and how much. When you reach another step in the progress of your training, marksmanship, promotion, we hear about it and see to it that you get the proper credits on your records. And, the additional pay! But when we read, "Ashore, France," stamped on your card—well, it is but a little hope, just a thought, but it is a prayer that God will watch over you and care for you, in the end delivering you safely home.[18]

Private Leibrand also wrote with feeling about her ride in a Marine hydroplane at Quantico, VA.

> The pilots told me to hold my mouth tightly closed to insure the imprisonment of my heart as the plane would leave the water. . . . [They] listed all the different antics they would perform once they got me into the air. But I did some quick thinking and just smiled back at them, for wherever they sent me they had to go, too. . . . All of a sudden we were off. I didn't realize we had left the water until I saw it receding below me. Then up, up, up. O, Boy! There's not a single adjective in the United States that has the power to express it.

The rhapsodic Private Leibrand was also the first to make a training film for the Marine Corps, All in a Day's Work. With film sent from the front lines in France, she worked under armed guards at the Smithsonian Institution, developing, drying, and editing the bloodiest footage in the world. It was said that she sometimes worked eighteen to twenty hours at a stretch.

Many women Marines filled important jobs in the Washington, DC, offices of the adjutant and inspector, the quartermaster, and the paymaster. A few who looked particularly sharp in their uniforms were assigned as messengers to make trips throughout Headquarters Marine Corps and various offices of the Navy Department. Special permission was also given to enroll women for duty in recruiting offices across the country—in New York City, Rochester, Boston, Philadelphia, Indianapolis, Denver, Spokane, San Francisco, and Portland, OR.

The women enlistees also were used for publicity in bond drives and rallies, in newspaper photographs, and as recruiters' aides. Often, however, the female Marines were posed in bogus situations such as learning to execute a drum roll during a visit to Parris Island's Drum and Bugle Corps or pictured with large pots of glue, pasting up recruiting posters in New York. Harmless, perhaps, but denigrating to women who wanted to be of serious service to their country at war.

"I had a lot of fun in the service," said Minnie Arthur Kistler. "I did recruiting in Indianapolis and Chicago." She was the "bait" for recruiting campaigns, as her husband later described it. "I did promotions—Victory Bonds, for instance—and met celebrities," she said.[19] Corporal Arthur was also taken for an airplane joyride. She recalled that flying over Indianapolis, "we dropped Victory Loan literature and several coupons good for $2 payment on a $50 bond. It was cloudy when we went up, but we went away above the clouds where the sun was shining. It was mighty cold, but I was dressed good and warm. Lt. Ballard [the pilot] cut a lot of capers in the sky, but he said his passenger was 'dead game.' " Asked when she would go up again, Corporal Arthur replied, "First time I get a chance. I'd go up again today if they'd let me." That flight earned Minnie Arthur the distinction of being the first woman to fly in an airplane in Indiana.

Another young recruit, Violet Van Wagner, age eighteen, was assigned to handle correspondence connected with casualties. "We would get the muster rolls, with the information about a man's death, and enter it onto record cards, with other details," she said. "The carnage was awful in those last months of the war, from the battles at Chateau Thierry, Belleau Wood, and the Meuse Argonne.[20] The most difficult part was writing the next-of-kin letters for the commandant's signature, telling the families what had befallen their young men. "It was not a fun job," Violet Van Wagner remembered. "We instinctively developed a flair for words in such cases—'It is with heartfelt sympathy that I have to advise you . . . ' We tried to share with the loved ones their grief, and also the pride of sacrifices made for our country."[21]

Florence Gertler was twenty-two when she enlisted in New York on August 13, 1918. As secretary to the assistant adjutant and inspector of the Marine Corps, she used White House stationery to prepare lists of officers for promotion. Those were sent on for President Woodrow Wilson's signature before they were submitted to Congress. "Each sheet of that stationery had to be accounted for," she recalled. "If a sheet was spoiled, it had to be listed and turned in for replacement. I never spoiled a sheet."[22]

In contrast to the reluctant Philadelphia recruiter Sergeant Kase, most Marine men were happy to have the women on duty and tried to help them with their work. But the women Marines doubtless suffered a lot of good-natured teasing, and even some petty harassment from the men of the Corps who felt that the service had "stepped down" when it enrolled women. Most of the female reservists believed that they were treated as equals by male Marines. "The men did not look down or frown on us," Pfc. Edith Macias recalled. "Actually, they were glad to have us. We were given a job to do and we did it. We were definitely not considered decorative rather than practical. We were treated as professionals."[23]

But even professionals had to have a roof over their heads, and there were no military barracks available for the female recruits in Washington, DC, where most of these first women Marines were stationed. Indeed, their dress and their conduct were strictly circumscribed, but curiously, they were on their own with their subsistence allowances when it came to housing. They wound up scattered throughout the city, some in single rooms in private homes and boardinghouses, others in rented apartments with small groups of friends. In seeking accommodations, the Marine women faced many of the same problems as their Navy counterparts, the Yeomen (F), and often found similar happy solutions in their camaraderie. One kind soul in the Maryland suburbs temporarily set up her sun porch "dormitory style" to accommodate a discouraged group of six new women Marines who had spent a whole Sunday fruitlessly searching for housing.

On occasion a few of the young women with suitable quarters would entertain groups of wounded from the nearby naval hospital. "Several of them were brought over in a truck," said Pearl Chandley Oagley, who attended one of these parties. She recalled:

The men with good legs carried the less fortunate on their backs up the one flight of stairs [to the apartment]. We brought home-made cakes and ice cream to serve, and one of the other girls, Lela Leibrand, had obtained a movie film to show. We used ironing boards and other furniture to make room to huddle together so we could all see the film through the archway into another room.

One Marine with a very crippled arm in a sling had undergone 22 major operations to save it. He stood behind me and rested his chin on the top of my head so he could see the movie. This turned out to be a rather long story. We went out to dinner later and he ordered a steak, so I had to cut his meat for him. This got to be a habit. Before he left for his home to get established in making a living, he asked me to wait for him, promising rather convincingly that he could take better care of me with one good arm than anyone else could with two.[24]

After the Armistice of November 11, 1918, there was, of course, a gradual decrease in the need for the women reservists. Eventually, by July of 1919, most of them were ordered to inactive status. But before they returned to civilian life, a grand ceremony was arranged on the White House lawn, where the commandant, General Barnett, reviewed the Marine women for the last time. The irrepressible Josephus Daniels, still secretary of the Navy, then stepped up to give the farewell address. Cpl. Elizabeth Shoemaker vividly recalled the occasion:

We stood proudly in front of him in our uniforms, listening to every word of his eloquent speech; he said we had been good Marines and he was proud of us. Then, in his closing statement, he said, "We will not forget you. As we embrace you in uniform today, we will embrace you without uniform tomorrow." All down the file of men standing at strict attention, the line broke, and everyone roared with laughter. The Secretary of the Navy forgot he was talking to women.[25]

In 1919, General Barnett said of the women Marines, "It is a pleasure, but not by any means an unexpected one, to be able to state that the service rendered by the reservists (female) has been uniformly excellent. It has, in fact, been exactly what the intelligence and goodness of our countrywomen would lead one to expect."

Gradual "disenrollment" continued until, by 1922, all of the female Marines had packed away their uniforms. Some of the women reservists remained on duty as civilians in government service, and others returned home—all with the same full veterans' benefits as their male counterparts. All received a Good

Conduct Medal and World War I Victory Medal when they were discharged from the inactive reserves.

One of the women Marines who chose to remain in government service after the war, Pvt. Alma Swope, served in the Supply Department for more than forty-four years. Of the World War I Marine reservists who accepted civil service positions, she was the last to retire from her government duties.

Minnie Arthur, who had flown over Indianapolis in the Victory Loan campaign, was made a sergeant in the Marine Corps Reserve in May 1919, an appointment heralded as a first by her hometown newspaper. She also joined the American Legion, claiming to be the first woman in the United States to do so. "A man I knew told me it was something being organized by one of Theodore Roosevelt's sons, and I said if he was [in] back of it, I'd join up." She took an active part in her Legion post in Indianapolis, IN, serving as treasurer, vice-commander, and assistant adjutant.

Violet Van Wagner Lopez wrote many poems in the years following the war, possibly trying to blot out the memories of those next-of-kin letters she wrote in 1918. "That war was really a terrible, horrible, stupid thing," she said seventy years later. "It still gets me crazy when I think about it today."[26] She faithfully attended the annual conventions of the Women Marines Association over the years and was highly honored by her colleagues as she advanced into her nineties.

Pearl Chandley married her Marine with the disabled arm and fondly remembered that "it was a challenge to see that he kept all those promises about taking care of me with his one good arm. . . . It took both of us full time working together to achieve our modest ambitions and to make our dreams come true as we raised our son and daughter."[27]

Lela Leibrand also saw dreams come true following the war. She married a veteran of the Argonne Forest campaign in France and they settled in Texas. Later she watched proudly as her pretty young daughter, Virginia, grew up to become the motion picture legend Ginger Rogers.[28]

For other World War I Marine women, the slogan "Once a Marine, always a Marine" had special meaning. Two of them returned to the Corps to serve as officers in the Marine Corps Women's Reserve during World War II. Lillian O'Malley Daly, one of the eight women who came into the new Women's Reserve directly from civilian life in early 1943, served as West Coast liaison officer. Martrese Thek Ferguson, a Marine veteran of the Great War, rose to the rank of lieutenant colonel in World War II, commanding more than 2,000 women at Henderson Hall in Arlington, VA.

After two wars, when she was close to eighty, one of those first female Marines, Pearl Chandley Oagley, observed, "There is so great an opportunity and real need for women to put their strength behind every move toward world peace and fellowship. So much may seem just talk, but talking is better than shooting."[29]

Notes

1. Capt. Linda L. Hewitt, USMCR, Women Marines in World War I (Washington, DC: History and Museums Division, Headquarters, U.S. Marine Corps, 1974). Unless otherwise noted, the historic details in this chapter about the first women Marines are taken from Hewitt.

2. Sgt. George W. Kase, unpublished memoir, Personal Papers Collection, History and Museums Division, Marine Corps Historical Center, Washington Navy Yard, Washington, DC.

3. Ibid., 82.

4. Author telephone interview with Florence Gertler Miller, Dunedin, Florida, 1988.

5. Marine Corps circular dated August 14, 1918, U.S. Women in World War I file, History and Museums Division, Headquarters, U.S. Marine Corps, Washington, DC.

6. Newspaper clippings, 1918–1958, and family records of Minnie Arthur Kistler, loaned by her daughter, Mrs. Ted Rand, Seattle, WA.

7. Hewitt, 9.

8. Pearl Chandley Oagley, unpublished memoir, 1975. Personal Papers Collection, History and Museums Division, Marine Corps Historical Center, Washington Navy Yard, Washington, DC.

9. Hewitt, 25.

10. Ibid., 36.

11. Ibid., 21.

12. Ibid., 22.

13. Ibid., 21.

14. Ibid., 35–36.

15. Ibid., 31.

16. Author interview and correspondence with Violet Van Wagner Lopez, Kew Gardens, NY, 1988.

17. Oagley memoir.

18. Pvt. Lela Leibrand, "Fair Marine Tells of Flight in Hydroplane," Leatherneck newspaper (Quantico, Virginia), Jan. 2, 1919.

19. Kistler family records.

20. Lopez interview and correspondence. The carnage she refers to was the heavy casualties in the famed Fourth Marine Brigade serving with the Second U.S. Army Infantry Division. The Marine Brigade included the Fifth and Sixth Marine Regiments and the Sixth Marine Machine Gun Battalion.

21. Ibid.

22. Miller interview.

23. Hewitt, 31.

24. Oagley memoir.

25. Hewitt, 41.

26. Lopez interview and correspondence.

27. Oagley memoir.

28. Ibid.

29. Ibid.

Crowds of eager women flocked to Marine Corps recruiting offices when enlistment was announced in August 1918. This group, sworn in at the New York office, borrowed jackets and hats from men Marines for a publicity photo. One of the recruits recalled, "There was great consternation among veteran Marines who objected to the picture of women wearing sharpshooters' badges, Good Conduct Medals, and other ribbons on the tunics." (National Archives photo no. 127-G-530552)

Two sisters of the Macias family of Jersey City, NJ, enlisted together in the Marine Corps early in September 1918. Pictured here is Pfc. Edith Macias, standing proudly during a review of the women reservists by Maj. Gen. George Barnett, Marine Corps commandant, in Washington, DC. (National Archives photo no. 165–WW–598–A–10)

A few Marine women reservists were assigned as messengers to Headquarters Marine Corps in Washington, DC, carrying official communiqués and intraoffice correspondence. Among these were Pfc. Mary Kelly, left, secretary to Col. Albert S. McLemore, in charge of Marine Corps recruiting; Pfc. May O'Keefe, center, of New York City; and Pfc. Ruth Spike, also of New York City, youngest of the reserve enlistees. (National Archives photo no. 127–G–530266)

Minnie Arthur, age twenty-one, became the only woman Marine enlisted in the state of Indiana. Until the Armistice, she served as a recruiting aide in Indianapolis and Chicago, and she later joined the American Legion, claiming to be the first woman in the United States to do so. (Lettie Gavin collection)

Pvt. (later Sgt.) Lela Leibrand, assigned to the Marine Corps Publicity Bureau, was given a ride in a hydroplane at Quantico, VA, and wrote an enthusiastic report of the publicity stunt. (National Archives photo no. 127–G–518553)

Secretary of the Navy Josephus Daniels, center, with his assistant secretary, Franklin D. Roosevelt (holding the hat), are pictured with Marine women reservists, left, and Navy Yeomen (F) in white uniforms at their final parade at the Ellipse in Washington, DC, February 3, 1919. (National Archives photo no. 127–G–530164–A)

= 3 =

The Army Nurse

Several thousand skilled and patriotic U.S. nurses went to France in 1917–1918 to tend the sick and wounded of the American Expeditionary Forces (AEF).[1] Perhaps many had signed on with a romanticized notion of what nursing entailed. Popular illustrations depicted a pretty young woman wearing a crisp white uniform emblazoned with a scarlet cross, a halo cap and flowing veil covering her hair. She hovered daintily over a smiling wounded soldier sitting up in bed, a spotless bandage wrapped around his head, his left arm trussed up in an immaculate sling. He smiled gratefully at his nurse, and probably fell in love with her on the spot.

Nothing in this popular fantasy could have prepared the nurse for the reality: lice-infested, mud-crusted uniforms, bloody bandages, gaping shrapnel wounds, hideously infected fractures, mustard gas burns, frantic coughing and choking from phosgene inhalation, groans and shrieks of pain, trauma from exposure, fatigue, and emotional collapse. Could the nurse have imagined her own horrified reaction when she saw that "every available spot—beds, stretchers and floor space—was occupied by a seriously wounded man. The overflow cases lay on the wet ground, waiting their turn to be moved under cover: We stood, tears mixing with the rain, feeling anger and frustration."[2] "A steady stream of patients [was] carried into the X-ray room . . . where the plates all showed foreign bodies and often the bubbles . . . of the dreadful gas gangrene."[3]

The nurses of 1917–1918 could not possibly have guessed the extent and nature of the work ahead of them, nor the conditions of their own service in France: the raw, cold weather; the bundling up in drab, gray uniforms, leather vests, wool sweaters, boots, and knitted hats; the shortage of water for baths and shampoos; the cold dormitory barracks; and the dreary, monotonous food. Nor did the nurses have the authority, prestige, and security of rank and appropriate pay. They were neither officers nor noncommissioned officers during the Great War. Although they were given "relative rank" (rank in name only) in 1920, they did not receive pay, status, and benefits equal with men until 1944.

But in spite of the shock and dismay, the exhaustion and discomfort, these women and their counterparts in the Army Medical Service and the U.S. Navy provided the best care that had ever been accorded to an army in the field. More than 12,000 nurses were on active duty on June 30, 1918; of these, 5,350 were serving overseas. The Army Nurse Corps (ANC), established in 1901, reached a peak strength of 21,480 by November 11, 1918, when the Armistice was signed.[4]

They gave the best care that science had to offer, plus a devotion that transcended the popular ideals, and their patients recovered and returned to duty at an astonishing rate. Odd as it sounds, many of the surviving soldiers recovered because of the war, not in spite of it. They lived due to advances in medical treatment forced by the war. A man with a sucking chest wound, for instance, would probably have died on the spot in 1914. By the end of the war, however, medical science had concentrated on such potentially fatal conditions and devised appropriate and effective treatment.

U.S. doctors, nurses, and hospital corpsmen went to France to man the base hospital system devised by distinguished surgeon George W. Crile on his return from a visit to the French battle front in 1915. Dr. Crile's plan, proposed as a preparedness measure before the United States entered the Great War, was heartily approved and supported by the Army's surgeon general. But because of the peacetime austerity imposed upon the military, the Army did not have the money to implement the plan at that time. To resolve this dilemma, the military enlisted the assistance of a civilian organization, the American Red Cross. With supervision by the surgeon general's office, the Red Cross agreed to establish and finance fifty base hospitals under the sponsorship of parent civilian hospitals. Complete hospital units, including all necessary personnel and full equipment, were to be organized in civilian medical communities, ready for transfer to the government in case of emergency.

The most obvious advantages to such a plan were that the base unit was assembled and equipped without expense to the government, its staff was composed of men and women who had worked together in civilian life and were familiar with each other's abilities and methods, each unit had the moral and financial backing of a large and interested body of supporters from its hospital, and its personnel were stimulated to their best efforts by the desire to do credit to the parent institution. During 1916, many of the great civilian hospitals throughout the country began to organize these hospital units, usually with the financial aid of the local chapter of the American Red Cross.

Much of the medical planning at this time was augmented by the ideas and opinions of the hundreds of U.S. volunteers who had served with the British and French overseas during the thirty-three months before the United States entered the war. Such organizations as the American Fund for French Wounded, the American Committee for Devastated France, the American

Women's War Relief Fund, and many others had sent medical and other volunteer personnel to Europe from the outset of the war in 1914, and these people contributed considerable expertise in formulating the base hospital plan for the United States.

Not only was the Red Cross the moving force behind the establishment of the base hospitals, but it also was responsible for the several thousand trained nurses who had been examined, registered, and prepared for service as the United States entered the European war. Enrollment had begun several years before when the National Committee on Red Cross Nursing Service began to organize and maintain a register of well-qualified nurses for service in time of disaster or war. These women were available to serve, and they were eager and enthusiastic as well. Irma Tuell of Seattle, WA, was typical of the nurses. "Our 1918 graduating class at Seattle General Hospital was dedicated to the government," she recalled. "So when they asked for volunteers we jumped at the chance. Nobody had to recruit me." Miss Tuell and her sister both served at the huge Mesves Bulcy Hospital Center in France before the war ended in November.[5]

During the first decade of the century it had been said that many training schools for nurses were opened simply to provide cheap—rather than well-qualified—labor for hospitals. Recognizing this situation, Jane A. Delano, a nurse administrator of wide experience, had for several years worked diligently to improve the training of nurses and to establish professional standards. Miss Delano had served as chairman of the Red Cross nursing service committee and as the second superintendent of the Army Nurse Corps since 1909. In 1912, she resigned her Army position to devote all her time to the development of the Red Cross nursing enrollment plan. This plan made an important contribution to nursing education by demanding above average qualifications that became even more stringent as time went on.

Working tirelessly, Miss Delano built up an extensive pool of nursing talent until it became the recognized reserve of the Army Nurse Corps, the main avenue through which U.S. nurses might respond in time of national crisis. An imposing woman, dignified and gracious in appearance, Miss Delano in time had the satisfaction of seeing her roster of well-trained nurses meet the enormous demands of 1917–1918: the Red Cross supplied the majority of the nurses who served with the U.S. Army during the Great War.

Until the civilian base hospitals were called into active service, they were under the immediate jurisdiction of the Red Cross. But when the units were mobilized and taken over by the government, they became part of the Army or Navy, subject to the orders of the surgeon general. When the United States entered the war on April 6, 1917, only twenty-five of the proposed fifty base hospitals were ready to go, or at least in some stage of organization. This number was, of course, completely inadequate.

To meet the urgent need, other large medical institutions quickly began to assemble their own units. As each was established, it was officially authorized by the War Department, and a commanding officer, an adjutant, a quartermaster, and other officers were appointed as required. Each base hospital also was given a number (in order of its authorization) by which it would be known. Thus New York's Bellevue Hospital unit, authorized in January 1916, became U.S. Army Base Hospital No. 1. Additional New York hospitals, and others in Cleveland, Boston, Philadelphia, Chicago, and Detroit, quickly followed. In the first seven months after the United States joined the war, seventeen base hospital units were rushed to France; the rest were held in readiness for immediate departure.

The first call for U.S. aid overseas came in 1917 through the British Commission, requesting doctors and nurses. Dozens of U.S. doctors were dispatched to serve as medical officers with British infantry units at the Front, and six of the waiting base hospitals were assigned to duty with the British Expeditionary Forces. Among these was Base Hospital No. 21, organized by Washington University Medical School in St. Louis, MO. That unit was sent to Rouen, France, with Julia Catherine Stimson as chief nurse. A Massachusetts native and a graduate of Vassar College and the New York Hospital Training School for Nurses, Miss Stimson had been appointed superintendent of nurses for the Children's Hospital and the Washington University Hospital in St. Louis in 1913. She joined the Army Nurse Corps on May 15, 1917, and served in France with her unit until April 1918, when she was named to head all Army nurses with the AEF in France.

During the war years, Miss Stimson wrote often to her parents from Rouen, where her base hospital was stationed at a racetrack that had been converted with tents and huts into a British military receiving hospital. From her quarters in the jockey room under the old grandstand, she described the arrival of British wounded:[6]

> The other night at midnight I went down to see a convoy coming in. . . . The big marquee has about two feeble electric lights in it; it was all very dim and spooky. The ambulances backed up near the door . . . and the stretchers are brought in and laid on the dirt floor as close together as possible. Another group of men begins at once to examine the tickets fastened to the coat of each [wounded] man, and assigns them to particular tents where men with similar injuries or in similar condition are taken care of. A couple of orderlies hand out steaming hot soup, and the doctors talk to the men a little, but do not examine them there at all. Then very quickly the stretcher bearers

come and carry out the men that have been assigned . . . off to a bed in some comfortable tent where a nurse and an orderly are waiting to get the poor tired creature into bed. The doctors have found that the men are much more in need of a good sleep than of a doctor's care at first, and unless absolutely necessary, dressings are not changed until the morning.

That night, 64 men, most of them stretcher cases, were brought in, assigned, given soup, and taken off to their wards (tents) in 25 minutes, which you see is pretty speedy work. The men have very little to say when they first come in. They are tired out and forlorn and often in pain and dazed . . . but later some of them tell the most awful stories.

One of them told the other day of getting caught on a barbed wire entanglement on which he was thrown by the explosion of a shell, and of hanging there all day before he was rescued. . . . Another told of lying out between two lines of trenches [for] three days. He was hurt in the hip and could drag himself only a few inches at a time. His only drinking water came from the bottles of the dead soldiers around him.

September 1917 was a busy time at Base Hospital No. 21 as casualties poured in from the British offensive at Ypres in Flanders. Miss Stimson wrote, "We began in the operating room about 4:30 p.m., taking out foreign bodies and incising and draining. I scrubbed up and helped, not so much because they needed me but because I wanted to be in it. We kept three [operating] tables going all the time. Out in the little hall there were always three or four patients [waiting] on stretchers on the floor. We took pieces of shell out of necks, hips, knees, skulls, ankles, shoulders, and out of the spine of a poor paralyzed man."

The situation worsened in the spring of 1918, when the Germans launched an overwhelming counteroffensive, first against the British Fifth Army on the Somme, and in April against the British forces in Flanders. German divisions struck deeply into the British rear areas, overrunning and forcing evacuation of aid stations, headquarters sites, supply dumps, ammunition parks, and hospitals. As Miss Stimson wrote home from Rouen in March 1918, "patients began to pour in upon us. . . . Day before yesterday we operated on 50 cases, yesterday 51, today they had 73 scheduled. . . . They have at least 40 more cases to operate on tonight. . . . More convoys are due tonight. The doctors are about dead. They are working in shifts as much as they can. The stretcher-bearers are dead tired, but as cheerful as monkeys."

Often, when heavy casualties threatened to overwhelm a hospital in the battle zone, other units would be ordered to send an "emergency group" or surgical team to supplement the staff. Base Hospital No. 21 received such assistance that spring. Miss Stimson reported, "Yesterday was the first day in two weeks that any nurse had any time off duty. Because of reinforcements that arrived, we were able to send every nurse off to rest for three hours. . . . We received a mobile unit from the AEF, 15 nurses and 30-odd enlisted men. You may be sure we were glad to get them." Like an anxious mother, Chief Nurse Stimson agonized over the bone-weary women of her staff. On April 6, she wrote, "I don't mind for myself, but it breaks my heart to see my children get hollow-eyed and white, and see them one by one succumb, at least temporarily, and have to be sent to bed. Still, they have done wonders." A few days later, she observed, "We have had no convoys and are catching our breaths. . . . There were so many deaths and so many awful cases and such pitiful things going on all the time, it was hard to keep steady, especially as everyone was much over-worked."

The winter of 1917–1918 in France was extremely cold—some said the worst of the war. Miss Stimson reported that her people were funny-looking nurses, wearing knitted caps, sweaters, and wristlets with their gray dresses and aprons. Most wore knickerbockers under their uniforms and often wore their raincoats, leather gaiters, and rubber boots while on duty. "Some, I know, have knitted sleeveless Jimmy shirts on top of two sets of underwear," she wrote.

Keeping clean was as big a challenge as keeping warm. "Just think of the problem of enough hot water to bathe five or six hundred patients in a camp where all the hot water has to be heated on camp stoves after being drawn from about a single pipe," wrote Julia Stimson. There was scarcely enough water to clean up the muddy wounded men, leaving little to none for the nurses' personal hygiene. Most nurses wore their long hair twisted up into a "pug" on the backs of their heads and dreamed of the luxury of a soothing shampoo. One of their special visions was of relaxing in a warm, marble bathroom, with plenty of hot water and soft, fluffy towels.

Stocking of supplies and equipment furnished further problems for the base hospitals. One British hospital telegraphed to London a shopping list of desired equipment that included "3,000 roller bandages; 1,000 each abdominal, chest, shoulder, hip, elbow, head triangular and T bandages; 200 each splints; 200 sand-bags [used to weigh down the traction device when treating fractures]; three dozen pairs crutches, 500 limb pillows, 1,000 pneumonia jackets, 500 arm slings, five cases each absorbent wool and absorbent gauze, also unlimited gauze dressings."[7] Miss Stimson wrote, however, that "so far we seem to have enough of the necessities. We have long since ceased to attempt to change sheets between patients. A good many patients have been in beds without any sheets at all, but that is a minor matter."

Once wounded, a soldier retreated by any means possible—on foot, by litter, or by animal-drawn or motor ambulance, depending on the severity of the injury and the difficulty of the terrain. His next stop was the dressing station, which might be 3,000 yards or more behind the line. One medical corpsman from New York, Frederick A. Pottle, of Evacuation Hospital No. 8, described how the wounded were sorted and treated:

> Besides giving first-aid treatment to the men, the dressing station also provided shelter and served as a collecting and classification center for the ambulance service: The wounded were then carried back by ambulance to the triage, or sorting station, which was usually a field hospital, normally two to four miles back. Here the wounded were carefully sorted out according to the seriousness and urgency of their injuries. Gassed men were sent to the gas hospital, seriously wounded to an evacuation or mobile unit, slightly wounded farther back to the railhead. The field hospitals operated on some of the most desperately wounded men—those with abdominal and chest wounds, for instance—but the first definitive surgical work was performed principally by the evacuation hospitals and mobile units. These units were usually smaller, did most of their work under canvas, and had much of their equipment fitted in trucks so that they could move easily on short notice."[8]

The base hospital was one of the final links in the chain of progress for the recovering U.S. soldier. From here, recuperated troops were returned to duty. Convalescents were sent farther back behind the lines to special rest-and-recreation camps located at considerable distances from the Front. Some soldiers, judged unfit for any further military duty, permanently disabled, or seriously diseased, were returned to the United States as soon as possible. Early in their overseas duty, Pottle's unit was set up in an old school, the College de Juilly, Seine-et-Marne, where they arrived on a June morning in 1918. He found the big old stone buildings, plus a number of brown ward tents, jammed with casualties from the great battle of Belleau Wood. Hundreds of wounded U.S. Marines filled the rooms, cloisters, dormitories, and halls of the ancient school. As he looked on the scene with shock and horror, the novice corpsman noticed a woman, an Army nurse, stooping over a patient. She rose and came over to him.

He recalled that she was ready to drop with fatigue, her hair escaping from under her cap, her face gray and suffused with perspiration. She was so glad to see him that she nearly cried.

During the last four days, the hospital had treated nearly 2,000 desperately wounded men. On June 2, it had only the personnel of a Red Cross base hospital of about 250 beds: two surgeons, 20 Red Cross nurses, a few civilian employees from the nearby French village, and a handful of French soldiers unable to serve at the front. During this period, hardly anyone at Juilly had worked less than 20 hours a day.[9]

A U.S. nurse, Laura Frost, had similar vivid memories of her first encounter with the wounded at a hospital near Paris in the summer of 1918. "If it hadn't been the amputation ward, maybe the shock wouldn't have been so devastating, but helping dress those quivering stumps and hearing the men's laughter and jokes in spite of their misfortune, was too much for me and I cried all that first day."[10]

Miss Frost, a native of Massachusetts, had gone overseas with Base Hospital No. 44 from Boston, but soon after arrival in France, she was reassigned to Evacuation Hospital No. 5 (known as Evac 5) and equipped with a helmet, gas mask, mess kit, and canteen. "Meanwhile, the Americans were fighting their first big action [the Aisne-Marne offensive], trying to turn back the German advance on Paris," Miss Frost recalled.

> We heard that the fighting was intense and that a French general had ordered the Marines to retreat. . . . An American officer responded, "Retreat? Hell, no, we just got here." It was then that our troops snatched the initiative from the Germans at Chateau Thierry, and it was here that Evac 5 came into the picture. We set up our first mobile tent hospital near the ruins of a town on the River Marne, with a total of about forty nurses in our unit.
>
> When the wounded began to come in, the stretchers were laid on the ground and the corpsmen stripped them of their muddy clothes and deloused them, usually before we received them in the operating tent. I can still hear the sound of a leg being sawed off and remember the boy who had one side of his face blown away, asking: "Do I look bad?"
>
> We worked eight hours on and eight hours off, around the clock. By the time we got up and got into bed, it was more like six hours off in the twenty-four. The patients were given only necessary operations in our evacuation hospital, and then were sent back to the base hospitals as soon as they could be moved. It was a long way back to the base on a jolting train, but it was the first leg of their journey home for some.

Because evacuation hospitals followed behind the line of battle, Miss Frost, with Evac 5, was dispatched next to Villers Cotterets, on the Oise-Aisne front. As she recounted:

> We nurses lived in tents. They were large, each one with room for twenty of us. Our lockers fit under each cot, with a box between our beds to keep our things. A cone-shaped stove called a Sibley [used during the U.S. Civil War] was in the middle of the tent. It took off some of the chill. A wooden floor

kept us out of the mud, for it rained a lot and there were many tramping feet. We had to walk everywhere outside on slippery duckboards laid down over the muck.

The operating tents were covered with khaki blankets to keep the lights from showing at night, and we couldn't have any light showing in our own tents, which made it hard to find our way back and crawl into bed. One nurse used to make herself a cup of tea on her little alcohol lamp when she came off duty. She kept a small pail of water under her cot, also another pail in case she had to get up in the night. One late night we were awakened by her cussing—she had mistakenly used the wrong bucket for her tea.

For washing and bathing, when a big push was over, we used a basin and pitcher of hot water that we heated over a bonfire in a big can. The only real bath we had was when we were taken back to Rest and Rehabilitation.

About that time, Miss Frost wrote home to her parents about a swim in the river. "One of the officers loaned me a suit, so I accomplished one ambition and incidentally, a bath. The bath was no small part of the swim, either. Do you know, you don't mind being dirty over here. It is quite the thing, and if you wash too much, you are considered odd."

Evac 5 moved next to the Meuse-Argonne sector, where the German army had been living for some four years. They had built some clever housing for themselves in the area; many of the dugouts were deep underground, nicely furnished, and even included running water and toilets. Here the U.S. First Army (totalling a million men, including some French soldiers) launched their attack with a rolling artillery barrage against the German lines on September 26, 1918, at 5:30 A.M.

Next, Evac 5 headed by train to the Belgian front. The men rode in "40 hommes, 8 chevaux" boxcars (designed to carry forty men and eight horses), and the nurses traveled six to each compartment in the passenger cars. "The trains were so slow you could get off at each village and go shopping," she observed. "To pass the time, we sang all the popular songs of the time, 'Pack Up Your Troubles,' 'Long, Long Trail,' and our own twist to the lyrics to 'The Rose of No Man's Land'—'Mid the war's great curse, stands the Cross Red Nurse. She's the rose of no man's land.' "

Eventually Evac 5 arrived at a village near the battered medieval town of Ypres. "The Germans were getting desperate and using more and more mustard gas," Miss Frost remembered.

Our casualties were 20 and 30 percent gassed. It caused huge blisters on the men, and they suffered painfully. . . . We became very fond of one of our patients, a young fellow with a bullet hole right in the middle of his forehead. We kept trying to get him to talk. All he could say was "glass," but he wasn't paralyzed. When he wanted something, we would keep asking him until we hit the right thing and he would nod his head. One day Margaret sang "Over There" to him and he followed along, saying all the words. That was a great day for us. When he was evacuated, we went to the train with him and sat by his litter until the train pulled out.

Canadian Margaret Erb was among the nurses who remained with Base Hospital No. 44 when Laura Frost was dispatched to the muddy, drafty tents of the evacuation hospital.[11] During the last week of July 1918, Base 44 proceeded from the port of Le Havre to the ancient spa town of Pougues-les-Eaux, a picturesque resort in the Loire valley. Their experience at Pougues was typical of U.S. efforts to convert existing schools, hotels, villas, religious establishments, and athletic and recreational structures all over France into hospital stations and huge medical centers. Pougues was famous for its mineral springs and had been for many years a popular summer resort for those who wanted to "take the cure." There were a number of fine residences in and near the town, as well as several luxurious Victorian hotels catering to the summer trade.[12]

Some of the hotels had been used by the French as hospitals early in the war, and when the United States later entered the hostilities, arrangements were made to lease about twenty of the buildings to the U.S. Army Medical Department for the care of U.S. soldiers. Included were the Hotel Splendide with its fine grounds, chalet, casino, tennis courts, gymnasium, and baths; three hotels; and six villas; as well as the new Mairie (city hall), the Maison Clement, and two private residences.

Base 44 was assigned the daunting task of cleaning, remodeling, and equipping those buildings so that they could be used for hospital purposes. Freight trains bearing their supplies and equipment soon arrived, and the U.S. personnel went to work feverishly. The unit's history describes the scene: "Beds were set up in all available places; furniture was moved about and rearranged in a weird fashion; carpenters, electricians, plumbers, and painters ripped, tore, scraped, altered, and rebuilt the interiors of buildings, while details of detachment men and civilian employees scrubbed and cleaned. Laboratory, dental, eye, ear, nose and throat, and the X-ray departments were organized and rapidly put in condition for work."[13] The unit's nurses, including Miss Erb, arrived August 4, and a week later the unit received its first patients: 159 convalescents from the large U.S. hospital center at Mesves, about twenty miles away. The men were practically all ambulatory, and their chief cry was, "When do we eat?"[14]

Early in September, as the U.S. First Army prepared for attacks at St. Mihiel, Base 44 was ordered to enlarge its capacity from 1,200 to 1,750 beds. Cots were set up in attics, hallways, and sheds; beds were crowded into wards already considered full; mattresses were laid out on open floor spaces; and the unit's personnel were squeezed into attics and dugouts.

Six hundred patients were transferred to Pougues from the Mesves center in mid-September, and after the first phase of the U.S. Army's attack in the Meuse — Argonne commenced September 26, wounded men began arriving directly from the Front. The first long hospital train rolled in carrying 350 "sitters," who were walked to their quarters; the rest were "liers" on stretchers.

By the end of the first week in October, Pougues was full to overflowing, the daily census showing well over 1,700 patients. Many of the men were dangerously sick or wounded, and a number of deaths occurred. Every member of the unit was working overtime. Nurse Margaret Erb remembered the twelve- and fourteen-hour shifts at "the Splendid," as the Americans called the Hotel Splendide. "Even the bath house was needed to place these men," she recalled.

Seventy years later she remembered, too, a wounded lad who had been shot in the chest. "It was a nasty wound. It would show signs of healing, then break down and discharge. After some three weeks of dressing this, I probed rather deep and struck something I thought was not bone. I called one of our surgeons to have a look. After his probing and some surgery, we found the soldier's name tag. A fitting souvenir. It probably had saved his life."

Not far from Base 44 at Pougues-les-Eaux, in the scenic, rolling foothills of the Vosges Mountains, another grand old summer resort, Vittel, had earlier received its own contingent of U.S. medical personnel in November 1917. Base Hospital No. 36, originating at the Detroit College of Medicine, was the first of the larger units of 1,000 beds to be dispatched overseas, and the group made itself at home in five of the elegant old spa hotels built around the famed mineral springs of the Grand Source and the Source Salée, known and enjoyed in antiquity by the Romans. "We took over in the midst of winter," wrote the unit's organizer and director, Dr. Burt R. Shurley. "With meager supplies and under enormous difficulties we opened for the reception of 400 patients three weeks after our arrival."[15]

The unit's 100 nurses reached Vittel after a tedious, cheerless forty-hour trip from Le Havre on the infamous French railroad. "None of us will ever forget that long, cold journey through France," wrote Nurse Alice Evelyn Cooper. "We were given Army rations of bully beef and hard tack, beans, and coffee soaked in cognac, which was too stiff for us. . . . At one long stopover we got off the train and purchased a bottle of 'vin rouge' and carried it back to the train. The journey seemed interminable and we became stiff and cross, getting what sleep we could curled up on the seats. No lights were allowed, so the night seemed never-ending."[16] Nurse Eva Belle Babcock recalled being shipped by "40 and 8" railroad cars, "with just board seats in the compartments; no heat, no water, no toilets. The boys crammed into the cars ahead could relieve themselves out the doors, of course. But we just had to hold it till they made a stop. Then we all rushed for the bushes!"[17]

The nurses were cheered somewhat and took courage en route when told they would be stationed at the famous French summer resort. Eagerly climbing off the train at Vittel, one nurse "anchored her good vin rouge around her waist; in her hurry she missed the step and fell. The bottle, loosed from its moorings, clattered onto the platform and was smashed to pieces. This is recorded as the first tragedy in Vittel, Nov. 17, 1917."1[18]

After being marched through the dark streets to their quarters, Miss Babcock and her colleagues found their rooms

> cold and very damp . . . not equipped with stoves, nor fire places. . . . [There were] no bath tubs, so we were obliged to depend upon basins and small pitchers of "eau chaude," which our landladies were able to spare. Two of the nurses had purchased a collapsible rubber bath tub in New York; it was rather hard to manage, but proved popular. It had a way of syphoning itself off onto the floor after one got folded into it, which was most annoying. We squandered our substance on small kerosene stoves, paying fabulous prices for kerosene, as it was scarce. We could then cook a little.[19]

The unit spent three weeks of hard work sprucing up the resort's run-down buildings, but the hospitals were still not quite ready when the first trainload of patients arrived. "These men were not wounded, they were mostly cases of measles, trench foot, mumps and battle fatigue. But they were so excited to see American women," Miss Babcock recalled. "They just shouted, 'She speaks English,' and they grabbed us and kissed our hands. I told them, 'When you get to the elbow, you stop there!' " One of the first patients she tended was

> a lad dirty and muddy and lousy as a pet coon. We gave him a bath, got him all cleaned up and disinfected, washed and combed his hair, which was full of cooties [body lice]. But the next day, he was scratching again. So we gave him another bath and worked him over a second time. Next day his cooties were as thick as ever. Then I had a hunch. I went over and unbuttoned his shirt, which embarrassed him. But there around his neck was his rosary. I said, "Give me that rosary," and I took it and dropped it into a batch of hot soapy water. That water just turned black on top with all those lice. Every bead of that rosary was packed full of cooties![20]

In June 1918, the hospital received a trainload of wounded English soldiers fresh from the line between Soissons and Reims. In July, the first U.S. wounded were brought in. Over the summer the work increased, paralleling U.S. battle action, reaching its height late in September. At one time there were 10,000 patients at Vittel, and often the staff had more than it seemed possible to handle. "The nurses often worked 40 and 50 hours at a stretch, but I never heard them complain," the hospital historian wrote.[21]

Early in October, "our beds were filled to overflowing and as the casualties continued to pour in [probably U.S. wounded from the Meuse-Argonne offensive], we were obliged to line our corridors and halls with cots," wrote Col. Henry C. Berry, of Hospital D at Vittel. "In spite of the terrible suffering which these men were enduring, they maintained a brave front, and only by suppressed moans and facial expressions of pain could one appreciate their agony."[22]

Those last months before the Armistice of 1918 were filled with anguish for the doctors and nurses as well. Miss Babcock never forgot it. "When the trains came in full of wounded, we knew it was time to get into the harness and start pawing the air," she recalled.

> During the long hours, we couldn't stop to eat. Just grab a bite off the mess cart, or a cup of coffee. It was awful to see those poor kids strapped on a board with their backs broken, or an arm or both legs off. It was terribly trying on your nerves.
>
> I got so nervous, I couldn't relax when it was over. I couldn't sleep. They found me walking in the street wearing just my pajamas, saying I had to get back on duty. . . . That's when I wound up in the hospital myself. They gave me warm baths and some sedatives. About then, my father hadn't heard from me in a long time, so he wrote to Washington. They wrote back that I was in the hospital suffering from "shell shock" [see Appendix A].[23]

Frequently the U.S. Army had to build hospital space for itself in areas where there were no sturdy French buildings to convert to medical facilities. In such cases the AEF was quick to take over acreage close to a main thoroughfare or a railroad, where dozens of temporary wooden buildings and rows of tents were constructed to house the hospital units. "The hospital consists of many wooden barracks clustered around an old chateau, each building having 48 beds, up to a total of 1,400," wrote Capt. Bertram Bernheim, an Army doctor assigned to Base Hospital No. 18, which was built by the Army in Bazoilles-sur-Meuse, France, in the fall of 1917. "The staff is housed in a long barrack which is divided into little [semi-private] rooms, about eight feet by ten, by partitions that go two-thirds of the way to the ceiling. Each cubicle has a door and a window, and an electric light, a bed, kitchen table, and an iron wash-stand with the usual basins." But the nurses had no such accommodations, spare as they were. "The nurses are wonderful sports, fine women; [but] their lot is a sad one. They have beds side by side like the enlisted men, and their barracks are cold as can be, nights and early morning."[24] He observed further that the Army hadn't learned to treat nurses as well as the male officers are treated.

Dr. Bernheim continued, "We came over in summer, and until December the nurses had to wear white uniforms, no others having been provided. Many of them have chilblains [inflammation caused by exposure to cold], and never are there less than five, out of the 65, sick in the infirmary. Once 15 were ill, and one died of scarlet fever." He added, however, that "the country here [in the foothills of the Vosges Mountains] is beautiful, quite hilly and deeply wooded, but I have never known such a climate. It rains most of the time, clears up frequently during the day, only to cloud up again and pour."

Bazoilles-sur-Meuse, humorously referred to by the Americans as "Bacillus on Mush" or "Bazwillie Sure Moose," was a village of 412 souls. Eventually, the "U.S. city" of Bazoilles contained some 11,000 inhabitants, most of whom were patients in the seven hospitals built there. All of these medical units arrived between April and October 1918, along with engineers, quartermaster units, labor battalions, and a motor transport unit. A nurse in one of the Bazoilles hospitals recalled

> the panorama of wood-crowned hills, a river and three of the most noted roads in France. One road was tree-bordered, a silver line where trucks and motors passed up and down endlessly. The second was the railroad on which our boys went to the battlefields, singing, waving, and cheering; and on which they returned to us, silent, broken, but undaunted. The third road was the last road of all for the boys we left in France. It was a short road, ending in a plot at the foot of the hill where the sun's last light touched the white crosses "row on row."[25]

Base Hospital No. 49, organized at the University of Nebraska in Omaha, was stationed at another of these vast U.S. hospital centers, this one some 150 miles southeast of Paris, covering about eighty acres near the tiny French village of Allerey. Here the U.S. Army engineers had laid out a great medical camp, with special railroad tracks running through the heart of the installation. Ten hospital units and 20,000 beds were included in the plans.[26]

In July 1918, as U.S. divisions joined the great French counteroffensive against the Marne Salient, activity turned furious at Allerey. Various other hospital units were rushed in. Engineers, doctors, nurses, and hospital attendants worked night and day, setting in order all the appliances and instruments for modern hospital work.

The Nebraska unit, Base 49, arrived at Allerey in August and early September, just as the St. Mihiel drive got under way. Losses in that action were less than a quarter of the estimates. Later in the month, however, the Meuse-Argonne attack produced losses far greater than expected. The Allerey complex received more wounded men during the Argonne battle than any other U.S. hospitals: more than 40,000 casualties. Of these, 4,844 were cared for by the Nebraska unit. The highest number of patients under treatment at any one time was 1,934, an impressive record for a unit originally organized to provide beds for 1,000 patients.

During large-scale attacks and offensives, the base hospitals in the rear areas often were ordered to send surgical teams or emergency groups forward to the casualty clearing stations, which were advanced aid stations or field hospitals close to the lines. Here those teams provided extra hands to help care for the vast flow of casualties. The teams usually included a surgeon, an assistant surgeon, an anesthetist, two nurses, and several orderlies. More than 200 of those crews, modeled on teams already organized by the French, were dispatched to the forward medical areas, where they were desperately needed during the last seven months of the war.[27] Most nurses were eager for assignment to such emergency groups. They felt it was a chance to "get close to a great war; close enough to wear a gas mask; to see day break through a mist of smoke and in a din of conflict; and to admire the mettle of the American doughboy, his fortitude, his sympathy with the buddy whom he considered worse off than himself, his philosophic endurance and unfailing sense of humor," wrote nurse Edith Medhurst.[28]

In May 1918, Miss Medhurst got her chance. She was out picking daisies to decorate soldiers' graves at Vittel, some fifty miles behind the front lines, when she was called in and asked if she would go on special duty closer to the battle. She rushed to get ready and drove off in an ambulance with other members of the team. Their destination was an evacuation hospital—two brick school buildings and several tents—on the outskirts of Baccarat, a French city famous in peacetime for its beautiful cut crystal. The nurses soon learned that the reason for their emergency summons was a "severe attack during the night of gas shells mixed with high explosive—a new trick which had cost the Americans a good many lives."

Miss Medhurst described the situation:

I had a ward of 20 beds; seven of the men were on oxygen the first day, administered for 20 minutes of each alternate hour; each man had at least one alkaline bed bath per day, and none were allowed to do a thing for themselves, even though they felt equal to do so. . . . The water supply around the hospital was badly polluted, so very little was used, and this not until the top sergeant had emptied a whole tube of Chlorine into each small bucket. It was no use; you might call it "coffee" for breakfast, or "tea" for supper, but it was just plain Chlorine to the taste.[29]

Miss Medhurst was happy to get back to the relative civilization behind the lines at Vittel.

In early July 1918, another Base 36 nurse, Ethel Lickley, was part of a team sent to Coulommiers, near Chateau Thierry. Hospital facilities were located in an old chateau surrounded by tents. She wrote: "We were working all the time, night and day, for two weeks, helping to take care of that endless line of wounded which was constantly pouring in. Some days . . . we worked as fast as possible, and still were not able to care for some of the men before they died."[30]

Another team, one of three organized by Base Hospital No. 46, was sent early in July 1918 to Field Hospital No. 12 of the Army's First Division. One of those nurses reported, "The sight that greeted us, none will ever forget. About 1,500 wounded men on stretchers all about the grounds in the shade of the immense chateau, and surgical teams working in 24-hour shifts. Only the men severely wounded were treated at this hospital, the remainder being transferred back, eventually to the base hospitals. We had Americans, French, British and a considerable number of Boche pass through our hospital each day."[31]

In September, a crew of extra nurses, Emergency Group E, arrived in the Verdun area, where the final offensive of the war was raging. Nurse Elizabeth Campbell Bickford remembered that the rain was "cold and continuous, the mud like glue. . . . Our destination was Evacuation Hospital 11, where hundreds of seriously wounded men lay on the wet ground, waiting their turn for attention." Nurse Bickford was assigned to surgery, where she was astonished to find

a spectacle, never pictured in my wildest dreams . . . a long, dirty looking room with seven surgical tables, each occupied by a seriously wounded man, with seven surgical teams working feverishly. On a heavy night, three hundred or more wounded would be brought to us. . . . Fortunately, in all the mud and filth, there always seemed to be large packing cases of neatly folded gauze squares, large sponges and pads and other surgical dressings which had been put together with loving care by the women back home.[32]

The first phase of the Meuse-Argonne offensive ended October 1, when a blessed quiet settled over the sector. But the battle began again three days later and continued, in all its horror, for yet another month.

Meanwhile, as hundreds of U.S. Army nurses were working frantically among the sick and wounded in Europe, another thousand or more Red Cross nurses, fully trained and eager for duty overseas, were not permitted to sail for France. Because of their color—they were black—they were ignored or refused the chance to serve by the Army Medical Department.

With pompous officialism, the department reported the deplorable story of the black nurses in its 1927 history of service in the Great War: "Before the World War, no colored nurses had ever served in the Army Nurse Corps. Many of them, however, were anxious to join the corps and were . . . offering their services, as early as December 1917." These nurses were permitted to enroll with the Red Cross, but "the question of separate quarters for them was the greatest problem in connection with their appointment" to the ANC. "However, in July, 1918, tentative plans were made to send colored nurses in groups of 20 to several posts [in the United States] which had large numbers of colored troops . . . [but] delays in the provision of separate quarters and mess for these women resulted in their not being assigned to duty until after the signing of the Armistice, when Camp Sherman, Ohio, and Camp Grant, Illinois, were each supplied with nine colored nurses."[33]

One of the group who went to Camp Sherman was Aileen Bertha Cole, a 1917 graduate of the nurse training program at Freedman's Hospital, Washington, DC. "Our class was the first in which each member was already a high school graduate," she recalled proudly. "The Red Cross recruited us before we graduated, and we were hoping for overseas assignment. We wanted very, very much to go 'over there.' President Wilson had told us this war was to make the world safe for democracy, and we were patriotic and we were all fired up. We were eager to go."[34] But the black women—it is estimated that some 1,800 black nurses were certified by the Red Cross for duty with the military—were not called up by the Army.

In August 1918, Army surgeon general William C. Gorgas issued a public plea for at least 1,000 nurses to enroll each week for the next two months for immediate assignment to duty. But the black nurses still were not called up. Two months later, another fervent request for more nurses came, this time from the Red Cross: "The Army needs at least 8,000 additional trained nurses between now and January 1st. . . . The present needs are so great that the surgeon general of the army has called for 1,500 to be sent overseas immediately."[35]

Still the hundreds of black nurses continued to cool their heels in the United States. The Red Cross later rationalized that they "had no control over the black nurses' assignments to hospitals, which meant that unless a 'colored cantonment' had need for them, their services were often not utilized. . . . The Red Cross encouraged all races to give service," said Henry P. Davison, chairman of the American Red Cross War Council during the Great War. "We can show you in the Red Cross as fine a collection of Baptists, Methodists, colored people and every other kind of people as there is on the face of the earth." However, the military units were segregated, he explained, and the racial composition of volunteer services at the Red Cross chapter level reflected the prevailing attitudes of the community.[36]

The situation changed, however, when the flu epidemic of 1918–1919 swept around the world and medical help was even more scarce, the need more desperate. As Miss Cole remembered, "The Red Cross finally asked us to help during the flu epidemic in 1918. People were dying everywhere. Some of us were asked to go to West Virginia to work among the coal miners, where the epidemic was very serious. We were told, 'We've got to save the miners' lives to keep the transports moving. If we keep the transports moving, we can keep our boys crossing over. The outcome of the war depends on them, and on you Red Cross nurses.' "[37]

Miss Cole was stationed in two little West Virginia towns, visiting the miners' homes with a Red Cross physician, taking temperatures and dispensing aspirin and a cough mixture. "About the only medicine we had was whiskey," she recalled. She was still working in West Virginia when the war ended, and she was urged to stay on at the mines. "But I turned it down," she said. "We had learned that there were vacancies in the Army Nurse Corps and we had waited a long time to get in."

Shortly after the Armistice, November 11, 1918, Miss Cole received the long-awaited letter: "The Surgeon General has called on a limited number of colored nurses, enrolled in the Red Cross, to be available for service about December 1." On November 22, she was assigned "to active service in the military establishment," one of eighteen black nurses, a history-making contingent, the first black women to serve in the Army Nurse Corps. None of the black nurses was ever sent overseas, and none ever received any benefits or pension from the Army because they were sworn into service after the Armistice.[38]

As the war rolled to an end in November 1918, the white nurses overseas continued to work at full capacity and beyond. A few broke under the strain, and others seemed to perform automatically, snatching rest when exhaustion overcame them, Elizabeth Bickford recalled. She always believed that the Armistice came just in time for her worn-out group of emergency nurses in the Meuse-Argonne evacuation hospital. Later they were reviewed by the commander of the AEF, Gen. John J. Pershing, and "we were granted the privilege of wearing a little bronze star on our service ribbon, to show that we had served in an offensive sector."[39]

In the French spa town of Pougues-les-Eaux, where Base Hospital No. 44 was in residence, news of the Armistice caused a mighty celebration. "It was wonderful, but it was tragic," recalled Army nurse Margaret Erb. "The village folk—old men and women, young people and children, the widows—they all paraded on the main street, the Rue Nationale. There were no young men left to parade. It was a pathetic little parade. My heart ached for them. Those of us who saw it were saddened and we wept, knowing many fathers, husbands and young men would not likely return to their homes."[40]

Nurse Laura Frost, on duty with Evacuation Hospital No. 5 in Belgium, remembered the first week in November, when "we began to hear rumors that an armistice was being planned. We didn't believe it, for we still heard the guns, and the wounded were still coming in. Finally one day, the 11th of November, there was a sudden silence about 11 o'clock in the morning. We wondered what was different. It was the silence. There wasn't a sound. We heard the good news, but we were too busy for any hilarity."[41]

In time, Miss Frost and her friends seized upon the peace and quiet to do some sight-seeing while they waited to be relieved and sent home. They visited the canal city of Bruges and the ruined medieval town of Ypres, some twenty miles away. "The devastation was unbelievable. Houses just a pile of rubble, dead cows in the fields, bloated bodies of horses along the muddy roads where big rats were scurrying out of the way," she recalled. Many of the nurses toured Paris, "once without leave," Miss Frost remembered with a grin. "We got away with it because, one M.P. told us, there was no jail available for us [women]." Another time they overstayed their leave one night and paid "nearly a month's wages" for tickets to a performance of Aida at the Paris Opera. The nurses felt it was "well worth the bawling out we received when we returned late to camp."

Finally, they headed home. Arriving in New York Harbor "was an unforgettable event. Tug boats and fire boats came out to meet us and in my exuberance, I flung my blue straw hat right at the Statue of Liberty," Miss Frost recalled. "Bands were playing and toilet paper was strung all over the ship like confetti on a happy cruise ship."

Nurse Eva Belle Babcock brought home a most unusual souvenir from her wartime experience—a spiritual presence that remained with her for the rest of her long life. "I hear from Kramer every October," she explained.

In spirit only, of course. He comes to me just as strong as if he had actually written me a letter. . . . He was a sergeant, head of a platoon of soldiers advancing toward the Front, when he stepped on a mine. He was blinded and dreadfully cut up on his body. He kept saying as soon as he got his bandages off, he wanted to see what his nurse looked like. I babied him a lot because I knew he wasn't going to make it. He questioned me, asking if I thought he was going to die. I told him, "My dear, that's a question nobody can answer. Able-bodied as I am, who knows if I'll be here tomorrow morning. When one of those German planes goes over, we might all go together."[42]

A nurse who came home from France with high honors was Julia Stimson, who had gone overseas as head nurse with Base Hospital No. 21. In April 1918 she was named to head all Red Cross nurses in France. After the Armistice, in December 1918, Miss Stimson also became director of nursing service of the AEF, in charge of the Army Nurse Corps. She received the Distinguished Service Medal from General Pershing on June 5, 1919.

Ordered back to the United States in July, she was appointed acting superintendent of the ANC (later becoming full superintendent) and dean of the Army School of Nursing. When Congress amended the National Defense Act in 1920, authorizing relative rank from second lieutenant through major to Army nurses, Julia Stimson became the first woman to earn the rank of major. Although the Act allowed Army nurses to wear the insignia of relative rank, the secretary of war did not prescribe full rights and privileges, such as base pay, for nurses until nearly twenty-five years later.[43]

When the Great War ended, Jane Delano, the stalwart of the Red Cross, could look back on her almost superhuman efforts, which included the registration of 18,989 graduate nurses for Army, Navy, and Red Cross service during the war. By 1919, she felt that she could finally relax a little from her duties. She wanted to visit the battlefields and have a look at various Red Cross activities, and she planned to attend an international health conference in Cannes, France. Before the trip, she admitted that she was very tired, and her photographs showed signs of excessive strain and fatigue. But she sailed for France in the spring of 1919. Her tour ended abruptly in a military hospital at the huge Army medical center at Savenay. "Poor old Miss Delano," wrote nurse Elizabeth Ashe, "has had a mastoid operation and I fear there is little hope for her. She has been ill ever since her arrival." Miss Delano died April 15, at the age of fifty-seven, and was buried at Loire, France, with full military honors. Her government awarded her the Distinguished Service Medal posthumously. Later, her body was brought home and re-interred in the nurses' plot in Arlington National Cemetery.[44]

Miss Delano probably died of complications from the pandemic of Spanish influenza believed to have originated in the United States in late August 1918. The deadly virus raced around the world with the speed of a prairie fire. Military camps at home and overseas were particularly hard hit, and the Medical Corps was severely taxed to provide care for the stricken. Although remedies, elixirs, and nostrums abounded, effective medications were few. Nurse Margaret Erb recalled treating the sick with hot sponge baths and aspirin. "That was all we had," she said. "And you felt so helpless. You had to stand there and watch them slipping, slipping away. All you could do was pray for them."

The public was ordered to wear gauze face masks to avoid inhaling or spreading flu germs, and there were laws against public coughing, sneezing, and spitting. Churches, theaters, libraries, and other public gathering places were closed in an effort to prevent the spread of the disease. Eventually the medical world concluded that nothing much could be done for the flu victims except to keep them isolated, warm, fed, rested, and protected against the deadly complications, particularly pneumonia, that might arise.

The dreadful epidemic finally seemed to wear itself out by the spring of 1919, but not before it had killed twenty-one million people around the world, including more than 500,000 Americans, ten times the 53,513 who died in the battle in France. Of the 102 Army nurses who died overseas and the 134 nurses who died in the United States from April 1917 to November 1918, most were victims of the flu and pneumonia.[45]

A particularly poignant casualty of the flu was Nellie Dingley, an Army nurse who had been a small-town librarian in Kent, OH. Enlisting in 1918, she was thrilled to be assigned to the Army's First Mobile Operating Unit, which was sent to France in July "to work close-up to the fighting lines, caring for cases that without prompt attention would greatly increase the death list."[46]

Before she sailed, Miss Dingley marched with other Red Cross nurses in the huge wartime Fourth of July parade in New York City, the last time she was seen by friends in the United States. A couple of weeks after her arrival overseas, Miss Dingley wrote home to a friend in Ohio:

> Regardless of anything else that has been or shall come into my life—my work here in France will ever remain the pot of gold at the end of the rainbow for me. There is a touch of the divine in the manner in which these American boys face everything—wounds, sickness and death—they die smiling. It seems so small a thing for a woman to do—all she can do—and she should do that nobly—stand by them in their last great hour.

If war has done one thing well, it has been the bringing out of qualities that have lain dormant in the race for years, and this is no small matter. I shall return to old Ohio with a greater love and a finer feeling for the state and country. . . . Somehow you get the feeling that death is not such a terrible thing over here. To lie in death facing the stars in France is almost a privilege, especially in a cause so noble, and there are lads like yourself to whom life has not been gentle. They face death gladly—and why should not I, to whom life has given so much.

Was it a premonition that prompted Miss Dingley's comments? Within the month, Nellie Dingley contracted a bad cold that became pneumonia. She was sick only nine days and died August 28 at age thirty-seven. She was buried with military honors in the U.S. cemetery at Suresnes, France, not far from Paris. Miss Dingley is remembered today by a plaque, shaded by a maple tree, on the lawn of the Kent Free Library, in Kent, OH, where she served as its first librarian.

Nearly half of the overseas deaths of U.S. nurses probably were due to complications of influenza but were listed as pneumonia, according to Army statistics. Twenty deaths were attributed to meningitis, four to influenza, and two to unspecified "disease."[47] But overall, the casualty rate for the Army's nurses was amazingly low, considering the conditions of much of their service overseas: cold, damp, crowded barracks, irregular meals and poor food, long hours of overwork, and little rest and recreation. The first to die were two nurses with Base Hospital No. 12 from Chicago. Edith Ayers and Helen B. Wood were killed by brass fragments from the faulty discharge of a gun aboard the *USS Mongolia* en route to France in May 1917, shortly after the United States entered the war.[48]

Only two Army nurses were seriously wounded on duty in France. The first was Beatrice Mary MacDonald, a member of Base Hospital No. 2 from Presbyterian Hospital, New York City. She had been sent forward late in July 1917 as a member of a surgical team to a British casualty clearing station near St. Sixte's Convent in Belgium. There she worked with Helen Grace McClelland, who was on duty with a U.S. team from Base Hospital No. 10, a Philadelphia unit. When Miss MacDonald was hit in the face by shrapnel, Helen McClelland rushed to her friend's assistance and stopped the hemorrhage from severe wounds in the eye and cheek. According to reports, Miss McClelland worked swiftly and efficiently, disregarding the danger to herself from the bombardment by German airplanes. The wounded nurse lost the sight of one eye and was evacuated to the AEF ophthalmic center at Boulogne, France. Later she was returned to duty and remained with her unit until two months after the

Armistice in November 1918. Both nurses were awarded the Distinguished Service Cross for extraordinary heroism.

The second Army nurse wounded by enemy action, Isabelle Stambaugh, was also a member of Base Hospital No. 10 from Philadelphia. She was sent to a forward casualty clearing station near Peronne, France, during the great German drive of the spring of 1918 and arrived when the location was under heavy air attack. The clearing station team retreated to Amiens but found no respite there. Despite the bombardment, team members tried to go about their duties, ministering to the wounded and operating on the emergency cases. In the midst of her work in the operating room, Miss Stambaugh was struck down with a deep shrapnel wound in the leg. She was evacuated but returned to duty later in July. She, too, was awarded a Distinguished Service Cross.[49]

In addition to the three Distinguished Service Crosses conferred on Army nurses, this decoration also was awarded to a Red Cross nurse, Jane Jeffery of American Red Cross Hospital No. 107. While on night duty at Jouy-sur-Morin, July 15, 1918, Miss Jeffery was struck by shell fragments of an airplane bomb and was severely wounded. According to her citation, "she showed utter disregard for her own safety by refusing to leave her post, though suffering great pain from her wounds."

A Distinguished Service Medal was awarded to Edna M. Coughlin, another member of a surgical team and one of twenty-four nurses to receive this high award. In addition, the Allies awarded many decorations to U.S. nurses, both those singled out by the War Department and those recognized for meritorious service in the advanced zones. The British honored about 90 nurses, and the French decorated more than 100 of those in the AEF. Romania, Belgium, Greece, and Russia also decorated a few nurses, and there were a great number of base hospital and division citations for nurses, both from the Allies and from U.S. commanders.

No nurses were killed by enemy action. One nurse died in an airplane accident (and all nurses were thereafter forbidden to joyride with the daring aviators). Another nurse was run over by a train, one was thrown from a horse and fatally injured, and a number were killed in automobile accidents.[50]

One nurse reported she was saved from possible death, or at least a painful wound, by the heavy corset she was wearing. "German planes occasionally flew low over us [probably mapping the area]. We would wave and the pilot would wave back and shout greetings to us," said Mildred Brown, who served with Evacuation Hospital No. 7 in 1917–1918. "This one time, he turned and came back and shelled us. I was hit in the backside by a piece of shrapnel, and it bounced off a stave in my corset. I picked up the bit of metal, still hot. It broke the skin, but nothing serious. A soldier asked why I was crying, and I told him I'd been hit. He asked where. I answered, 'On Verdun Hill.' That was really funny, since I was actually hit on the 'derriere.' "[51]

A bizarre accident claimed the life of a sightseeing U.S. nurse several weeks after the Armistice. "We were allowed to go to see the battlefields where our men had fought so bravely for four years," wrote nurse Leila Hamerton (later Williams) in her memoirs. "Everyone had been warned not to pick up any shell cases, old hand grenades or other weapons lying about. One day an ambulance-load of nurses was taken to the Verdun sector to see the trenches, and one of the girls picked up an empty shell case. As they examined it on the way back to camp, the thing exploded, setting fire to everything. Five nurses were badly burned, and one died. I shall never forget that graveside service. A doughboy sang, 'The Rose of No Man's Land.' "[52]

The Rose of No Man's Land

There's a rose that grows on No Man's Land
And it's wonderful to see,
Though it's sprayed with tears, it will live for years,
In my garden of memory.
It's the one red rose the soldier knows,
It's the work of the Master's hand;
'Mid the war's great curse stands the Red Cross Nurse,
She's the rose of No Man's Land.

Notes

1.   This chapter recounts the history of Army nurses in great detail; there is, however, no corresponding history of Navy nurses. It was not my intention to overlook the contributions of women who served in the United States Navy Nurse Corps, but historical research on this organization is sadly lacking. What is known is that Congress established the Navy Nurse Corps on May 13, 1908, with Esther Voorhees Hasson as superintendent. The first small group of Navy nurses is fondly called "the Sacred Twenty."

When World War I broke out in 1914, the Navy had no hospitals in Europe, but two of their nurses, J. Beatrice Bowman, one of the Sacred Twenty, and Katrina T. Hertzer, were released from Navy service temporarily to sail overseas in September 1914 with medical relief units on an American Red Cross mercy ship. These units were withdrawn due to lack of funds in 1915.

A U.S. Naval Reserve force was created in 1916, with a provision for reserve nurses. When the United States entered the war in April 1917, there were 160 Navy nurses, and by July 1918, their number had increased to 1,082, reaching a total of 1,476 by Armistice Day in November 1918. Navy nurses wore an outdoor uniform described as "Navy blue Norfolk suit, Kitchener pockets, tan gloves, black shoes or tan boots, and a sailor hat." For nurses going overseas, the Red Cross provided complete equipment, including such interesting items as sleeping bags, ponchos, black tights, heavy wool underwear, long-sleeve knit corset covers, and a small U.S. flag.

When the United States entered the European war in April 1917, Naval base hospital units (similar to Army organizations) were established at several civilian hospitals in the United States. Units, consisting of fourteen officers, forty nurses, and about 100 enlisted men, were recruited as a group. These units were sent to Brest, France; Strathpeffer, Scotland; Leith, Scotland; Queenstown, Ireland; London, England; and L'Orient, France. Some Navy nurses were loaned to Army field units and served with operating teams near the Front in France, as well.

Other Navy nurses served on various troop transports, where they received excellent reports on their services at sea. Their performance had a distinct influence in the later acceptance and assignment of nurses to regular duty on Navy hospital ships. Three hundred and twenty-seven nurses served overseas and on transports during 1917–1919. Most Navy nurses, however, were deployed in five foreign stations—the Philippines, Guam, Samoa, Haiti, and the Virgin Islands—and in twenty-five mainland hospitals in eighteen states and the District of Columbia.

The first Navy nurse to die in the service was Nellie M. Sherzinger of Columbus, OH, who was serving at a training school for native women on Guam. Miss Sherzinger was interred with full military honors on Guam, August 29, 1916. During the war, thirty-six Navy nurses died. Twenty-five succumbed to illness contracted in the line of duty, mainly during the influenza epidemic of 1918. Three of these women were posthumously awarded the Navy Cross "for distinguished service and devotion to duty" during the epidemic. Following the war, Lenah Sutcliffe Higbee, the second superintendent of the Navy Nurse Corps and one of the Sacred Twenty, also was awarded the Navy Cross, the only woman to have been so decorated during her lifetime. Six other Navy nurses received citations from the Army and Navy.

I am indebted to the following sources for information on Navy nurses: Dermott Vincent Hickey, "The First Ladies in the Navy: A History of the Navy Nurse Corps, 1908–1939" (master's thesis, George Washington University, 1963); "The Navy Nurse Corps: A Pictorial Review," U.S. Navy Medical Newsletter 55 (May 1970): 6–7; and J. Beatrice Bowman, "History of Nursing in the Navy," The American Journal of Nursing 28, no. 9 (September 1928): 1–7.

2. Elizabeth Campbell Bickford, Army Nurse Corps, Medical Department, Eleventh Evacuation Hospital, unpublished memoir, World War I Survey Collection, Archives of the U.S. Army Military History Institute, Carlisle Barracks, PA.

3. Julia C. Stimson, Finding Themselves: The Letters of an American Army Chief Nurse in a British Hospital in France (New York: Macmillan, 1919), 122.

4. Details on the history of hospital units and the Army Nurse Corps are taken from Col. Robert V. Piemonte, ANC, USAR, and Maj. Cindy Gurney, ANC, eds., Highlights in the History of the Army Nurse Corps (Washington, DC: U.S. Army Center of Military History, 1987); Portia Kernodle, The Red Cross Nurse in Action (New York: Harper, 1949); The Past Was Valorous, pamphlet printed by the American Red Cross Nursing Services, A.R.C. 1640–A (February 1949); and from the histories of various U.S. base hospital units.

5. Author interview with Irma Tuell Lynn, Seattle, WA, 1987.

6. Stimson, 42; subsequent quotes from Stimson are from pp. 48–226.

7. Ibid., 226.

8. Brederick A. Pottle, Stretchers: The Story of a Hospital Unit on the Western Front (New Haven, CT: Yale University Press, 1929), 141.

9. Ibid., 101–102.

10. The following quotations are from Laura G. Frost Smith's unpublished memoirs, letters to family, and author interviews since 1988.

11. Information about Nurse Erb is from author correspondence and telephone interviews with Margaret C. Erb Schreiter, Kitchener, Ontario, Canada, 1987–1988.

12. Frederick M. Dearborn, ed., "The Battle of Pougues-les-Eaux," in American Homeopathy in the World War (New York: Globe Press, 1923), 43.

13. Ibid., 69.

14. Dearborn, 69.

15. A History of United States Army Base Hospital No. 36, organized by the Detroit College of Medicine and Surgery in April 1917 (n.p., n.d.), 9.

16. Ibid., 142.

17. Author telephone interviews with Eva Belle Babcock Austin, Buena Park, CA, 1988.

18. History of Base Hospital 36, 142.

19. Ibid.

20. Austin interviews.

21. History of Base Hospital 36, 135.

22. Ibid., 107.

23. Austin interviews.

24. Capt. Bertram M. Bernheim, MCUSA, Passed as Censored (Philadelphia: J. B. Lippincott, 1918). Confirming Dr. Bernheim's opinion is the finding of the Committee of Nursing of the U.S. Council of National Defense, which recognized as early as October 1917 that Army nurses were limited in their effectiveness by the lack of military rank. Bestowing official military status on nurses, the committee believed, would dignify the nursing profession and place military nurses alongside military men, not behind them.

    As Jo-Anne Mecca stated in "World War I Army Nurses: Our Forgotten Healers," a fall 1994 article in Women on Campus, the newsletter of the Jersey City State College Women's Center and Women's Studies Program:

    > U.S. Military authorities never doubted the propriety of permitting nurses to endure combat conditions and related dangers. Nor did they doubt the importance of the services that these women provided. What was in doubt was the recognition—through rank—and the compensation they deserved.
    >
    > When nurses began returning from the war early in 1919, the battle for rank became heated. The Army Reorganization Act of 1920 contained a section relating to the rank of nurses. It provided military and social rights and privileges, including the right to wear the insignia of commissioned rank. But it did not provide the same pay scale as that of male officers. It took 27 years, until 1947, for

military nurses finally to achieve regular commissions in the U.S. Army and with them the acknowledgment, long overdue, of their professionalism and entitlements.

25. On Active Service With Base Hospital 46, U.S.A. (Portland, OR.: n.p., n.d.), 152.

26. Reba Benschoter, "Base Hospital 49" (1919), Nebraska History and Record of Pioneer Days (1980): 152. Archives of the University of Nebraska Medical Center, Omaha.

27. The Medical Department of the United States Army in the World War, vol. 8, Field Operations (Washington, DC: Government Printing Office, 1925), 201–204.

28. History of Base Hospital 36, 155–156.

29. Ibid., 154.

30. Ibid., 134.

31. On Active Service With Base Hospital 46, U.S.A., 101.

32. Bickford memoir.

33. Julia C. Stimson, ANC, The Medical Department of the United States Army in the World War, vol. 13, part 2, The Army Nurse Corps (Washington, DC: Government Printing Office, 1927), 292.

34. Author interviews with Aileen Cole Stewart, Seattle, WA, 1987.

35. Kernodle, also a 1918 American Red Cross Department of Nursing pamphlet, 56.

36. Patrick F. Gilbo, The American Red Cross: The First Century (New York: Harper and Row, 1981), 68.

37. Stewart interviews.

38. Ibid.

39. Bickford memoir.

40. Schreiter interviews.

41. Frost memoirs, 9.

42. Austin interviews.

43. Piemonte and Gurney, 17.

44. Kernodle, 181–182.

45. Elizabeth A. Shields, ed., Highlights in the History of the Army Nurse Corps (Washington, DC: U.S. Army Center of Military History, 1981), 9. See also statistics in Chapter 10.

46. Information on Nellie Dingley was obtained through the kind cooperation of her family in Painesville, OH, and the staff of the Kent Free Library, Kent, OH, who sent information about this nurse.

47. Army Nurses Who Died Overseas, Women's Overseas Service League survey, May 1922, Liberty Memorial Museum, Kansas City, MO.

48. Piemonte and Gurney, 8.

49. " Daughters of Valor," American Legion Magazine (May 1939): 49–52.

50. Stimson, Medical Department, 350–351.

51. Letter from Mildred Brown Byers to Lettie Gavin, December 24, 1984.

52. Leila Hamerton Williams, Memoirs of the First World War (privately published, 1966), 23.

The staff of Base Hospital No. 20, University of Pennsylvania, Philadelphia, prepares to sail for France. Three of the nurses demonstrate their "safety suits," to be donned in case of submarine attack on their convoy en route. Special funds had been raised by the public to purchase these clumsy lifesavers, which cost $60 each and had "everything in them but hot and cold running water," as one observer reported. (Courtesy of University of Pennsylvania Archives)

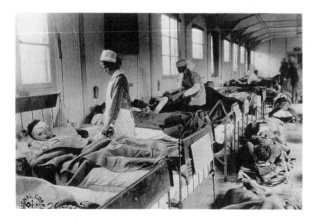

Nurses often worked to the point of exhaustion in crowded hospital wards like this one at Evacuation Hospital No. 114, Fleury-sur-Aire, France. Notice wounded lying on litters on the floor, awaiting bed space. Because the large hospitals were usually miles behind the firing line, the wounded often had to wait for many hours, sometimes days, until the overworked staff could get to them. (U.S. Army Military History Institute, Carlisle, PA)

Scene from the compound fracture ward at Base Hospital No. 50, Mesves-Bulcy Hospital Center in France. Many of the beds are fitted with elaborate frameworks of wood ("Balkan frames") that kept broken limbs under constant tension while they healed. Note hanging bottles and tubes of Dakin's solution, used to irrigate wounds. (Lettie Gavin collection)

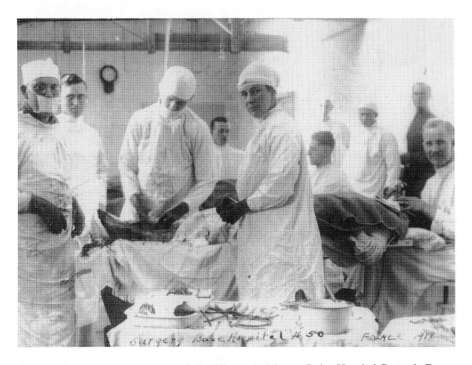

A surgical team operates on a wounded soldier at the Mesves-Bulcy Hospital Center in France, 1918. Base hospital operating rooms usually contained three or more tables, which were often busy night and day during the last few months of the war. The team members pictured here are part of Base Hospital No. 50, University of Washington, Seattle. (Lettie Gavin collection)

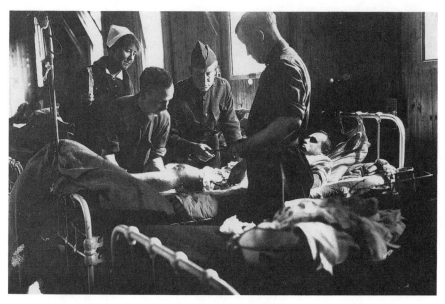

Dressing a soldier's wounds is this team of doctors, corpsmen, and a nurse of Base Hospital No. 18, Johns Hopkins Unit, in Bazoilles, France, May 1918. It was said that few soldiers could have afforded the care at home that they received from the corps of enlisted specialists in the Army Medical Department. The medical crews often worked under primitive conditions, but their wounded recovered in surprising numbers, and relatively few died in the process. (National Archives photo no. 111–JC–11889)

Overall view of the Mesves-Bulcy Hospital Center, France, where several base hospital units were stationed in 1917–1918. The Army built thousands of these temporary wood and French brick barracks to house U.S. hospital units, usually far behind the lines, where they could not be damaged or destroyed by air raids or moving battle lines. The occupants, both staff and wounded, suffered a great deal from the French weather—cold, rain, and mud. (Lettie Gavin collection)

Keeping clean was a constant problem for nurses. There was never enough time and never enough water for baths, laundry, or shampoos in the battle areas. These nurses, members of Evacuation Hospital No. 5, scrape the mud off their shoes before entering their dormitory tent. Nurse Laura Frost, right, went overseas with Base Hospital No. 44 from Boston, MA, but was transferred on arrival in France to the evacuation hospital unit, which lived in tents and moved by truck. (Lettie Gavin collection)

Nurse Eva Eger was the envy of her colleagues because she had had the foresight to bring along a washboard to do her laundry. The nurses were serving in Evacuation Hospital No. 11, situated in 1918 on the border of the Meuse-Argonne battle area. One nurse, Elizabeth Campbell Bickford, wrote later that their chief nurse was the only one who had an extra uniform, "which we took turns wearing, while we washed our own in the one-half pail of water we were allotted." (U.S. Army Military History Institute, Carlisle, PA)

After the Armistice was declared in November 1918, thousands of troops and medical personnel had only one thought in mind, as voiced in a popular song of the day: "I Wanna Go Home." But for many, it would be a long wait before transport was available to take every American back to the United States. Pictured here is Nurse Annette Munro with some of her happy convalescents at Gievres Hospital Center, the last to be evacuated in 1919. (U.S. Army Military History Institute, Carlisle, PA)

More than 1,000 black nurses were trained, registered with the Red Cross, and eager for overseas service during the war years, but the Army refused to send them to France because "separate but equal" accommodations could not be provided. Meanwhile, some served on home soil with the Red Cross during the flu epidemic, and after the Armistice, eighteen were sworn into Army service. This group was assigned to Camp Sherman, OH. (Lettie Gavin collection, donated by Aileen Cole Stewart, front row, left)

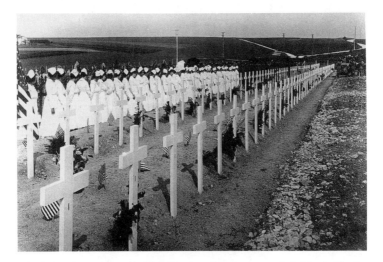

Many Army nurses remained in Europe after the war ended, interred in the huge U.S. collection cemeteries built by the American Battle Monuments Commission. These nurses attend the funeral of one of their own in one of the new burial grounds. No nurses were killed by enemy action, but more than 100 died of other causes, especially during the great influenza epidemic of 1918–1919. (Lettie Gavin collection)

Julia Catherine Stimson, director of nursing service for the AEF, is pictured at her desk in Paris, France, 1919. Miss Stimson went overseas in 1917 as chief nurse with Base Hospital No. 21 and eventually became superintendent of the Army Nurse Corps. General Pershing personally presented her the Distinguished Service Medal for her work during the war years. (U.S. Army Military History Institute, Carlisle, PA)

= 4 =
The Hello Girls of the Army Signal Corps

Soon after he arrived in France with his American troops in April 1917, Gen. John J. Pershing concluded that he could not fight the Imperial German Army while he was battling the atrocious French telephone system. That system, never very efficient, had suffered during the three years of conflict and was incapable of meeting the vast wartime demands placed upon it. The problem was humorously stated in a popular doughboy lyric of the time: "If you want to get hold of a friend to talk, the phones are there, but it's quicker to walk!" Pershing quickly realized that he would need an entirely new communications network, plus highly skilled people to operate the system.

As Col. Parker Hitt, chief signal officer of the U.S. First Army later noted, "Since the early days of the American Expeditionary Forces, it had always been the contention . . . that an Army telephone central would have to have American women operators to be a success. Our experience in Paris with the untrained and undisciplined English-speaking French women operators, and experience elsewhere with the willing but untrained men operators was almost disastrous.[1] Thus, in November 1917 Pershing asked that the War Department send him 100 French-speaking U.S. telephone operators. Because telephone operators at the time were exclusively female, this meant that Pershing was asking for women to operate the Army switchboards. These women would not be armed or assigned to combat, he specified, but "the women who go into the service will do as much to help win the war as the men in khaki."

This was not the first time the commander-in-chief had asked for American women to be sent to France. He had observed early on the splendid contributions made by British women in the war zone, and he was also aware that thousands of U.S. women already were overseas with the various volunteer service organizations. In addition, he had previously requested the services of other U.S. women, especially those with clerical skills, so that male office workers could be moved to duty at the Front.

Pershing was not the only member of the military to see the need for qualified female help. The surgeon general wanted women doctors, and the Quartermaster Corps, Ordnance, Central Records Office, and Central Post Office all would have greatly benefitted from the assistance of skilled women.[2] (The latter two departments did, in fact, employ hundreds of British WAACs—members of the Women's Auxiliary Army Corps—at their headquarters in Bourges, France.) The War Department, however, seems to have strongly resisted the formation of a women's corps. Even though enabling legislation had been introduced in Congress earlier, it was never passed.[3] Such legislation, however, might have become a necessity if the war had continued into 1919.

By the end of 1917, Pershing's request could no longer be denied. Nor could the stipulation for bilingual recruits. This requirement was no idle whim: these women would function not only as operators, but also as interpreters—often on vital military matters, where a mistake might mean irreparable loss.[4]

The War Department immediately began recruiting the necessary personnel. 1st Lt. Ernest J. Wessen of the civilian personnel section of the Signal Corps was given charge of the proposed unit of telephone operators. True to his reputation as a man of action, he quickly gathered the needed women. But his methods remained open to question for many years to come.

The official authorization creating the telephone units undoubtedly intended the women to be civilian employees of the Army, but the evidence is overwhelming that, in fact, the women were not told that they were being hired as civilian employees. Indeed, they believed that they were enlisting as bona fide members of the military establishment. The resulting confusion was not addressed at the time, but it led to a long-smoldering battle between the Army and its female telephone operators, a struggle that continued for some sixty years.

The U.S. Division of Woman's War Work, Committee on Public Information, reported that at first an effort was made to fill the quota of telephone operators with women of French descent from Canada and Louisiana. But from more than 300 of those applicants, the committee selected only six, probably because few of the volunteers could meet both the language and technical telephone requirements. Next came a national newspaper announcement requesting female telephone operators, and more than 2,400 applications were received. From those, the Signal Corps chose its first female personnel.

By the spring of 1918, more than 7,600 applications were in hand. One hundred fifty of those chosen were assigned to training schools, and a reserve force of 400 was listed "on call" for possible future training. When the war ended in November 1918, 450 civilian women had undertaken the special training in both local and long-distance telephone operating, and 223 of them were sent abroad.

Explaining the process of selection, The Associated Press wire service reported in May 1918 that "each applicant's character and ability were certified by her previous employer before she was considered. A psychologist gave tests . . . using methods employed in judging qualifications of officers. Also, since the work was largely of a confidential nature and would give the operators access to carefully guarded information as to troop movements, each candidate's loyalty and motive for applying for service were investigated by secret service agents."[5] Wives of Army officers and enlisted men liable for duty abroad were forbidden by existing laws from membership in telephone operator units.

Training centers for the operators were established in New York City, Chicago, San Francisco, Philadelphia, Jersey City, Atlantic City, and Lancaster, PA. On January 12, 1918, the first group of selectees entered training. They practiced telephone procedure in the largest city exchanges and were dispatched to Army cantonments to learn military methods and terminology.

Of those carefully selected and trained young women, the First Unit of thirty-three operators from the United States and Canada set sail for France on March 1, 1918, to be followed by a second group on March 16 and a third in late April.[6] Two other units went to France before the war ended. The first contingent was headed by Chief Operator Grace D. Banker, a graduate of Barnard College and a former instructress in the operating department of the American Telephone and Telegraph Company.

Overseas, the telephone operators were affectionately christened "Hello Girls" and were quickly assigned to U.S. Army offices in Paris, to Pershing's headquarters at Chaumont, and to the Service of Supply center at Tours. Later they also served in seventy-five other towns in England and France, and in several instances during the closing battles of the war, they were sent forward to operate communications equipment immediately behind the front lines.

Their pay was the same as for male soldiers in comparable positions: chief operator, $125 per month; supervising operator, $72; operator, $60; substitute operator, $50. The Signal Corps did not authorize funds for uniforms, however, and each operator recruit was expected to provide the $300 to $500 needed to purchase her own dark blue wool Norfolk jacket and matching long skirt, black hightop shoes and brown Army boots, hat, overcoat, rubber raincoat, woolen underwear, and black sateen bloomers. The latter, deeply resented by some of the young women recruits, were presumably to be worn in case the long skirts should be blown up by the wind.

News that the Army wanted French-speaking telephone operators was perfectly timed for a young woman of French descent, Cordelia Dupuis, who lived in the small town of Rolla, ND. Throughout the first years of the war, she had been plotting a trip to France, where she intended to enlist as an ambulance driver or find some other way to help the French people. She felt eminently qualified for the Signal Corps service: she was chief operator for Rolla's telephone company, and she was fluent in three languages: English, German, and French. Miss Dupuis signed on as a Hello Girl without delay. She was enthusiastic and eager to "do her bit," but she felt vaguely depressed at the thought of leaving her little prairie hometown and her large family, which included seventeen children. As she wrote in her diary, February 9, 1918,

> I wonder why I feel so sad this morning. I got up very early and went to breakfast, and every one of my sisters and brothers looked very sad and stared at me with eyes full of tears, which made me feel I would very much hate to part with them. When I kissed little Blanche, she said, "Are you going to war today?" . . .
>
> My, such a crowd of people at the depot. I was amazed. I never realized the Rolla people would take so much interest in me. . . . They loaded me down with boxes of chocolates, magazines, and other gifts: a watch, a petticoat, a $5 gold piece, two handkerchiefs and two corset cover drawstrings, and a statue of the Blessed Virgin Mary, a swell pendant, and the cutest and smallest watch I'd ever seen. My darling sister Zelda [gave me] a leather toilet case, and Papa paid my fare to Grand Forks. . . . The men started a collection and collected somewhere near $60 for me. . . .
>
> Then we heard the train whistles and every body was giving me a tight handshake and a hurried kiss and some were crying and telling me to be sure and write, and if I saw any of their boys in France to let them know how they were getting along.[7]

Early in March, Cordelia Dupuis sailed from New York with thirty-two other Signal Corps enlistees, surrounded by secrecy on a darkened ship behind blackout curtains, to join the American Expeditionary Forces (AEF) in France. This was the First Unit, ranging in age from nineteen to thirty-five and drawn from country towns and big cities alike. After they had been accepted by the Signal Corps, they had received telegrams from the Office of the Chief Signal Officer instructing them to be sworn into service by either a notary public or a justice of the peace, as required under the provisions of the Articles of War and Army regulations. Arriving in New York, they were given physical examinations and were measured for uniforms. Then, although they had all taken the oath previously, the women were sworn into the service a second time.

Grace D. Banker, chief operator, who had charge of the First Unit, had many vivid memories of her first days in the Signal Corps, waiting in a cold and cheerless boardinghouse in Hoboken, NJ, for transport overseas. And then:

> Twelve days of lifeboat drills at sea, aboard the old White Star liner *Celtic*, converted to a troopship. Three nights of obeying orders and sleeping in our

clothes. Stuck on a sand bar at the harbor of the Mersey River just outside Liverpool, England, a target for German submarines all one moonlit night. A week in Southampton, adjusting ourselves to wartime rations. . . . Two days on a little Channel packet caught in a dense fog between Southampton and Le Havre. Running into a submarine net and narrowly missing being rammed by a French cruiser. The girls in that First Unit were good sports, taking every thing in their stride. They were the pioneers.[8]

The First Unit of Signal Corps women included California sisters Louise and Raymonde Le Breton, who were born in France and had lived in San Francisco only four years when war broke out in Europe. Louise recalled:

> My sister and I felt very strongly moved by patriotism and we had tried to join various organizations to take part in the war. The Red Cross and the Y.W.C.A. wouldn't take us because we were under 25 years of age. I was 19 and Raymonde was 18 months younger. . . .
> Everyone wanted to enlist. We wanted to fight for freedom and democracy. We were inspired by the [German] invasion of Belgium and the fight the French and British put up. Of course, we had known there would be a war someday because my grandmother, who had lived through the War of 1870, used to say: "We have lost Alsace and Lorraine, but we will get them back." It came suddenly, however, in 1914; no one was prepared.[9]

When they read the appeal for women telephone operators, Louise and her sister applied and were accepted. "We were ordered to telephone school for three weeks of intensive training, and then on to New York, where we were fitted for uniforms, and prepared to sail."

Arriving in Paris on March 24, 1918, Cordelia Dupuis recalled that she and her colleagues were quickly indoctrinated into the rigors of war. They had no sooner settled into their hotel rooms than the building next door was hit by an aerial shell and went down in rubble. "We didn't know enough to be frightened," Cordelia recalled. "We were tired and wanted to go to sleep, but the French maids made us go to the cellar, five flights down. We slid down the banisters in our nightgowns. But we were plenty scared the next day when we saw that huge hole next to our hotel."[10]

Cordelia Dupuis went on to Tours with eleven other Hello Girls. Eleven more went to Chaumont, and ten remained in Paris. One of those remembered starting work immediately at the U.S. headquarters in the Hotel Mediterranée:

> The French girls whom we replaced had been in the office since its infancy, so they knew all the numbers and did not feel the necessity of having a

directory. They resented our coming, as it put them out of good jobs, and all but two left that morning. This made it doubly difficult for us. . . .

Oftentimes, during the early days, after saying, "Number, please," there would be a silence broken by an awed, "Oh!" Sometimes it would be, "Thank heaven you're here at last!" One man called for the American ambassador and added, "God bless you."

Used to the efficiency of phone service in the United States, this Hello Girl and her colleagues had to learn great patience in France.

Most of our toll calls had to go over the French lines, and that sometimes made things very trying. When you wished to call over the French line, you said, "J'écoute." ('I listen.') After a quarter of an hour, the conversation would begin with an exchange of pleasantries. "Good morning, how are you? Are you tired today? If you please, I should like to get _____ [a certain town]." All this had to be in honeyed tones, otherwise there wasn't the slightest chance of getting any attention. And mademoiselle would reply, "Ah, oui," in a languid sort of way, as if the call were of no particular moment, but might as well be handled, now that she was about it. If you asked for one place too often, you committed a serious blunder, for the result would be something like this: "You are unbearable, you ring too much, it gets on my nerves. Je coupe! (I disconnect)" and—bing, the line would be lost and that was an end to that.[11]

The Hello Girls who went to Chaumont loved the charming hilltop town overlooking the beautiful valleys of the Suize and the Marne Rivers. U.S. Army offices were located in a large old French army barracks surrounded by a tall iron fence. The three wings of the building enclosed a courtyard used in peacetime as a drill field. Nearby was a French chateau with smartly uniformed U.S. guards at the doors, the wartime residence of the U.S. commander-in-chief, General Pershing. The town streets were full of American officers and enlisted men serving in the various branches of AEF headquarters.

The ancient stone barracks had once been the headquarters of the Russian Army in France. In 1918, a small room on the first floor served as the U.S. telephone office, and the first group of Hello Girls moved in, taking over from the male operators. Louise Le Breton recalled the conditions. "As we were the first women to arrive in Chaumont, we lived in a room with French families [for the first few weeks]. We lived out of our suitcases, worked ten hours a day, and came home to cook our own dinner. It was tough going. The exchange had to be enlarged and it was a headache working in the office [while the work went on]. It was drilled into us that every single call was so important."[12]

Grace Banker, the chief operator, described the first days at Chaumont. "Many of the calls had to be routed over the local French lines. The French exchanges in the rear were handled by French women in the Civil Service. They had an easy, unhurried philosophy of life, perhaps to be admired, except in times of stress. A simple request to the French ladies would bring nothing.[13] She added, "When we met French soldiers on the lines nearer the Front, they gave us the towns quickly. Perhaps they knew only too well the difference a few minutes might make."

The Hello Girls in Chaumont were soon ensconced in a pleasant stone house that boasted one of the few bathtubs in town. "To be sure, during several shortages, there was not enough water to use it," Miss Banker recalled. "Still it did give such an air of respectability and we were very proud of it. Often after office hours, we would walk in the beautiful valleys. There the violets bloomed in March, and in April we found the lily-of-the-valley growing wild."

Throughout the spring and summer of 1918, more units of Signal Corps operators arrived overseas and opened new offices in the advance section of the battle area. Additional U.S. telephone lines were laid out, and the work settled down to a fairly steady routine.

The Third Unit of Hello Girls landed in France in May 1918. Among them was Adele Hoppock, who had joined the Signal Corps while she was a senior honor student at the University of Washington in Seattle. Five other female members of her senior class joined up with Miss Hoppock; all were fluent in French and had been active in various campus organizations.[14] From Paris, Miss Hoppock wrote home:

> We arrived at 10:30 P.M., and from there we were taken to another city. I can't mention any names of places (except Paris) so you will have to be satisfied when I tell you that it is a beautiful place and we all loved it on the spot. Some of us lived in a convent for a couple of days, a quite novel and interesting experience. The place was thick with American soldiers and we felt quite at home. . . .
>
> Every important place where headquarters and large camps are located has a switchboard worked by our girls. This allows the officers to be connected with anyone in their own camp and also with other camps and cities all over France.[15]

Like many of the other Hello Girls, Miss Hoppock wanted to be as near the front lines as possible. "You can imagine my delight to find four other girls and myself stationed in the nearest place to the Front that our girls are located," she wrote. "It is not in the danger zone, of course, but it is not nearly so far away as it might be. They are going to rent a house for us and have it furnished. There will be a YWCA Secretary to live there and arrange things. It is a small town which I had never heard of before. It is the place above all others that I would choose."

While awaiting transport, Miss Hoppock described what life was like for the telephone operators:

> The girls work only eight hours or less and are taken to the office every day in a Winton Six [automobile]. The girls make friends with the officers and they have dances and all sorts of good times. Certain rules, however, must be kept. They cannot be out after dark without a pass, and then there must always be two girls together, "with or without male escort." One rule is quite foolish, I think. They cannot associate with privates or civilians. . . . If I stayed here, I am afraid I would have too good a time. I didn't enlist to be treated like a queen. I expected to rough it and be really in things. I never want to forget the fact that I am here to work hard. We are so proud to be in the service and we feel as though it is our privilege, not our duty, to do our utmost.

A member of the Fifth Unit of Hello Girls, Merle Egan of Helena, MT, remembered the day she sailed for France, marching proudly to the Hudson River docks with thirty other young women in the sweltering heat of the New York City summer of 1918. "Just two weeks earlier we had been gathered from widely scattered areas of the United States and welded into a closely knit platoon. We had been fitted with uniforms, filled with necessary shots, properly vaccinated, and subjected to such military drills as time permitted."[16]

The four preceding units had been composed mainly of college women who spoke fluent French but had only brief telephone training. As the AEF telephone system expanded in France, however, the Signal Corps needed more experienced operators, regardless of language abilities. When Miss Egan, an employee of the Mountain States Telephone and Telegraph Company, applied, she was immediately accepted by the Signal Corps and was twice sworn into the service, once by the adjutant general of Montana and again by an official of the telephone company. Within a month she was headed for France aboard the *USS Aquitania*. She recalled, "Our ship, carrying 7,000 men and 200 officers, was one of the few to sail without a convoy, and as we left New York in the twilight, we had no inkling of a German submarine that had somehow eluded the harbor defense and had us as its target. It was not until years later that I read in a magazine article how close we had come to eternity at the hands of that enemy U-boat."

In France, Miss Egan was dispatched to Tours, one of the most important telephone centers in the AEF. But "the weeks that followed were hardly the war experiences I had expected," Miss Egan confessed. "I felt further from the war in Tours than I did back in Montana. At home we had lived in a feverish war atmosphere—meatless days, wheatless days, war bond rallies and 'all out to defeat the Hun.' "

Life in Tours was very quiet. The Front was 200 miles away, and there was no fear of air raids. "Our only contact with the fighting was when we handled a long distance call from some harried officer trying to order up some needed equipment. Then we could hear the roar of the guns in the background. We discussed this feeling of distance from the fighting, and we decided that, no matter our location, we were there as important links in the chain of command."

Eventually, men were needed to operate frontline communications, and as Miss Egan recalled,

> I was soon teaching classes of a dozen or more soldiers how to operate our switchboards, which were of the magneto type found in small Montana towns with which I was familiar. Some of the men were disgusted with a female instructor and greeted me with such remarks as, "Where's my skirt?" I just reminded them that any soldier could carry a gun, but the safety of a whole division might depend on the switchboard. I had no more trouble. Except for one hard-boiled sergeant who refused to report to a woman until he spent a week on K.P. duty and decided that I was the lesser of two evils. In the end, he was my prize student.
>
> Just before the Meuse-Argonne offensive in late September, I was given the seemingly impossible job of training 60 men in three days. Those sessions were long and grueling, but the task was accomplished.

The sixth and last unit of Hello Girls to travel overseas experienced a rough crossing of the Atlantic; many had the flu, and one woman was so ill that she had to be left in a hospital in England. One member of that unit was Oleda Joure, born in Michigan, the daughter of French-Canadian parents. "Having always lived in a small town with a close-knit family, lonesomeness never entered my mind," she said later. "But aboard ship, I realized a person can be lonesome and homesick even among hundreds of strangers. At night I used to go up on deck and crawl underneath a lifeboat to cry out loud." Homesickness was not the only hardship to be endured on that crossing.

> A great many cases of the 1918 flu epidemic developed as we sailed for Europe. There were not enough facilities to take care of them all, so their mattresses were placed on deck. I used to play the piano to entertain them. When we arrived in Southampton we were quarantined for two weeks and then we were ferried across the Channel by a British troopship, a night

crossing—as was the custom in war—and a rough one. It was plenty rocky, and the seasickness started with a vengeance. One girl said they would have to build a bridge to get her back to the States. Sadly, that girl was Cora Bartlett. She died later in Tours of pneumonia, and her body was returned home a year later, so she didn't have to repeat the agony of the seasickness.[17]

Another member of the Sixth Unit, a twenty-five-year-old chief telephone operator from Emmett, ID, was actually invited to join the Signal Corps as she was working at her switchboard at home. "One afternoon in 1918, I placed a long-distance call that changed my life," said Anne Campbell Atkinson. "The lines were very noisy and I had to repeat the conversations between the two parties. They completed their business and I hung up and went back to other chores. Within minutes, one of the operators called me on the line and a voice said, 'Madame, if you are the lady who just assisted with the call to New York, I'd like to hire you for the U.S. Army. I'm a recruiter for General Pershing, and your voice is so crisp and clear—would you be willing to go to France as an operator for the Army? Your country needs you.'"[18]

After some consideration, Miss Campbell accepted the offer, "partly out of patriotism, partly curiosity, and mostly because my sister was already in France as an Army nurse," she said. Buying the uniform, however, was a problem for Miss Campbell. The price—$300 to $500—was a considerable sum for the average young woman in 1918. But help came from the Commercial Club of Emmett, who stepped in and held a community benefit picnic one hot afternoon in August. At the end of the day, the club president handed her enough money to purchase her Army wardrobe.

Miss Campbell was stationed at La Belle Épine, the telephone toll office outside the gates of Paris, and she recalled that General Pershing often visited the communications center. "He seemed very stern and didn't talk much," she recalled, "but we always had everything we requested. He always asked if we were all right and if the equipment was operating. And sometimes at the end of his visit, he would smile and tell us to keep up the good work."

In September 1918, as the last contingent of Hello Girls reached their stations in France, General Pershing was preparing the American Army to attack at St. Mihiel to reduce the long-standing German salient there. A call went out to the Hello Girls, requesting a unit of six operators to serve at the Front. At once every one of the 225 operators offered to go. "We were all just dying for a chance to go up," wrote one who was not chosen for the assignment. "And the mean things would allow only six of us to go."[19]

Chief Operator Grace Banker was one of the chosen. She was ordered to proceed to the First Army headquarters, along with two other operators,

Suzanne Prevot and Esther Fresnel. "Where these headquarters were, I did not learn until later, when we were told that we were headed for the little town of Ligny-en-Barrois," Miss Banker recalled.[20] Three more operators, Helen Hill, Berthe Hunt, and Marie Lange, were added to the group as they proceeded to Ligny.

The six plucky Hello Girls took up their duties in a house on Ligny's main street. "Sandbags were piled high on the outside; within, the office was bare enough: a few switchboards behind which were still piled rolls of wire and kegs of nails," Miss Banker wrote.

> For days a large packing box served me as a combination chair and desk. Once up on it, I felt as though I were on a mountain top, for I could see over and around everything else in the room. Later on someone took pity on me and rounded up a real chair and desk.
>
> All night long, the streets of Ligny gave back the sound of marching feet, and the camions and artillery added their rumble. We were told we were about five miles south of St. Mihiel. One night we walked out to a French observation post where we could see the star and caterpillar signals [flares] over the trenches.[21]

One of the other operators, Berthe Hunt, wrote of her impatience. "My! How we did long for that drive to begin; we were weeks waiting for it, watching the troops pass, the artillery rumble by, the trucks constantly going day and night—supplies and men passed continuously until we thought all America had been sent over." Her letter continued:

> Special lines, called "operation lines," were put on our switchboard and were to be used only in connection with the drive. It was most thrilling to sit at that board and feel the importance of it. At first it gave me a sort of "gone" feeling for fear the connection would not be made in time and a few seconds would be lost.
>
> The night the drive began we were called to the office—before that, men operated [the switchboards] between 10 P.M. and 7:30 A.M.—and for the three days during the attack we were on four hours and off four hours.[22]

Another operator, Esther Fresnel, wrote to her parents about the St. Mihiel campaign:

> Before and while this "stunt" of ours [the campaign] was pulled off, we were rushed to death; we worked day and night. The strain was pretty bad;

officers were all on edge, and it was rather hard to keep our tempers at times because everything came at once. . . . The lines would go out of order [because of] bombs or thunderstorms. . . . All together we were all very excited and just strained to the utmost.

Then, all at once, something seemed to come over everybody. Their voices were not so harsh—they almost said funny things to us over the lines. We would call for places in the most dulcet of tones, even though we were dead tired, and we knew—even before we were told—that the whole thing had been successful.[23]

As Miss Banker recalled, "Everybody worked hard, yet no one seemed to complain. The excitement carried us along." Things, however, did get a bit confusing. "Much of the work was in codes which changed frequently. Ligny was 'Waterfall.' Toul might be 'Podunk' one day, and 'Wabash' the next. The Fourth Corps was known as 'Nemo.' Once in the mad rush of work I heard one of the girls say desperately, 'Can't I get Uncle?' And another, 'No, I didn't get Jam.' It all sounded like the Mad Hatter in 'Alice in Wonderland.' "[24]

The six Hello Girls remained at Ligny throughout the St. Mihiel drive, as the American First Army drove the enemy out of the salient. The telephone operators had handled an average of 40,000 words a day over the eight lines leading out of the Ligny switchboard.[25] But they believed the hard work was worthwhile when they "saw the prison pen filling up with German soldiers," said Grace Banker. "We were thrilled; we hadn't yet seen enough of the gruesome side of war."[26]

To the men of the army, the service of the Hello Girls was more than worthwhile. One wrote, "Not the least part of the credit for the brilliant finesse with which the St. Mihiel salient was pinched out in the brief course of 48 hours, is due to the marvelous ease and facility with which the telephone communication at Army Headquarters was handled, and this glorious bit of American history was written by six plucky girls who eagerly jumped at the chance of doing their bit in the fighting area in and about St. Mihiel."[27]

On September 20, the First Army headquarters moved north through Bar-le-Duc to Souilly, near Verdun, where they took over the Armée Adrienne barracks, old wooden sheds, remnants of 1916 when the French had held the fortress of Verdun against the terrific German assaults. The Hello Girls from Ligny, together with a new arrival, Adele Hoppock, were rushed to the Souilly headquarters. "It was the experience of experiences," Berthe Hunt recalled.

We arrived at headquarters on Sept. 26, ready to do our part in the great Argonne drive. The barracks were flimsy things that had been lined with old newspapers and maps to keep out the cold. The YWCA helped us out by giving us a blanket each, a rug, oilcloth and other comforts. In fact, our sitting room (which we acquired later) was furnished with a piano and other things taken from Boche dugouts in the vicinity. The 27th Engineers helped us get settled and made us shelves for our various belongings, wash stands, wooden tables and benches, etc. This was an advance area, where we could see the red and yellow glare from the shelling and feel the reverberations caused by the booming of the big guns.[28]

Miss Banker described the dilapidated barracks, which were

set down in a sea of mud at the edge of the village of Souilly. Instead of glass windows they had frames covered with a sort of oiled paper. In the daytime these could be pushed out, like the windows in a chicken coop. At night they were hooked down and covered with a black cloth called "the camouflage," lest a stray beam of light announce our presence to the raiding German planes. We had an "abri" [dugout] for a shelter, and there was another abri far down in the ground where a single switchboard stood ready for any emergency.[29]

At first the women operators had charge of the operating boards only, handling routine calls concerning supplies, transportation, and other relatively minor matters. Very soon, however, they handled the entire exchange, including the "fighting lines," connecting the fighting units with the commanders directing their movements. Every order for an infantry advance, for a barrage preparatory to the taking of a new objective, and in fact for every troop movement, came over those fighting lines.[30]

In a few weeks, six more Hello Girls arrived at Souilly to bolster the speed of Franco-American communications in that final campaign of the war. The new arrivals included Louise Beraud, Berthe Arland, Hennie Young, Marie Belanger, Leonie Peyron, and Marie Flood.[31]

Winter came early to the hills around the old battleground of Verdun, and cold autumn rains began to fall in Souilly. By October there was ice on the water pails in the morning, and Miss Banker froze her feet badly while she was sleeping—dead tired—inside the barracks. It happened "one night when I tumbled into bed, exhausted," she recalled.

I never noticed anything until my feet began to swell. Then I discovered a leak in the roof of the old barracks. Of course I moved the bed, moved it several times, in fact. But I never found a place where there wasn't at least one leak. It was a long time before I could wear shoes again. But I kept thinking of the boys out there in the trenches in that awful weather. They were so much worse off. We didn't really suffer; we had plenty of warm food; we were happy in our work, and we had fine officers to work for. They watched over us carefully.[32]

Miss Banker remembered the planes flying low over the barracks, usually Americans from Chaumont-sur-Aire, but "sometimes the Boche came over, too. Once a bit of shrapnel dropped beside me as I watched a German plane soar overhead. It looked as harmless as a dragonfly in the peaceful blue sky. . . . Day after day the ambulances drove past our headquarters to the evacuation hospital in the woods beyond. Once when I had to go over there for treatment, I saw too much. There is no glory in war!'"

At about noon on October 30, a catastrophe occurred that threatened to demolish the communications system of the continuing Argonne campaign. A fire broke out in one of the old barracks buildings, and before it could be controlled, the flames spread until the blaze had consumed eight more buildings, including the Signal Corps center. "The officers and men worked like mad, but a bucket brigade was powerless," Miss Banker recalled. The Hello Girls were ordered to vacate their switchboards but refused to leave until they were threatened with disciplinary action. They returned an hour later to find two-thirds of the lines had been ruined or cut, but they immediately resumed operation on the remaining lines.[33] Grace Banker remembered:

Only smoldering embers remained of our office in Barracks No. 8. Wires were down; the telephone line was out. Fortunately the headquarters had just been moved to another barracks, and it was saved. When at last the flames died down, we gathered up our scattered belongings and carried them to new quarters in an unfinished shed behind the rest. My toothbrush turned up in an old shoe and a prayer book came back sitting on a piece of steak in a frying pan.[34]

Very soon, new orders came for Miss Banker: she was to proceed forward with a small group of Hello Girls to Dun-sur-Meuse, headquarters for the next Allied action. But three days later, November 11, 1918, the war came to a close and her orders were countermanded. Her work with the First Army at an end, the exhausted chief operator was assigned a rest leave in Nice on the Mediterranean coast of France. Hardly had she landed in Nice, however, than she was ordered to report to Paris, headquarters for the Allied Peace Conference. There Miss Banker took charge of the telephone operations conducted by a crew of Hello Girls in a huge house on the Avenue des États-Unis, the temporary residence of President Woodrow Wilson, who had arrived to participate in the peace negotiations.

The young U.S. women enjoyed Paris and life in a posh hotel, but "we missed the First Army with its code of loyalty and hard work," she recalled. Indeed, this was not very exciting work for the woman who had dodged shrapnel and had seen the war firsthand. "So when the choice came to stay or go to the Army of Occupation at Coblenz, Germany, I left Paris and went to the Rhine," she wrote.

It was while she was stationed in Coblenz that Miss Banker received the Distinguished Service Medal, the citation reading, "For exceptionally meritorious and distinguished services. She served with exceptional ability as Chief Operator in the Signal Corps Exchange at General Headquarters, American Expeditionary Force, and later in a similar capacity at First Army Headquarters. Through untiring devotion to her exacting duties under trying conditions, she did much to assure the success of the telephone service during the operations of the First Army against the St. Mihiel salient and the operations to the north of Verdun." Early the following September, with three service stripes on her sleeve, Grace Banker sailed for home after twenty months' duty in the Signal Corps.

Operator Cordelia Dupuis heard about the Armistice while on duty at Nevres, south of Paris. "Today Germany ceases hostilities. The Armistice was signed at 10 a.m.," she noted in her diary, "and at 4:30 p.m. every church bell in France will ring at the same time."[35] At four o'clock the bells began to ring, and "everybody in Nevres went wild. The French people were screaming in the streets. All the engineers got together and paraded up and down the Rue de Commerce with tin pans and sticks pounding them, making all the noise they could."

In Tours, where Merle Egan was on duty in November 1918, there had been rumors of peace for several days. "We knew about plans for the Armistice," she recalled, "but we were warned that any messages we might overhear were confidential, and any leakage would mean instant dismissal. Then on November 11 at 11 a.m., came the wonderful news, the war was over! An hour later a long line of French citizens singing 'La Marseillaise' wound through our grounds." She continued, "In our office we were warned to keep a low profile and do no 'American boasting.' Three of us felt we must celebrate in some small way, so we wandered down to the main square where the celebration was in full swing. The French had gone mad and the French soldiers were more amorous than usual. They felt since America had saved them, Americans must be kissed."[36]

Two weeks later, Miss Egan went to Paris as a chief operator of the American Commission to Negotiate Peace. Headquarters were in the Hotel Crillon, one of their twin mansions facing the Place de la Concorde that had been leased by the U.S. government to house peace commission personnel. In preparation for the negotiations, the famous and beautiful Grill Room of the Crillon had been transformed in just five days into an up-to-the-minute telephone exchange with eight switchboards and two chief operators.[37] A visitor described the scene at the Crillon:

> There on their high stools before the maze of plugs sat eight American girls.
> . . . Everything was running like an oiled spindle; not a voice raised, not an instant of confusion as the flying fingers threaded among the green and red bound wires. Occasionally one of the operators put a question in purer French—for they all speak it—and now and then a low laugh from one of the girls marked the efforts of an unseen and gallant American to pay homage to a real American voice.[38]

Paris was a thrilling experience for Merle Egan, the young woman from a small town in Montana, and others like her. After President Wilson arrived in France in January 1919, there were daily calls from his residence to Prime Minister Lloyd George of England and Vittorio Emanuele Orlando, prime minister of Italy, and "no one realized that the young men listed in our directory as John Foster Dulles and Christian Herter would later become famous as American secretaries of state."[39]

The Hello Girls stood awestruck before the historical monuments in the City of Light and spent weekend leaves traveling to the Chateau Thierry battlefields and to the beautiful, though battered, Reims Cathedral. There were Red Cross dances and entertainments, and frequent visits from homesick soldiers from the States, eager to see a familiar face.

When the Peace Treaty was signed and the Crillon offices were returned to their peacetime uses, Merle Egan sailed from Brest on the *Graf Waldersee* in May 1919. Back home, Miss Egan soon became Mrs. Anderson and settled in Denver, CO. "My husband, who always was proud of my service, wrote to the government, asking for my Victory Medal," she recalled. "We were astonished to be told that I was not eligible for an honorable discharge or a medal for service, since I had not been a member of the armed forces. They said the Hello Girls were considered 'civilians,' or 'contract employees' of the Signal Corps, not military."

For Merle Egan Anderson, this was a rude awakening. "We had signed no contracts. We had proudly worn the Signal Corps uniform, black bloomers and all. We had served in a war zone under military orders and military discipline, and we had been constantly reminded of our duties and responsibilities as 'Army women.' Now that the war was won, they wanted to forget us."[40]

To the veteran Hello Girls, the Army's attitude was unjust, and above all, unacceptable. Thus began a new war, a war with the Army Signal Corps for recognition for the Hello Girls, with Merle Egan Anderson leading the charge.

This new war turned out to be a discouraging, frustrating sixty-year struggle. During most of that time, there was no progress, despite support from such prominent members of Congress as Senator Hubert Humphrey and Representative Margaret Chase Smith and from such high-ranking military personnel as Gen. Mark W. Clark, a famed World War II commander. (Merle Anderson always credited at least part of General Clark's support to the fact that he had fallen in love with one of the Hello Girls when he was a young officer in France in 1918.)

More than fifty bills granting veteran status to the Hello Girls were introduced in Congress over the years, but none was passed. Then a young Seattle lawyer, Mark Hough, saw a newspaper article about Mrs. Anderson's battle with the Army bureaucracy and volunteered his services—at no charge. Hough's expertise and diligence did much to win the long, arduous struggle.[41]

At length, with the national backing of the Women's Overseas Service League, the Veterans of World War I, and the fledgling National Organization for Women, plus powerful support from Senator Barry Goldwater of Arizona, the women of the Signal Corps won their battle. They were among several groups of women approved for veteran status under S. 1414, the G.I. Bill Improvement Act of 1977. Processing of the new statute took another two years; it was not until 1979 that ranking Army officers were dispatched across the country to present discharge certificates, Victory Medals, and full veterans' benefits to the handful of Hello Girls still alive.

By that time, of course, most of the Hello Girls were gone. There were only eighteen women surviving of the 223 who had so eagerly left home to serve in France in 1918. But the survivors expressed no bitterness over their long fight for recognition. One of the Hello Girls, Esther Fresnel Goodall, reminisced, "I really felt it was my mission to talk on the telephone. When I was off duty I sometimes spent the whole night talking on the phone with the boys at the Front. I kept thinking it might be their last night."[42]

Looking back, the soldiers of the AEF reported great pleasure and satisfaction in having the telephone women working side by side with the troops during the Great War. Although there had been some initial skepticism, any doubts about the female operators were quickly dispelled as the women quietly joined their male colleagues to get the job done. A story often told involved a busy American officer who lifted his receiver one day in 1918, groaning at the difficulties he expected from some impudent French "central." When he heard the familiar "Number, please" in English, he was so overjoyed that he shouted, "Thank God" into the ears of the amazed Hello Girl at the switchboard.

Echoing that sentiment, Col. Parker Hitt, the chief signal officer of the First Army in France, observed in his report to the secretary of war in 1919, "The use of women operators throughout the entire war was decidedly a success; not only are they more skillful in the manipulation of a board than are the men, but there is also a psychological consideration. Officers were inclined to put up with vexatious delays because of the fact that women were on the switchboard, and that feature alone has much to do with the smooth and efficient functioning of a telephone system."[43]

The day after the Armistice, November 12, 1918, Brig. Gen. Edgar Russel, chief signal officer of the AEF, sent his compliments to each of the Hello Girls: "I desire . . . to congratulate you on the large part you have had in our glorious victory. . . . By your ability, efficiency, devotion to duty and the irreproachable and businesslike conduct of your affairs, personal and official, you have not only justified the action taken in assembling you, but have set a standard of excellence which has been responsible for the success of our system of local and long-distance telephone communication."

AEF commander-in-chief General Pershing, who had originally requested the services of the women telephone operators, always remained proud of his decision, and often referred to the "switchboard soldiers who accepted hazard, without reservation, to serve their country." Pershing awarded testimonial citations to a dozen Hello Girls, and Meritorious Service Citations to fifteen. He later remarked that "no civil telephone service that ever came under my observation excelled the perfection of ours [in France]. The telephone girls of the A.E.F. took great pains and pride in their work, and did it with satisfaction to all."[44]

Notes

1. Report of the Chief Signal Officer to the Secretary of War (Washington, DC: Government Printing Office, 1919), 540.

2. June A. Willenz, Women Veterans: America's Forgotten Heroines (New York: Continuum, 1983), 17.

3. Ibid.

4. A. Lincoln Lavine, Circuits of Victory (Garden City, NY: Country Life Press, 1921), 273.

5. Associated Press article, San Francisco Bulletin, May 16, 1918.

6. Lavine, 277.

7. Unpublished 1918 diary of Cordelia Dupuis Davis and author interview with Mrs. Davis, November 1979.

8. Grace Banker Paddock, memoirs, World War I Survey Collection, Archives of the U.S. Army Military History Institute, Carlisle Barracks, PA, 2.

9. Michelle A. Christides, "Women Veterans of the Great War, Oral Histories Collected by Michelle A. Christides," Minerva: Quarterly Report on Women and the Military 3 (Summer 1985): 103–127.

10. Davis diary.

11. Lavine, 279.

12. Christides.

13. Paddock memoirs, 2.

14. "Prominent Senior to Be Phone Girl," University of Washington Daily, February 6, 1918.

15. Letter from Adele Louise Hoppock Mills to her mother, May 16, 1918, World War I Survey Collection, Archives of the U.S. Army Military History Institute, Carlisle Barracks, PA.

16. Merle Egan Anderson, "The Army's Forgotten Women," unpublished memoir.

17. Christides.

18. "Hello Girl Recalls WWI Telephone Service," interview with Anne Campbell Atkinson by the Associated Press, no date.

19. Lavine, 491.

20. Paddock memoirs, 3.

21. Ibid.

22. Lavine, 493.

23. Ibid.

24. Paddock memoirs, 4.

25. Lavine, 492.

26. Paddock memoirs, 5.

27. Lavine, 490.

28. Ibid., 564.

29. Paddock memoirs, 5.

30. Lavine, 565.

31. Ibid.

32. Paddock memoirs, 6.

33. Lavine, 576.

34. Paddock memoirs, 7.

35. Davis diary.

36. Anderson memoir.

37. Lavine, 608.

38. Ibid., 613.

39. Anderson memoir.

40. Ibid.

41. "The Army's Forgotten Women," speech by Paula M. Cheatham at the Women's Overseas Service League national convention in Louisville, KY, June 24, 1980.

42. Karen L. Hillerich, "Black Jack's Girls," Army 32 (December 1982): 48.

43. Report of the Chief Signal Officer, 541.

44. Lavine, 610.

In 1917, Cordelia Dupuis (opposite page) was chief telephone operator in her small hometown of Rolla, ND, when she heard that the AEF needed French-speaking telephone operators. She rushed to enlist and within months shipped out with the First Unit of Hello Girls. She is pictured here in an identification photo taken in Hoboken, NJ, her port of embarkation, just before she sailed for France in March 1918. Soon after reaching France, she visited Paris and was pictured, (here), in her new French tailor-made uniform, complete with smart bow-tied, low-top shoes. (Courtesy of Cordelia Dupuis Davis family, West Covina, CA)

A large contingent of Hello Girls went on duty at Chaumont, headquarters of Gen. John J. Pershing and the AEF. These four, left to right, Rose Langlier, Minerva Nadeau, Marie Gagnon, and Suzanne Prevot, are pictured in front of GHQ in April 1918. Of the more than 7,600 who applied for the service, some 223 women volunteer telephone operators went overseas and served in seventy towns in England and France. (U.S. Army Military History Institute, Carlisle, PA)

In preparation for the U.S. attack at St. Mihiel in September 1918, six Hello Girls were chosen to serve at the Front. Chief Operator Grace D. Banker, front row, third from right, proceeded to First Army Headquarters at Ligny, near St. Mihiel, with five other operators. A number of others pictured here soon followed to work the switchboards at Souilly, near Verdun, in the Meuse-Argonne campaign. (Lettie Gavin collection)

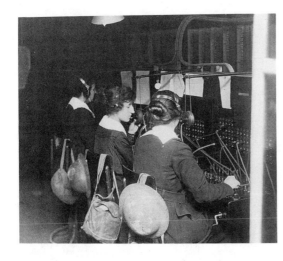

Hello Girls pictured at the switchboard at Souilly-during the Argonne drive: from left, Berthe Hunt, Esther Fresnel, and Grace Banker, chief operator. The emergency equipment—tin trench helmets and gas masks—indicate their proximity to the Front. (Courtesy of Liberty Memorial Museum, Kansas City, MO)

Grace Banker, chief operator, led the Hello Girls contingent during their entire eight months of service in the war zone. This snapshot of her was taken while she was on leave with friends at Ostende, Belgium, in July 1918. (Courtesy of Cordelia Dupuis Davis family, West Covina, CA)

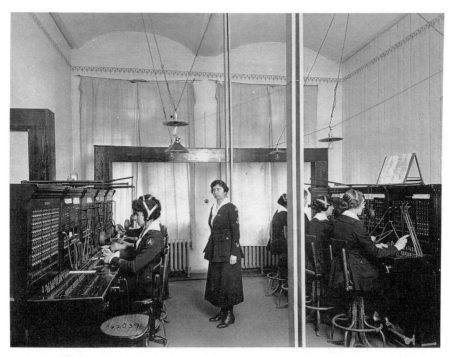

A view of the Signal Corps telephone exchange, code-named "Doodle Bug," at Third Army Headquarters, Coblenz, Germany, in June 1919. Standing center is Grace Banker, chief operator. (National Archives photo no. 111–SC–162039)

During peace negotiations in Paris following the Armistice, Hello Girls were on duty at the huge telephone exchange in the Elysées Palace Hotel. Another large telephone exchange was set up in the famous Hotel Crillon bar, one-time gathering place for English and U.S. expatriates in Paris. There were eight boards at the Crillon to serve the peace conference, with two chief operators. Seated left was Merle Egan, who later led the battle to obtain veteran status for the Hello Girls. (Lettie Gavin collection).

=5=

Reconstruction Aides

There is no subject which deserves more immediate consideration than the physical reconstruction of disabled soldiers.

—President Woodrow Wilson, 1918

Therapy in its ancient form probably originated when humanity first discovered the relaxing and rejuvenating qualities of the bath. Much later, the Chinese employed rubbing as a therapeutic measure as early as 300 B.C., and Galen, the famous Greek physician observed in A.D. 172 that "work is nature's best physician and essential to human happiness." But the ancients could never have envisioned the art of reconstruction, as therapy was then known, as it developed in the wake of the First World War. Few could have imagined how therapists, physical and occupational, would be able to treat so successfully those crippled in battle and return them to useful, happy lives.

The use of exercise or activity in treating patients was not, of course, unknown in the early twentieth century. Civilian hospital programs in the United States and abroad had offered the basics of therapy for many years. Remedial work had been used in the United States since the early 1800s in treating mental patients, and early in the next century such work became important in re-educating handicapped persons.

The disabled had always been supported by charity or philanthropy, but this support was limited to providing food, care, and shelter for these people; it did not extend to rehabilitating them. This philosophy changed at the end of the Victorian era, when society realized it would be more effective to train disabled people with new skills that would allow them to work and to live independently. This new concept of re-education would become the foundation of the U.S. Army Medical Department's reconstruction programs for the sick, wounded, and mentally ill of the First World War.[1] However, at the time the United States entered the conflict in April 1917, there were no formal reconstruction programs in place.[2]

Maj. Gen. William C. Gorgas, the Army's surgeon general, soon realized that reconstruction techniques would be necessary for the American Expeditionary

Forces (AEF), and he ordered a study of similar programs in English and French hospitals. As a result of this study, the surgeon general's office established in August 1917 the Division of Special Hospitals and Physical Reconstruction, which was given orders to investigate physical and occupational therapy programs and also to evaluate educational and vocational programs.

The only woman member of the new division was Marguerite Sanderson, an associate of Dr. Joel E. Goldthwait, a Boston orthopedic surgeon who was also a member of the division. Miss Sanderson, a graduate of Wellesley College and the Boston Normal School of Gymnastics, was a very vocal proponent of the reconstruction profession and one of the two outstanding women who guided the development of reconstructive treatment during and after the First World War. In 1917, working with several male physicians who were also pioneers in the field, Miss Sanderson organized the administrative details for the newly established reconstruction aide program. The following year, she transferred to Walter Reed General Hospital in Washington, DC, to oversee the formation of working units of aides.

Miss Sanderson and Dr. Goldthwait "put up a tremendous fight to get the reconstruction aide corps organized," wrote an early colleague, Mia Donner Jameson.

> She was a woman ahead of her time, but she was not able to overcome some of the objections of the "men on the Hill," i.e. the senators and congressmen. One of her aims was to get us "uniformed" in bloomers which she thought would be more practical than skirts for the mud and rain we might encounter [on overseas duty]. As you can imagine, in those days the bloomer idea was quite radical.
>
> She was an excellent organizer and disciplinarian, but we who knew her well . . . considered her one of us, and she was affectionately called "Sandy."[3]

Early in 1918, Miss Sanderson welcomed a new reconstruction aide to Walter Reed Hospital, a vital and charismatic physical therapist named Mary McMillan, who was to become the second guiding force behind the reconstruction profession. Born in Massachusetts, Miss McMillan grew up in England and was trained there in the early 1900s, working with Sir Robert Jones, a prominent orthopedic surgeon who used therapy extensively in his practice. Mary McMillan also had worked with British war wounded in a base hospital in England early in the war. She returned to the States in 1915, and Dr. Jones recommended her to the surgeon general's department, where she joined forces with Marguerite Sanderson in February 1918. A month later, Miss

McMillan was appointed head reconstruction aide when "Sandy" Sanderson began organizing reconstruction aides for service with the AEF in France.[4]

There were two specialties for reconstruction aides: physical (or physio-) therapists administered massage, electro or hydro treatment, and other therapeutic techniques; occupational therapists taught anything from crocheting, basketry, and weaving to reading and writing, math, typing, and mechanical drawing. But beyond these job descriptions, there was little that defined the occupation. "Reconstruction is a new word for a new work," Mary McMillan said at the time. "The profession was born in response to a brand new need."[5]

An early therapist, Mary J.J. Wrinn, wrote, "It had been found that men, wounded on the battlefield, recovered more rapidly when occupied; that the healing process was often hastened by massage and by the application of heat and light. Thus a call went ringing through a land at war [in 1918]. The Aide answered." Before that moment, "she may have been a teacher, an artist, a craftswoman, or a secretary, snatching odd moments to knit a sock or roll a bandage. But all at once she was none of these. She was something more. The same impulse that had sent the soldier to face death, now sent her to help him live again."[6]

There were few training centers for therapists at that time. Occupational therapy training was offered at Teachers' College, Columbia University, New York City. Courses at other schools had been approved—in Boston, in New York City, and a semi-official course in Washington, DC—but none were operating early in 1918. Columbia's curriculum included weaving, woodwork, basketry, block printing, knitting, crocheting, needlework and beadwork, applied design, practice teaching, and hospital routine.[7] The American Occupational Therapy Association estimates that 1,685 reconstruction aides graduated from fifteen schools or programs of occupational therapy between April 1918 and July 1921.

Physiotherapy students received emergency training in seven institutions throughout the country that were conducting such courses by April 1918. The largest program was at Reed College in Portland, OR, "the only college west of Michigan designed to train women to help restore our soldiers to their fullest capacity for a useful life," wrote Reed's president, Dr. William Foster.[8] Reed's first course—sponsored jointly with the University of Oregon Medical School—was a three-month session beginning March 1, 1918. Thirteen young women graduated in June. Mary McMillan, on leave from the Army, joined the Reed staff for two summer courses in 1918 and served as a teacher and director of the college clinics where students received their hands-on experience. Reed's curriculum included classes in anatomy, physiology, personal hygiene, psychological aspects of recovery, posture, theory of bandaging, massage, corrective gymnastics and other remedial exercises, practice in massage, and clinics in orthopedic surgery. French language was provided as an optional study.[9]

The Portland Oregonian reported in February 1918 that

> the psychological side of the [Reed] training is particularly broad in its scope. It teaches cheerfulness against adversity, and includes mental training to assist the badly wounded to "forget" lost functions and cultivate new ones, such as using one hand where two formerly were; talking as nearly properly as shattered jaws and throats will allow, and modes of living for those wounded internally but recovered bereft of certain original organs.

The college advised that "appointments" for training will be given only to women between the ages of 25 and 40, of good personality, good health and physical vigor, and citizens of the United States or of one of the countries allied with the United States in the war."[10] The Office of the Surgeon General announced further that "the aides must be women with powers of personal subordination, able to cooperate generally and capable of demonstrating team play, as it is essential that this new force have a standard and morale of the highest order. On this spirit, more than any other thing, will the physical re-education of soldiers depend."[11]

Another desirable quality in the type of woman sought by the Army was "the ability to associate with young men on friendly footing without encouraging undue familiarity."[12] It is estimated that some 150 of those modest young women graduated from Reed College's physiotherapy courses and served in the Army during the war years and after. Reed was later recognized by the American Physical Therapy Association as the first organized accredited school of physical therapy in the United States.

After weeks of arduous training, the First Unit of reconstruction aides arrived in New York in June 1918 to receive uniforms, medical shots, and last-minute instructions before departing for France. Each aide was expected to provide her own street uniform, consisting of a bulky dark blue serge "Norfolk suit" ($32.50) and accessories, including one ulster overcoat ($5) and one full, flowing cape lined with maroon silk (optional, $30), shoes, gloves, and a round beaver or navy straw hat with a cockade of maroon and white. "But not purses. We were never issued purses," one aide recalled. "And no colored shirts. White shirts only were worn, along with black four-in-hand tie." The Red Cross provided additional clothing, including a sou'wester raincoat and rubber boots, one gray sweater, two pairs woolen tights, three pairs flannel pajamas, four suits woolen underwear, and merino and cotton stockings. Each aide also received the pale blue chambray duty uniform that came with twelve sets of white collars and cuffs.

The First Unit, fully equipped, soon sailed for France, with Louisa C. Lippitt as head aide. One of the aides vividly recalled a visit from pioneer reconstruction aide Marguerite Sanderson just before the twenty-four hand-picked trainees steamed out of Hoboken, NJ, bound for the Great War:

> We were certainly ripe for a visit of inspiration. . . . We were fed up on snubs and mismanagements, on petty tyrannies and on piffling viewpoints. [But] with the first word that Miss Sanderson spoke, the clouds and cobwebs blew away, and the wholesome sun of clear purpose came out. She spoke of the big need overseas for P.T. [physical therapy] work, and of our good fortune in being the first to set sail in the high adventure. She spoke of what our work in the war would mean to post-war physiotherapy. During her talk, that elusive quality, morale, rose like mercury in a midsummer noon. [There was] not one of the 24 of us but who felt heartened and freshened by it, braced again to the big task ahead.[13]

It was a task that had some massive problems, in view of the fact that the eager reconstruction aides, or "re-aides," as they came to be known, were not always enthusiastically welcomed by the U.S. Army Medical Department. Perhaps because their profession was new, the aides sometimes were greeted with ignorance and misunderstanding in the hospitals, both at home and overseas, and the obstacles frequently seemed overwhelming. Re-aide Mary J.J. Wrinn felt that the very air in the overseas hospitals was thick with disapproval, impatience, and an irritating tolerance for the reconstruction philosophy. Indeed, it seemed the only ones who welcomed her and her colleagues were "an occasional farsighted ward surgeon, and the soldier himself, flat on his back." But "the need of the hour spurred them on."[14]

Another early re-aide recalled being lectured by an official in New York just before sailing for France: "You are Pioneers. Very few people 'Over There' know what you're for. Still fewer want you around. Don't get in the nurses' and doctors' way. Make yourselves scarce, if not invisible, until you have made such a place for yourselves on your wards that no ward will be complete without you."[15]

Occupational therapist Lena Hitchcock, arriving at a U.S. base hospital in France in the summer of 1918, remembered her welcome:

> The chief nurse greets us pleasantly enough, but is obviously puzzled and wishing us somewhere else. The commanding officer appears and has a pleasant greeting to us, at the same time telling us that he has told Col.

Goldthwait, when informed of our impending arrival, that he isn't running a boarding house, but if we are useful, we may stay until they can arrange for our transportation home.

The Head Aide, temper rising, advises the colonel that "we have every intention of making ourselves useful. That's why we are here." He turns on his heel and swaggers out, spurs clicking. The Chief Nurse tells us they will be glad to have us and assigns us to wards as nurses' aides, first giving us the rest of that day in which to orientate ourselves and settle our quarters, an unfinished barracks with a dirt floor and no glass in the windows.[16]

Anna G. Voris of the First Unit recalled a wearing journey overseas and finally arriving at a French railroad station, "weary and bedraggled from long hours in an uncomfortable train." Her group was greeted rudely by the officer in charge at the base hospital: "Reconstruction Aides! What do you expect to do? I didn't ask for you, we don't need you, I don't know where to put you," and so on.[17]

Even Maj. Julia C. Stimson, superintendent of the Army Nurse Corps in France, welcomed a group of aides heartily enough but admonished them not to get in the way of the nurses and doctors. Sometimes the aides were mistakenly perceived as nurses' aides, assistants badly needed to help the overworked doctors, nurses, and medical corpsmen in the overseas hospitals.[18] Although that was not their mission, the re-aides pitched in and worked wherever they could be useful in the overcrowded medical centers.

The medical officers, of course, had big problems of their own. One doctor, writing after the war, outlined the wartime trials of establishing reconstruction treatment for battle casualties. First was a lack of space to accommodate therapy programs.

> In other instances, it was necessary to sell the commanding officer of the hospital on this line of work [reconstruction]. I recall very distinctly my first visit to one of the largest tuberculosis hospitals, and was told by the commanding officer that he didn't want the ———— women messing around his hospital. After a long conference . . . he reluctantly said that I could send him a dozen [aides]. There was great care in the selection of those who were sent to this institution, and one month later we were requested to give him 35 [more] aides. From that day to this, reconstruction treatment has been successfully carried on in this institution. . . .
>
> Another obstacle was in securing supplies. There was a period in this early experience when we were not permitted to ship anything that was not directly or indirectly for combat purposes. During this partial embargo . . . absolutely no supplies could be shipped to aides [in certain areas].[19]

The First Unit of re-aides, all physiotherapists, arrived in Liverpool in mid-June 1918.[20] One of them, Mia Donner Jameson, a physical education teacher from Riverside, IL, recalled arriving at Base Hospital No. 9 at Chateauroux, in central France, in the middle of the night. "Base 9 was staffed by medical men who didn't know what we were or how to use us, so we spent several very frustrating weeks. Finally, three of us were ordered to Base Hospital 116 at Bazoilles-sur-Meuse, which we assumed would be an orthopedic center." Instead, the newly arrived re-aides found a bleak collection of barracks and tents, essentially an evacuation hospital, "where the men came in from the field dressing stations and as soon as they were cleaned up and [their wounds] dressed, were sent to bases further removed from the front line. Only the most seriously wounded, who could not be moved, were retained at Bazoilles." There was no opportunity here for the re-aides to practice their reconstruction therapy on recovering wounded.

Extra hands, however, were in short supply, and the nurses were very happy for any help the re-aides could provide. As Miss Jameson recalled,

> We really worked, dressing wounds, giving baths, sterilizing instruments, and so forth. It was a very unusual and satisfying experience for a physical therapist, even if it was not what we had expected to do.
>
> We finally were transferred to Base [Hospital No.] 8 at Savenay, where we were received with open arms by Major W.H. Orr, an orthopedic surgeon from Lincoln, Nebraska. He and his staff put us right to work, organized a clinic, and procured plinths [treatment tables], chairs and tables. We, of course, had no modalities [equipment], except hot water for packs and, I believe, hot paraffin.[21] As the hospital could not offer accommodations, we lived with a French family in the village—in itself an interesting experience.[22]

Re-aide Constance Greene remembered Base Hospital No. 8 as "an immense medical center on a hilltop near the little village of Savenay. [The hospital] was said to have a population of 25,000, including patients, doctors, nurses, reconstruction aides, engineers, Red Cross workers and others. It consisted of miles of brown prefabricated buildings, surrounded by mud, with a few roads wandering through." Conditions were far from ideal. "Men were brought in from the front line hospitals and then evacuated home as soon as they could safely travel—a long wait for some. I well remember my first assignment and the forests of wooden traction frames in those crowded wards. All those patients had femur fractures with unbelievably extensive wounds. And we had no antibiotics."[23]

The wounded remained a vivid memory for re-aide Nellie Godbolt Chilcote. "My most interesting patient was a young man with more courage than I had ever seen," she wrote.

> He had his leg bone below the knee fractured by shrapnel. He was not able to walk. But he felt that if the doctors would amputate his leg below the knee he could wear a wooden leg and would then be able to walk. He had pleaded with the doctors at every chance he had, but nobody would do the amputation.
>
> Knowing how he suffered because that leg was useless and painful all the time, I too believed that he would be better off with the leg off below the knee. So I took my courage in my hand and talked to the doctor (a dangerous thing to do in the physiotherapy department) and listened carefully to the lecture he gave me. And behold, a few days later the patient came in for his treatment all bubbling with happiness and announced that the doctor, a very conscientious and able man, had said he would operate. So he did and the patient wore a "wooden" leg and walked quite naturally for many years. And I was as happy as he was.[24]

The Second Unit of reconstruction aides left the Hotel Albert in New York early one Sunday morning in September 1918 and, "while church bells were ringing, proceeded to the old Hoboken wharf in New Jersey to go aboard the *George Washington*," wrote Maude E. Cook, physiotherapist. She especially remembered the "drowning drill."

> [This exercise] summoned us out so early to watch the gray water swish by, our eyes and ears alert for signs of danger [submarine conning towers]. Then the days and days of making and wearing influenza masks. At last the sight of land—the long line of transports and destroyers coming into the French harbor of Brest, and our greeting by real brother U.S. doughboys.
>
> Herded into the big army trucks, with standing room only, we were driven up the road skirting the harbor and outside the city walls to Camp Kerhuon. Those of us who had no nursing experience volunteered to work with the French maids, systematizing mess halls, etc., while the rest of us acted as aides to the overworked nurses. We heated water for bathing—the fuel was salmon cans filled with alcohol-soaked cotton. For long days, we turned and re-turned soiled pillow slips, washed towels and carried drinks—dressed always in our rubber boots and rain clothes. We carried our canteens to bed with us to have warm water for bath and laundry next morning. Our spirits rose in proportion to our hardships and we were a happy unit of girls.[25]

Four physical therapy re-aides, probably from the Second Unit, were dispatched in October 1918 to Base Hospital No. 20 at Chatel Guyon, France. They were assigned to duty in the Surgical Department, and a room was arranged for their work on the dispensary floor of the Hotel Nouvel, one of several spa hotels taken over by the AEF Medical Department.

The room contained "four couch tables, four small tables, desk, chairs and other necessary apparatus, including an electric vibrator and battery." Three days after their arrival, the four aides treated twenty ambulatory patients in this room in the morning alone. The work gradually increased until some mornings as many as fifty patients came in. In the afternoons, the aides visited the various wards to treat the bedridden wounded. In this manner, 3,127 treatments were given in ten weeks. These treatments included "stiff joints, paralysis, trench and flat foot, and various orthopedic conditions."[26]

Occupational therapists, meanwhile, worked in the wards with the bed and chair patients. They aimed to distract the patient by offering various projects, to maintain and improve function of an injured body part, or—in the case of amputation—to work toward skilled and dexterous use of the remaining extremity.[27] In the beginning, the occupational therapists taught "simple handcrafts in the form of knitting, beadwork, basketry, mat-weaving, block stamping, wood-carving and the like." As time went on, however, it was found that patients were much more interested in vocational training that might prepare them for the workplace after discharge.

"Consequently, stenography, typewriting, mechanical drawing, winding electrical armatures, academic and commercial study, and the more purposeful handcrafts were utilized."[28]

When craft supplies were scarce or nonexistent, aides improvised, using discarded boxes for making various toys, turning out small aeroplanes from wooden tongue depressors and swab sticks, and gathering pine needles from the woods around the hospital for making baskets. "The problem of getting supplies to work with seems to present itself in every war and, if nothing else, developed a talent for 'scrounging,' without which these workers could never have fulfilled the purpose for which they were sent overseas," wrote Alice R. DeFord, an occupational therapist who went to France in September 1918.[29] Describing her service at the huge hospital center of Savenay, Miss DeFord continued:

> We do both bedside and shop work, one girl managing a carpenter and tin-can shop, and three of us working in the wards. The fifth, our head aide, does the shopping and supervising. At Savenay, at first, everything had to be salvaged—old boxes for wood, dyed selvedges from bandages for weaving,

old tin cans (and there are quite a number in the A.E.F.) for vases, candle-sticks, and the like. It is very hard to get tools in France, even with the money to buy, for all the metal has gone into ammunition, and what's left is just impossible. . . .

The boys seem to have a great fondness for sewing. . . . They have embroidered or woven bags and hat bands, cross-stitched pillow tops and table-runners, and the like.

In knife work, they are doing a great deal of toy making. . . . They do block printing on goods or on paper, the latter usually little scenes to be water-colored later and mounted for post cards. Then there's crocheting and knitting and in some cases tatting and bead-work (when we can get the beads).

When supplies for crafts and projects were short, the soldiers could be as creative as the re-aides: "The other day we had one boy ripping up his 'issue' coat so that another, a tailor, could alter it; another gluing up a broken violin; another, digging out the hob-nails from his shoes so that he could go to a dance."

At Savenay, work was often rewarding, but not always easy. "We saw wholesale suffering; wholesale, but game, suffering. No motion pictures can ever show or lecturers tell; one must have been actually in the hospitals to know what this victory had cost." The injuries she saw, both physical and emotional, taught Miss DeFord that "there are far worse things than death. One boy I was working with today said he couldn't do anything because he couldn't work left-handed. He couldn't work right-handed, either, for the good reason that his right hand was gone. And the same machine gun took his right leg just below the hip. By the end of the day, though, he had embroidered a wool medallion and said he had had the best time he had had since the St. Mihiel drive began."

Lena Hitchcock was sworn in for re-aide service as an occupational therapist in March 1918 and began work at Walter Reed Hospital in Washington, DC. In those early days of the profession, Miss Hitchcock recalled, "we worked under great difficulties, teaching one another crafts. At first we had no uniforms, then we were given the hideous dark blue dresses. Katherine Semple suggested the apron, which was accepted. . . . Several of us, on the grounds that the dark blue hospital uniforms were depressing, succeeded in getting them changed to the present light blue chambray."[30] Miss Hitchcock considered the uniform "exceedingly ugly. It was designed by a man who believed that women working in the hospitals were a menace to the men patients."

Both physical and occupational therapists wore the pale blue uniforms, which earned them the nickname "Bluebirds." The only difference between the uniforms was that occupational therapists wore long sleeves, and physical therapists, short. Even devoted professional Mary McMillan was not thrilled with the uniform. "Would I dare say that the old army uniforms were like unto maternity gowns?" she wrote later. "Or had I just better say they didn't fit so well and let it go with that?"

In June 1918, Miss Hitchcock left Walter Reed and joined a group of twenty-seven re-aides in New York. They were there for several weeks, drilling in the Armory and kept under strict military supervision. The small band of re-aides, uncomfortable in their heavy uniforms, also marched proudly in the Fourth of July parade up Fifth Avenue. Miss Hitchcock described the scene:

> We swing into line behind the Army Nurses. When we turn into Fifth Avenue, a band strikes up "Onward Christian Soldiers." Flags of the Allies flutter from every window. My heart stirs, thrills—we are off to the Crusades. Hats are off as we pass. I overhear a comment from a man on the curb, "Say, them girls are a'goin' overseas." I want to shout but instead keep my eyes front, mouth sternly set. It's sweltering but I don't feel it. . . . On and on until we reach Seventy-Second Street, where we disband. Then, at last, I am aware of aching feet, bursting head, the trickles of perspiration pouring down my face, neck and back.

On July 30, Miss Hitchcock sailed for Liverpool aboard the *Walmer Castle*. Her group landed in France on August 11, 1918, and were sent to Base Hospital No. 9 in Chateauroux, where they discovered they were not wanted. At first, the duties they were assigned were not those they had been trained for. Miss Hitchcock recalled her arduous work schedule:

> I went on duty at 6 a.m., and until 9 a.m., did nurses' aide work—administered Dakin's solution to all patients receiving the treatment, swept out 70 beds with a whisk broom, washed 70 faces and prepared four dressing carts (assisting at one), did all sterilizing. Lunched from 11:30 a.m. to 12 noon, back to the ward until 6 p.m., interrupted by supper (1/2 hour) at 5 p.m. . . . Worked from 6 to 8 p.m. as nurses' aide, as well as three Sundays per month.

As summer 1918 faded into fall, U.S. attacks against the Germans intensified, and the wounded poured into Army hospitals. About one night, she wrote:

> A convoy of wounded has come in. . . . It's after eight. Men are lying on litters on the floor. Orderlies are pushing beds closer together; putting up cots and more beds in every vacant space, even in the supply room and foyer.

Two nurses and I make beds, beds, beds. As fast as we finish one, a man is popped into it. They are, many of them, still wearing the clothes they had on when wounded. The stench of gangrene and [mustard] gas is horrible.

I pass Major Todd, our new English surgeon. I'm carrying a basin filled with filthy dressings. "Sister," he orders curtly, "get that man's leg ready for dressing." I look at the "man," a boy no more than seventeen. I'm afraid I'm going to be sick; most of his leg has been shot away, the stump is wrapped in blood- and pus-soaked bandages. I meet his steady eyes, watch his smile tremble to firmness.

"Gee, nurse," he says apologetically, "I sure hate to bother you—I ain't very pretty." I smile back; how I manage to, I don't know. "You look pretty wonderful to me," I assure him. "I'm afraid that I might hurt you. I'm not a real nurse, you see, only a nurses' aide." Then I get busy—soaking the bandages first in a prepared solution to soften them. It's done. I feel harder, more competent.

And yet, in addition to assisting the nurses, the re-aides managed to make time for the work that had brought them to France. Miss Hitchcock recalled those busy days:

Work hums. The men become more and more interested. . . . I have an Italian soldier in my ward, misplaced, no one knows how. He is from Naples, has no English, and is very homesick. I have no Italian, but manage to make out a word here and there. I fix a wooden plaque for him to paint. I've included everything: Vesuvius, the Bay of Naples, a Neapolitan peasant girl. His mouth flashes in a smile, his black eyes sparkle, paint is everywhere— and the plaque, when finished, is fearful and wonderful. But he is pleased and content.

Hope [her friend Hope Gray, another occupational therapist] ponders a contrivance she is making for one of her boys who has lost both hands. He is dreadfully depressed and melancholy. She finally achieves an ingenious leather band with slits to hold paint brush, knife, fork or spoon, one for each wrist. The change in him is amazing—cheers!

One of the most important contributions made by occupational therapists during the First World War was in the care of neuropsychiatric patients, or NPs, as they were called. At first, therapy was considered only for those cases who were less disturbed mentally. As the re-aides became skillful in dealing with such patients and the benefits of therapy became more obvious, however, the scope of cases widened. The increased knowledge of how best to treat these cases brought substantial changes in their care.[31]

Mrs. Clyde McDowell Myres was among the first therapists sent overseas specifically to work with NP soldiers. Few people at this time knew what the aides were supposed to do, and "we were nondescripts," Mrs. Myres wrote. "We were pioneers going out with hardly the military status of scrubwomen."[32] The destination for those special aides was Base Hospital No. 117, a separate hospital for cases of war neurosis, located at La Fauche, a tiny village on the main route between Neufchateau and Chaumont, General Pershing's headquarters.

Mrs. Myres recalled the beautiful countryside, but she said, "the interminable passing of camions and troops, and the stark wooden barracks in the foreground, brought us sharply to our time and task. To us came the men with functional neuroses which showed in tremors, facial tics, strange twistings of the head and body, partial paralysis, deafness, dumbness, stuttering, extreme depression, etc."

Their orders were to set up a workshop immediately. "It was to be in a barrack, twenty by a hundred feet, cracks in the floor, cracks in the wall, door off the hinges, windows flopping, dust flying everywhere. At one end, the hospital carpenter had an office . . . at the other end the Red Cross Supervisor of Gardens." The re-aides were assigned a central location and soon attracted notice. "Up to the time of our arrival, there had been no women in the hospital. This little group of women reconstruction aides, seizing promptly upon mop and broom, attracted the curious; soon we were surrounded with khaki-clad soldiers. Holding our increasing audience, we began to open the boxes of equipment. Interested patients helped."

At length, the therapists, assisted by the NP patients, managed to improvise workbenches, a charcoal furnace for soldering irons, and—from discarded tin cans—three six-foot dishwashing tubs. Mrs. Myres remembered that "the eyes of the harassed commanding officer grew almost human. The kitchen sink had won him. Furniture was needed everywhere: for the doctors, rough boxes were serving for chairs and desks. Wards were barren of everything but beds; no bedside or ward tables, chairs or stools. Orders came from every corner, and there were more volunteers than we could manage." The re-aides had earned their welcome. "The doctors, as well as the commanding officer, began to look upon the work-shop with a kindly eye—kindly, or calculating," Mrs. Myres recalled.

Later the Red Cross provided a whole new building for the therapy workshop, and the work went on. "During that September and October [1918], the men poured in from the Front. They lined up at the door every morning before opening hour," Mrs. Myres wrote. The work the shop put out attracted buyers, a boon to men who had sometimes been for months without receiving pay. The

Christmas following the Armistice, the workshop was humming with activity, busily creating decorations for the huge Christmas tree given for the soldiers and for the French children of the neighborhood. "In the leisure of the passage home, when it all had settled into memory, I realized that we had had a great adventure," Mrs. Myres reflected.

From early June 1918 until the end of the war, nearly 3,000 cases of war neurosis passed through Base Hospital No. 117. Most of these took part in some kind of activity in the workshop as part of their treatment. One of the re-aides, Meta Anderson, observed:

> It was possible to judge, therefore, just what this sort of work was able to do for them, and how necessary a workshop is as part of the hospital for neuroses. The physiological and psychological needs were met by the use of muscular effort in the production of tangible articles.
>
> The handling of the tools and the various movements of sawing, nailing, screwing and hammering, and the finer and more coordinated movements of wood carving, metal work of various kinds, weaving and tinning, as well as much more delicate and more emotionally inspired techniques of painting, sketching and printing, supplied the essential training that the paralysis, tremors, and other symptoms needed.[33]

Reconstruction aides continued to join the AEF during the fall of 1918, and by December there were more than 200 of those women overseas working at twenty base hospitals, including Angers, Bordeaux, Brest, Nantes, Savenay, and Vichy. At that time, a new clinic was opened at Savenay, where the First Unit of re-aides had been warmly welcomed months before. The clinic was a delight to the aides—a large well-ventilated room with all equipment necessary for caring for the patients. Savenay's surgeons carefully diagnosed each of the wounded and worked out a plan of therapy with the re-aides. Injury classifications included gunshot wounds involving joints, gunshot wounds with fracture, gunshot wounds with resulting nerve injury, amputations, head injury, soft-part wounds, closed fractures, gunshot wounds with loss of bone substance, trench foot, and face wounds. In October 1918, 1,426 physiotherapy treatments were given at Savenay; by January 1919, the number had peaked at 6,568, tapering off to 4,218 in April.[34]

In 1917–1918, it is estimated that there were nearly 2,000 re-aides in service, almost 300 of whom were overseas. The work was carried on in all Army hospitals and was continued into veterans' hospitals in the United States after the war.[35]

As the wounded were shipped home after the Armistice and the need for reconstruction services decreased overseas, many of the aides were ordered back to the United States. Others had time to explore France and do some sight-seeing. Eva McLagan, an Oregon physiotherapist, never forgot the leave she spent near the notorious French battleground of Verdun:

> The work of salvaging was not yet complete and to our unaccustomed eyes, the desolation was almost unbelievable. Where graveyards had been blown up by exploding shells, human bones, partly clothed in some instances, were lying about, and the earth pock-marked by a mass of deep shell holes. Heaps of barbed-wire entanglements, wrecked tanks, piles of scrapped war machinery were in evidence, and as we followed along the line of advance, piles of bricks marked the places where houses had been.[36]

The last group of aides in France sailed for home late in May 1919. Many more aides, however, were still in the States, trained, equipped, and ready to serve overseas, when the Armistice intervened. One of them, Harriet Forest, had been a member of the first re-aide class at Reed College in Oregon, finishing the course in the spring of 1918 at the age of twenty-one. Because she was not yet twenty-five, the minimum age for re-aides at that time, Miss Forest did not go into service immediately. It was some months later, after considerable paperwork, that she received her re-aide appointment and was assigned to Unit 12, New York City, in October 1918.

She was still in New York, awaiting transport overseas, on the day of the "false Armistice," November 7, 1918, when rumors circulated that the war was over. In an unforgettable development that day, Miss Forest fell victim to the influenza epidemic and left her hotel "feet first" on a stretcher, along with an Army nurse also stricken. "We were sent by ambulance to the hospital, driving through huge crowds surging through the streets, celebrating the Armistice," she recalled. "They thought our ambulance was part of a parade and they surrounded us, cheering and shouting, all the way. I was still in the hospital when the real Armistice came on November 11."[37]

A few days later, Re-Aide Unit 12, including Miss Forest, was taken to the docks at Hoboken, NJ, to board a ship for France. Although the war was over, secrecy still prevailed. She recalled that the whole side of the ship was covered with canvas,

> so we couldn't read the name of the ship, and we entered through a canvas tunnel. We never knew which ship it was. We were on board for about three hours, and we heard the engines start. But they told us not to unpack. They brought us dinner on trays and we ate in our staterooms. At that point, an army orderly came and said, "Follow me." And we went over the side of the ship by rope ladder, into rowboats, and were taken ashore and back to our

hotel. That ship was full of army nurses, and the nurses went on to France. But we were sent back to our hotel.

Eventually, all re-aides who had orders for duty overseas were called together and given a choice: either to resign from the service and go home, or to accept assignment to an Army hospital in the United States. Miss Forest chose the latter. Assigned to Camp Gordon, GA, she went south by train, arriving in Atlanta in a snowstorm on the last day of 1918. One of her first patients, recently sent home from France, was a challenge for the devoted young therapist. "One of his legs, from the knee down, was so full of shrapnel bits. We worked and worked on that leg, massaging very gently, and eventually removed more than 100 pieces of shrapnel."

This patient was but one of the thousands of sick, disabled, and mutilated soldiers who were returned to the United States following the Armistice. The reconstruction aides did a great deal of outstanding work with those men. By 1919, physical therapy clinics were operating at forty-six Army hospitals. But as patients were discharged, there was a gradual cutback, and by June 1921 the number of treatment centers was reduced to six.[38]

Many re-aides remained in military service and worked on into the 1920s at Veterans Bureau (later Veterans Administration) hospitals and at public health facilities, military base camps and department hospitals, and national soldiers' homes. At Fort Sam Houston, TX, for example, the aides continued therapy in the psychiatric, tuberculosis, and surgical wards, "as busy in 1923 as in the days directly following the war. The P.T. work is extremely heavy," The Re-Aides' Post reported in January 1924. "The aides on duty, with the assistance of two trained ward men, average from 350 to 400 treatments a day. Treatments for the year 1923 will average near 100,000 [nationwide]."[39]

Occupational therapists, too, continued to work, teaching weaving, painting, basketry, printing, metalwork, and other arts. Several of these women opened boutiques and workshops where ex-servicemen could perfect their talents and sell their work.

The therapists organized in 1921 as The World War Reconstruction Aides' Association (WWRAA) and published a quarterly newsletter, The Re-Aides' Post, for many years, until the organization disbanded in July 1949. A list of all aides, prepared by the WWRAA in 1941, included 1,980 names, but because Army records of World War I aides were destroyed in a fire, it is impossible to determine the accuracy of this number.

Many aides were married after the war, of course, often to men who had been their patients. They became homemakers, started families, and struggled through the Great Depression. During those disastrous years, the middle-aged re-aides continued to worry about their onetime charges. An April 1932 editorial in The Re-Aides' Post made the following suggestion:

> In this day of great need, I am wondering if it would not be a fine thing for the different Units of our organization to provide in some way—work, food, or clothes—for a worthy ex-serviceman or such a man and his family.
>
> Some of the Units are doing that very thing. We who have worked with these men are in a position to do a very intimate bit of service to them, for we are sure of being understood. Old clothing is so acceptable to these needy families. A Bridge Party given as a benefit with a charge of a can of corn, a pound of coffee, etc., works magic. Now is your chance to "Carry On!"

Many of the veteran therapists themselves needed help. As The Re-Aides' Post noted in July 1922, "There have been some silent tragedies among our sisters who have contracted T.B. [tuberculosis] or who have lost the use of an arm from overwork in the clinic. And others who have sustained injuries through accident, and who did not know their rights under the Compensation Act because, perhaps, of the persistent bungling of the aide's status." This "bungling" was due to the fact that the re-aides, although sworn into the military in 1918, had been discharged not as military personnel but as civilians. As such, they were not eligible for veterans' compensation and benefits. Like the telephone operators of the Army Signal Corps, the aides were dismayed after the war to find themselves shuffled aside by the government they had served. It was "a grievance which was to ring down through the years until the coming of the Second World War."[40]

The Army considered the re-aides to have been civilian employees, subject, nevertheless, to Army regulations. Joining up in 1918, the women not only had to meet the requirements of the surgeon general's office, but they were required to take an oath and serve until they were released. They had to be between the ages of twenty-three and forty and be citizens of the United States or one of its allies in the war against Germany. In their department wards, the aides had stood inspection just like the camp soldiers, and like the nurses, they were not supposed to associate socially with enlisted men.

Through the WWRAA, the reconstruction aides tried a number of times to obtain recognition of their veteran status. One effort was to have themselves placed on Graduate Army Nurses' status, because nurses received full benefits and many aides had done nurses' work at various stations during and after the war. Aides pointed out, to no avail, that "upon being appointed a Reconstruction Aide in the Medical Department, U.S. Army," they had taken the oath of office. Their discharges, however, had been as civilians who had served "with" but were not "of" the military.

> This state of "being with but not of the army" became a grievance to the aides from the time they first realized their status, and the battle for recognition sometimes reached the ebullient stage. Several years after the war, they received from the Surgeon General's office some of the following arguments: The aides were too small a group to expect special consideration. There were "hundreds of thousands of other employees who were not receiving benefits, and the aides were no more entitled to military status than these others. This office is unable to perceive, however, why the particular classes of employees mentioned should be singled out for preferential treatment from all the employees connected with the military establishment during the war."
>
> This ratiocination, however, did not satisfy the aides. They still maintained that since they were "military" in everything but benefits, they also should have the benefits.[41]

The WWRAA also tried casting its lot with the American Legion and the Women's Overseas Service League, because the aides' association was considered too small and too weak on its own.

Legislation to accord veteran status to the re-aides was introduced in Congress a number of times over the years, but the women lacked a powerful lobby to press for passage. Indeed, in October 1933, the WWRAA Committee on Military Status reported in The Re-Aides' Post that "obviously this is no time to ask consideration for our group. . . . Those in authority are struggling under heavy burdens and perplexing questions concerning our common good. It is our duty to serve as we did in 1917—not to ask for service."

So the many enabling bills for the Great War re-aides died in committee in Washington, DC. Eventually, in 1942, physical and occupational therapists, along with dietitians, were organized into divisions of the surgeon general's office as the United States readied to fight yet another world war. In 1947, by act of Congress, these units became the Women's Medical Specialist Corps, later the Army Medical Specialist Corps. But it was not until the passage of the G.I. Bill Improvement Act of 1977—some sixty years after the Great War—that the re-aides of 1917–1919 were recognized as veterans. The same bill also granted veteran status and benefits to the Signal Corps telephone operators, clerks, and hospital dietitians of the First World War.[42]

Mary McMillan, one of the leading early physical therapists, ended World War I teaching at Reed College. She returned to the surgeon general's office in January 1919 and in March was named chief head aide in the Department of

Physiotherapy at Walter Reed Hospital in Washington, DC. During that period, she wrote Massage and Therapeutic Exercise, the first book by a physical therapist to be published in the United States. She went into private practice in 1920 and taught physical therapy at Harvard until 1932, when she went to China on a grant.

In November 1941, she set out to return to the United States but was caught in Manila in the aftermath of Pearl Harbor. She immediately volunteered her services at the Army hospital and was on hand when the first wounded were brought in. When the Japanese entered Manila, she was interned at Santo Tomas prison camp, where she was the only physical therapist in the prison population. For many months, ravaged by disease, privation, and abuse, she carried out treatment of her fellow prisoners. Her only equipment was a dishpan and two buckets, which she used for hot-pack treatments. After more than eight months, she was transferred to the Chapei prison camp near Shanghai, where she contracted beriberi, herpes zoster, and multiple neuritis. She was repatriated in 1944 and died in Boston in 1959.[43]

The pioneering Dr. Goldthwait summed up reconstruction aide service: "The war demonstrated . . . that even severe injury need not lead to serious disability. . . . Not only were many men saved to useful lives, who would otherwise have been crippled, but the principles of physiotherapy and occupational therapy were so definitely established that civil hospitals must [now] provide a staff of such workers, similar to those provided by the Army."[44]

Notes

1. Army Medical Specialist Corps, prepared and published under the direction of Lt. Gen. Leonard D. Heaton, surgeon general, U.S. Army (Washington, DC: Office of the Surgeon General, 1968), 69.

2. The Beginnings: Physical Therapy and the APTA (Alexandria, VA: American Physical Therapy Association, 1979), 15.

3. Ibid., 17.

4. Ibid.

5. Cora M. Howes, memoirs, Reed College Archives, donated June 10, 1968.

6. Mary J.J. Wrinn, "Why They Organize," The Re-Aides' Post (April 1925): 2.

7. The Medical Department of the United States Army in the World War, vol. 13, part 1, Physical Reconstruction and Vocational Education (Washington, DC: Government Printing Office, 1927), 75.

8. Reed College Record (May 1918): 68.

9. Ibid.

10. Ibid., 69.

11. Ibid.

12. "Courses for Reconstruction Aides, by Direction of the War Department," Reed College Record (May 1918): 68–69.

13. Beginnings, 16.

14. The Re-Aides' Post (April 1925): 2.

15. This was one of several lectures from Miss Lane (no other identification) as reported in The Re-Aides' Post (April 1928): 10.

16. Lena Hitchcock, "The Great Adventure," unpublished memoirs, Liberty Memorial Museum Archives, Kansas City, MO.

17. Letter from Anna G. Voris in The Re-Aides' Post (Jan.–April 1942): 10.

18. Cathryne Gooding Ledge, "Aides,!" The Re-Aides' Post (April 1927): 7.

19. Horace M. Evans, "The Reconstruction Aides of America," The Re-Aides' Post (Jan. 1929): 5.

20. Other members of the first overseas unit of twenty-four aides (all physical therapists) were Louisa C. Lippitt (head aide), Juliet O. Bell, Matilda Benjamin, Bertha Bowles, Florence Burrell, Minerva Crowell, Dorothea Davis, Ruth M. Earl, Jane Feinman, Rena Fisk, Sarah Fletcher, Ethel Gray, Myrna Howe, Elizabeth Huntington, Anne M. Larned, Blanche Marvin, Harriett McDonald, Magna Nash, Mabel Penfield, Frances Philo, Eunice Taylor, Anna G. Voris, Dorothy Wellington, and Juanita Wetherall.

21. Carroll J. McAllister, one of the first male reconstruction aides, described a complete list of treatments in Beginnings, page 37: "The modalities we regularly used included Morse wave (galvanic-sinusoidal low voltage), the ultraviolet ray (carbon-arc type), 1,500 W deep-therapy lamps, spark-gap diathermy, muscle training, massage, and exercise. Equipment we did not have as Reconstruction Aides were infrared lamps, mercury arc ultraviolet lamps, and many of the more modern electronic and radio frequency devices. In hydrotherapy, we did have electric light cabinet baths, whirlpools, sitz baths, Scotch douches, and showers. We also used wet sheet packs and fomentations."

22. Beginnings, 34–35.

23. Ibid., 32–33.

24. Ibid., 36.

25. Laura Brackett Hoppin, ed., History of the World War Reconstruction Aides: Being an Account of the Activities and Whereabouts of Physio Therapy and Occupational Therapy Aides Who Served in U.S. Army Hospitals in the United States and in France During the World War (Milbrook, NY: W. Tyldsley, 1922), 27.

26. History of Base Hospital No. 20 (Philadelphia: University of Pennsylvania), 60.

27. Army Medical Specialist Corps, 86.

28. The Armies of Mercy: Harper's Pictorial Library of the World War, vol. 7 (New York: Harper and Bros., 1920), 181.

29. Helene M. Sillia, comp., A History of Women's Overseas Service League (Newburgh Heights, OH: Women's Overseas Service League, 1978), 255–257. This organization was founded in 1921 by women who served overseas in World War I. Copies of this publication are available from Ms. Sillia, 3872 E. 38th St., Newburgh Heights, OH 44105.

30. Hitchcock memoirs, ix.

31. Army Medical Specialist Corps, 80.

32. Hoppin, 76–77.

33. Army Medical Specialist Corps, 90.

34. Medical Department, vol. 13, part 1, 66–67.

35. Beginnings, 61.

36. Hoppin, 70.

37. Author interviews and correspondence with Harriet Forest Moore of Corvallis, OR, 1988–1990. Mrs. Moore also kindly loaned her complete collection of The Re-Aides' Post and her copy of The History of the World War Reconstruction Aides.

38. Army Medical Specialist Corps, 91.

39. The Re-Aides' Post (Jan. 1924): 3.

40. Beginnings, 68.

41. Ibid., 61.

42. Groups approved for veterans' status under Public Law 95–202, Section 401 (the G.I. Bill Improvement Act of 1977): Signal Corps female telephone operators in World War I, engineer field clerks in World War I, Women's Auxiliary (Army) Corps, Quartermaster Corps female clerical employees serving with the AEF, reconstruction aides and dieticians in World War I.

43. Beginnings, 100.

44. Ibid., 53.

Mary McMillan, an American physiotherapist trained in England, is considered to be the founder of physical therapy in the United States. (Courtesy of the American Physical Therapy Association)

A Reconstruction Aide unit (these usually included both physio- and occupational therapists) posed for a group photograph at old St. Paul's Church, Hoboken, NJ. It was customary for groups of nurses and re-aides to gather at this historic church to attend a dedication ceremony and blessing of their flag before sailing for France. The officer pictured with them is believed to be the chaplain at St. Paul's. (Courtesy of the Medical Archives, New York Hospital–Cornell Medical Center)

Harriet Forest, a physiothera-
pist, was a member of Re-Aide
Unit 12, the last to head for
France after the Armistice. The
aides boarded a ship in New
York but never sailed. Harriet
Forest chose to remain in the
military and served at Camp
Gordon, Fort McPherson, and
Walter Reed Hospital. Harriet
Forest (Moore) died in early
February 1992, one of the last
of the surviving reconstruction
aides. (Lettie Gavin collection)

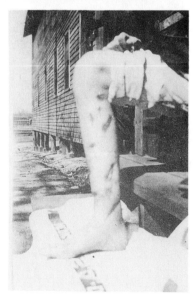

Harriet Forest Moore recalled
one wounded soldier whose
right leg was full of shrapnel.
"We massaged more than 100
pieces of metal out of that leg,"
she said later. (Lettie Gavin
collection)

A few of one aide's patients at a stateside hospital. One of the aims of reconstruction was to help the wounded forget lost functions and learn new ones. These wounded would have been given exercises teaching the use of artificial legs. They would also have received occupational training to teach skills necessary for professional success in the civilian world. (Lettie Gavin collection)

Occupational therapists at work in a tented hospital ward, 1918. Handicrafts were offered in the early stages of the program, primarily to divert a patient's attention from his disability. Later sessions offered vocational re-education training. (National Archives photo no. 111–SC–63988)

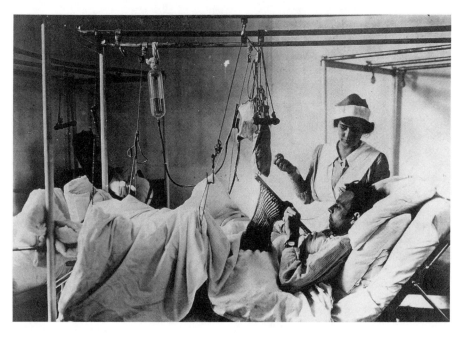

Re-aide Lena Hitchcock, an occupational therapist, encourages a wounded soldier as he learns weaving at Base Hospital No. 9, Chateauroux, France. (Courtesy of the Archives of the American Occupational Therapy Association, Inc., Bethesda, MD)

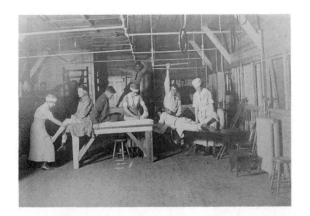

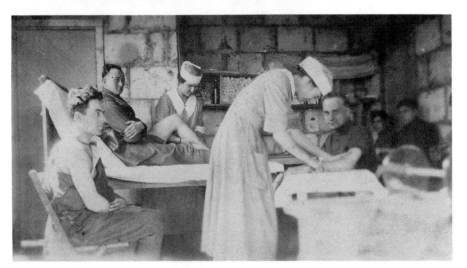

Re-aide physical therapists used a variety of techniques, including therapeutic exercise, massage and stretching, flexion and extension routines, resistive exercises, and special pulley weight apparatus, for treating the wounded. Hospital surgeons often worked with the therapists to set up a plan of therapy for such problems as gunshot wounds with fractures and nerve injury, amputations, head injuries, wounds with loss of bone substance, and face wounds. (Lettie Gavin collection)

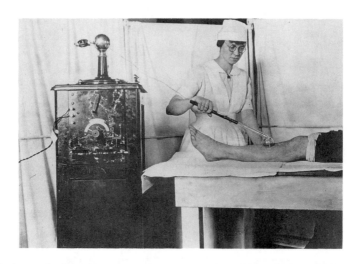

During and after the war years, reconstruction aides often used electrical currents to treat wounds involving nerve damage. This form of therapy was somewhat controversial, although the majority of aides believed it was a valuable adjunct to heat, massage, and passive movement. Above, Re-aide Jean Ewart uses high-frequency apparatus in treating a leg wound, while aide Evea Applegate, below, fits electrodes to supply high-frequency current to the damaged area of a wounded soldier's back. (Lettie Gavin collection)

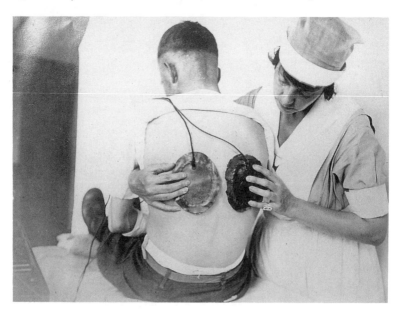

= 6 =

The Women of the YMCA

Service in World War I was but the latest chapter in a long history of cooperation with the military for the Young Men's Christian Association (the YMCA,
or Y), an English organization that opened its doors in the United States in
1851. During the Civil War, YMCA volunteers worked beside this country's
troops (both Union and Confederate), and in 1861 President Abraham Lincoln
commended Y leaders for their "benevolent undertaking for the benefit of the
soldiers." This undertaking involved establishing tents for social activities,
providing stationery and periodicals, ministering to the needs of prisoners of
war, and rendering other personal services for the soldiers. After the war, the
YMCA established the nation's first recreational, sports, and counseling services for U.S. soldiers and sailors. More than 500 Y workers participated in the
Spanish-American War, and when that war ended late in 1898 the YMCA's
governing body established a permanent Army and Navy Committee to oversee the group's work among the military forces. Within five months, the committee began constructing large, well-equipped buildings to house their work.
The first, located at the Brooklyn Navy Yard, opened in February 1899, and
soon they were found around the world.

In 1916, when 150,000 U.S. Army regulars and National Guardsmen were
dispatched to the Mexican border, Gen. John J. Pershing commander,
requested the help of 374 YMCA workers, who built forty-two temporary
buildings and provided portable equipment and supplies for educational, religious, and recreational purposes.[1] Thus, by the time the United States entered
World War I in April 1917, the Y had developed the knowledge, skills, and
experience to launch a massive program of welfare and morale services for the
military, both overseas and at home.

When U.S. involvement in the Great War began, each participating welfare
organization—the YMCA, YWCA, Red Cross, and Salvation Army among
them—worked independently.[2] To improve efficiency and coordinate the
work, General Pershing, by then commander-in-chief of the American Expeditionary Forces (AEF), placed all of them under military control, assigning
specific roles to each. General Order No. 26 directed that the Red Cross
should look after the sick and wounded, while the YMCA should concern

itself mainly with the instruction, amusement, and moral welfare of the troops.[3] General Pershing later estimated that the Y conducted 90 percent of the welfare work among U.S. forces in Europe during the war.[4]

YMCA service was conducted in "huts"—variations on the temporary buildings built along the Mexican border—that ranged in size and appearance from a tent—or even a large hole in the ground—to a variety of buildings that could serve as club, theater, gymnasium, church, school, post office, express agency, information bureau, and general store. The Y representatives, or secretaries, as they were known, created as cozy an environment as possible in those often flimsy structures, adding a colorful poster or two, a string of flags, a bunch of wildflowers, curtains, or a touch of paint. The hut was never exactly beautiful, but it looked like home to the thousands of American doughboys who flocked to these havens.[5]

In July 1917 the U.S. branch of the YMCA opened its service to females for the first time. These women were, the Y claimed, among the first to go to war, joining the nurses and Navy women who had begun to enlist in March 1917. Many Americans—military and civilian—objected to enrolling women, maintaining that they would be in the way and could not stand the physical strain of service in a war zone. Others argued, "You might send cooks and cleaners, but ladies would only embarrass the men, deprive them of freedom, and be themselves disgusted with contact with common soldiers."[6]

But the Y's national leadership believed otherwise and, backed by General Pershing, issued a call for female volunteers. In keeping with the times, these women were at first relegated to menial work in the canteens, kitchens, and cafes. The general plan was that the women would work in such "safe" areas as the ports, the Service of Supply (SOS) well behind the lines, and troop training camps, both at home and overseas.

In the summer of 1917, a small group of volunteers, mainly U.S. women already living in France, began YMCA work in two large French cities. Mrs. Vincent Astor opened the first canteen for sailors at the port of Brest in June, and Mrs. Theodore Roosevelt, Jr., organized the first canteen in Paris, which opened in July. These prominent matrons were the first of more than 3,000 Y women who followed in service to the AEF.

Mrs. Roosevelt soon put an end to the prevailing notion that a woman's place was in the Y kitchen, announcing that she was "eliminating all women from the dry canteen at the Pavilion Hotel in order to set women free for welfare service." Later, when William Sloane, chairman of the YMCA National War Work Council, went into the field and observed the expert and efficient work of the women, he immediately insisted that the Y drop the limiting title "canteen worker" and give the women the more dignified title of "secretary."[7]

Mrs. Roosevelt, whose husband was in command of the First Battalion, Twenty-sixth Infantry, First Division, of the AEF, had sailed for France just three weeks ahead of an official order forbidding military relatives from going overseas. She kept busy in Paris operating the YMCA canteen on the Avenue Montaigne during the day and teaching elementary French to a class of twenty-five soldiers in the evenings. "In August 1917," she recalled,

> the Y asked me to design a uniform for its women. I chose a gray whipcord jacket and skirt. The jacket had capacious pockets and a powder-blue collar with the YMCA triangle insignia embroidered in scarlet silk. The blue hat had a small brim and the same insignia. Instead of an overcoat, we copied an Italian officer's cape . . . in dark gray-green blanket cloth with a blue collar to match that on the jacket. Long and circular, it proved far better than an overcoat, as we could roll up in it when sleeping in camp or on unheated trains. The uniform was successful except when some of the girls, unused to discipline, persisted in adding lace collars, strings of beads, and hats trimmed with flowers.[8]

Among the first to wear the uniform were two pioneer Y canteen workers, Hope Butler and Dr. Marguerite "Daisy" Cockett, a U.S. physician, who together had organized the French Army's first U.S. ambulance unit to be driven by women. That unit had been appointed to the French Twentieth Army Corps, and the American women drove ambulances in the war zones of Amiens and St. Quentin. Later these two volunteers served in Serbia in a Red Cross unit working with the French Army. They also worked among war-zone refugees in France with the American Fund for French Wounded.[9]

But when the United States officially entered the war in April 1917, Miss Butler and Dr. Cockett joined the YMCA to serve their own country. The Y assigned them to establish a hut for the first detachment of U.S. troops, 6,000 men, in a small town near Chalons, which Miss Butler described as "little more than a mud hole with one winding street through it, and every other house a saloon." Undismayed, the women took over "a forlorn building with a mud floor and boarded-up windows" and, with help from an Army detail, proceeded to create a canteen. They cleaned the windows, covered the dirt floor, spread rough tables with checkered oilcloth, and hung red curtains. At first they served lemonade from two army buckets, but eventually they were able to expand their menu to include hot cocoa, coffee, pies, and cookies. That tiny hut, packed with doughboys throughout the miserable winter of 1917–1918, was one of the first of three wet canteens for U.S. forces in the field.[10]

Dr. Cockett later returned to Paris to serve at the Y headquarters, where, among other contributions, she wrote and illustrated a handbook for canteen workers. She and Hope Butler were sent home in the fall of 1918 to tour the country on behalf of a YMCA fund-raising and recruiting drive. Addressing a group of 500 Y secretaries about to go overseas, Dr. Cockett urged a better understanding and tolerance of the needs of the man behind the gun. "You must not consider it a bad thing to sell tobacco and cigarettes to the soldiers," she said, "and you must not be shocked if they play cards on Sunday. When they return from the horror of trench life and the hell of warfare, they need relaxation. They must get their minds off the scenes through which they have passed." She continued, "Your work is primarily to encourage and hearten the private soldier. . . . And don't mistake the interest shown you by the soldiers over there. To them you are but the symbol of American womanhood. They are not interested in you [personally], but in the woman at home that you represent."[11]

By early September 1917, many more Y women were arriving from the United States, including Gertrude Ely of Philadelphia and Martha McCook of Long Island, NY. These two intrepid volunteers came armed for their canteen work with three Victrolas, a quantity of popular music, and a tin lizzie automobile. Miss McCook later headed the Women's Bureau at the Y's Paris headquarters, and Miss Ely became one of the five women attached to the U.S. Army's First Division.

Miss Ely and her Y colleague Mary Arrowsmith were operating a canteen near the U.S. hospital at Froissy during the first U.S. engagements in the Cantigny sector in May 1918. At nearby Bonvillers, Frances Gulick and Dorothy Francis of the Y managed a similar service. In the aftermath of the doughboy attack, one observer wrote, "All four girls added regular nursing to their daily and nightly work. They made shields for the boys' eyes—for gassed eyes are terribly sensitive to light; they dressed wounds and mustard-gas lesions, they bathed the men, cooked for them, read to them, served them in every possible way."[12]

There never seemed to be enough nurses after a big push. "Therefore during and after any engagement, the women of the Y and the Salvation Army found throughout the fighting-line hospitals not only an opportunity, but a demand for nursing service, undisputed as it was imperative." During the Argonne drive, the Y women of the First Division assisted—at the Army's request—either in the triage centers or in the field hospitals at Cheppy, about three kilometers from the German line. There, the hospital consisted of a series of dugouts, along with a few tents. The Y women and the Salvationists worked in these areas, among the waiting men and even at the operating tables, sharing the work with Army nurses.[13]

Another of the First Division's Y women had arrived in Paris in March 1918 and was dispatched to Gondrecourt, a training area for U.S. troops. Life overseas was "tremendously interesting and full of the most wonderful opportunities," she confided with enthusiasm in one of her frequent letters home.[14] On her first assignment with the Eighteenth Infantry, she was billeted in a French home in the village of Saint Amand. She remembered it well:

> Madame conducted me to a sort of closet, which I was told was my room. It was on the first floor and opened onto a small back yard which I discovered served as a street for passing soldiers. As there was no chance for privacy, I went to bed practically as I was. As soon as I blew out my candle, several thousand mice (more or less) appeared. They dragged everything draggable about the floor until exhausted, when they sought my bed which evidently was theirs as well. The next morning a large white rooster appeared on my window sill—the cow didn't visit me, only because there was no cow. . . . I was determined not to complain, and I didn't.[15]

On April 8, she wrote again from Gondrecourt, "I was told unofficially that no women were to be allowed to rejoin the First Division. That the area was not a safe one and that we might be something of a nuisance."[16] Two days later she was transferred to Toul, and then on to Maron, a village where the Twenty-sixth Infantry was moving out to join troops massing for the Cantigny engagement. She wrote to her family:

> Supplies had been sent to the different villages where the troops were entraining, and we Y women were sent out to distribute them. Near the station was a small shed where we had two stoves, with two more outside. We heated water in large containers and made tea. The soldiers were in cattle cars, sometimes thirty men to a car, so that their chances of being comfortable were slim. They seemed delighted to get something hot, for it was rainy and cold with a penetrating dampness that made one shiver. Then we distributed a pack of cigarettes and a bar of chocolate to each man.[17]

Back with the First Division at the end of May in the village of Chepoix, and "happy beyond words to be there," the sturdy young Y volunteer wrote that she and her colleague had "a nice clean little room charmingly furnished with two mattresses, one table and two chairs. When we drive some nails into the wall to hang our clothes on, our apartment will be complete." She reassured her family, "Please don't weep over my discomforts, for they don't bother me at all. I know that I am the luckiest of women and I wouldn't exchange with anyone. . . . The country is wonderfully beautiful and the wild flowers magnificent—great fields of blazing poppies, corn flowers and clover. Surely this is a strange, strange world. Shells, bombs and poppies all in one field."[18]

When the First Division joined the offensive against the Marne Salient in July, the Y women were sent to Paris to wait until the troops were settled elsewhere. The anonymous canteen worker next wrote home telling of the hundreds of wounded arriving in the French capital "faster than they can be cared for." She promptly volunteered to help.

> I worked all night at the La Chapelle railroad station. The wounded are removed from the wonderful American hospital trains and placed in a long shed until ambulances arrive to take them to Paris hospitals. Sometimes they wait several hours. Many of them are from the First Division. I had rather dreaded the work, fearing I might break down or not be able to do it; but all thought of self disappeared when I saw them. Hundreds of them, long rows, stretcher after stretcher. It was the shortest night I ever spent!

The young U.S. woman was horrified by the sights and smells of the gangrenous wounds, but she was tearfully impressed by "the spirit of the soldiers, their endurance, their patience, their gratitude. . . . Wounded or not wounded, the American Soldier is unequalled for sheer courage, grit and sweetness."[19]

The first week in September found this Y girl setting up a canteen in the ruins of a chateau near the devastated village of Beaumont and making hot chocolate for the Third Battalion of the Twenty-sixth Infantry. Beaumont at the time was simply a collection of dugouts topped with slabs of sheet metal. One of these holes in the ground became her headquarters, and she settled in with her cot and two candles "which glimmer fitfully and throw dark shadows into the corners where the rats are playing about, making little squealing sounds."[20]

In the dark of one night, she shared her dugout with two doughboys looking for a dry place to eat their supper. "They sat on a box near the door," she wrote. "Sitting on my cot, I watched them and we talked, while the rats ran around like little dogs. The soldiers' faces stood out distinctly in the candlelight. As I looked at them I knew that as long as I lived I should remember them. It was one of those lightning flashes that come to us sometimes."[21]

Because the Army believed that the influence and support of the Y women were so important to the troops, the canteeners were permitted to remain with the First Division throughout the war,[22] and after the Armistice they marched with the troops into Germany. One of those women was Gertrude Ely, who had arrived in France in September 1917 bringing along her tin lizzie. U.S. writer Katherine Mayo described Miss Ely's activities as she traveled with the division. "Into that flivver, on the word to move, she packed a lot of rations, a cook-stove, a boiler, chocolate, a fiddle, some maps, a Y Red Triangle sign, writing paper, pens, ink, candles, her own bedroll, a lot of useful odds and ends, and all the cigarettes that room remained for. Then she started out a little ahead of the column." When she arrived at the next destination, "the billeting officer would give her a place, usually in the village saloon, because of the tables and chairs to be found there." Once assigned, "she would set up her stove, put on a pot of something good to cook, and prepare, meantime, to make hot chocolate. Then, if there was time, she would scour the place for a piano, commandeer or salvage it, and bring it in, at all costs. Then she would get out her fiddle, arrange her supplies, hang her Y sign in the window so that the boys marching in could find her," and wait for the troops to come down the road.[23]

Miss Ely, who was later decorated with the French Croix de Guerre for her work in the trenches, dugouts, and hospitals, was the first U.S. woman to cross the Rhine into Germany after the Armistice. Army sergeant Alexander Woollcott, then a correspondent for the official newspaper of the AEF, The Stars and Stripes, watched the U.S. occupation forces march over the river on a pontoon bridge that day: "First came Major Paul Daly of New York. . . . Then came Brig. Gen. Frank Parker and some officers of his staff. Then some French officers. Then a YMCA girl [Miss Ely] in a fur coat carrying a bunch of cookies and—bless her for a kind lady—three boxes of cigars."[24] Another Y woman secretary reportedly walked the entire distance with the troops, although her shoe soles did not survive the march.[25]

Mrs. Theodore Roosevelt, Jr., meanwhile, was assigned to the Savoy region, southeast of Paris, early in 1918. As she explained, "In August 1917 the chief secretary of the AEF-YMCA in France had offered to prepare plans providing leave centers for the troops, if General Pershing so desired. The need was clear. British and French soldiers could go home for the week's leave they were supposed to have every four months, military conditions permitting, but our men could not."[26]

In January 1918, the Army issued orders authorizing the first leave area, which was in Savoy and included the town of Aix-les-Bains. "I was one of a group of two women and ten men sent to Aix, a famous spa, to organize the leave area. The following May I was put in charge of the Y women in all such centers," Mrs. Roosevelt recalled. "By December, after the Armistice, we had ten Leave Areas which included 23 towns. Almost as many more were established later, to take care of the men awaiting demobilization."

The Savoy leave area could accommodate 4,000 soldiers at a time, with 600 arrivals and departures every day. "Our orders were to make it so attractive that the men would not mind missing Paris, a tough job indeed," Mrs. Roosevelt remembered. (Until after the Armistice, U.S. enlisted men were not permitted to go to Paris for fear they might get into trouble.) "We rented the Casino, or Grand Cercle, in Aix, a magnificent building with a theater, an elaborate bar where we had the canteen, and other vast rooms for various activities. In addition we leased a large field consisting of parts of eleven farms, to be used for athletics. As [each man's] leave was for seven days, we planned a program that offered different events each morning, afternoon, and evening, then would begin again."

Mrs. Roosevelt and her staff scheduled such outdoor activities as baseball, football, volleyball, tennis, golf, sight-seeing tours on bicycles, boating on the lake, fishing, hiking to places of interest, and picnics. Indoors there were professional and amateur theatrical performances, movies, religious services on Sundays, concerts, billiards, card tournaments, ping-pong, and dances. Unlimited hot baths, swimming, and water games were also offered at the Établissement des Bains at Aix.

Mrs. Roosevelt recalled that "the French people cooperated with enthusiasm and could not have been more helpful. The mayor issued proclamations . . . [and the residents] found us a cook, seamstresses to do mending for the troops, dishwashers, painters, carpenters, bicycles, and best of all a supply of milk. . . . [We used] nearly 500 quarts of milk a day."

At first, the soldiers deeply resented being forbidden to spend their leave in Paris and were fully prepared to hate Aix-les-Bains, which they called "Aches and Pains." "In spite of this," Mrs. Roosevelt wrote, "plans were successful. Before the war Aix had been the most fashionable of watering places, and many European royal families had been in the habit of going there 'to take the cure.' At length, American soldiers learned to delight in sleeping in luxurious hotel suites once occupied by Queen Victoria, King Edward VII, Emperor Franz Josef, Empress Eugenie, King Alfonso of Spain and others."

Among the group of Y volunteers who opened that first leave area at Aix was Alice Keats O'Connor, who arrived in France in February 1918. In addition to her work at the Aix canteen, Miss O'Connor had complete charge of the huge library there. In June she was assigned to an area in the Lorraine Sector, all that was left of the town of Baccarat, where the Forty-second Division was holding part of the line. There she set up a canteen a few kilometers behind the front.[27]

Although this was called a "quiet" sector, the area was gassed at least three days a week and bombed every other night. Nevertheless, Miss O'Connor carried on alone, maintaining her canteen as the Forty-second Division was replaced by the Seventy-seventh Division, and then by the Thirty-seventh

Division. When the troops were ordered out to participate in the St. Mihiel and Argonne drives, she moved with her regiment, the 148th Infantry.

Traveling in a camouflaged Ford truck carrying supplies and her bedroll, she established canteens for the troops at each stop along the march. She was given daily moving orders with the official road maps, and she generally reached the destinations ahead of the regiment, so that her canteen was ready when the troops arrived. In the St. Mihiel drive, Miss O'Connor was considered so indispensable to the regiment that she was permitted to remain despite the great danger. She often hiked on foot over miles of open roads to bring in supplies and newspapers, and she later drove a high covered wagon along the lines to distribute chocolate and cigarettes and any other treats she could scrounge. When her unit moved again, she operated a canteen south of the ruined city of Verdun.

After the Armistice, Alice O'Connor was sent into Verdun, where she worked with the Army and other volunteer organizations caring for the masses of Germany's former prisoners of war—British, French, and American—as they poured in. Each man was fed and given a bundle containing chocolate, cigarettes, and a copy of The New York Herald. She later worked with the U.S. occupation forces in Coblenz, Germany, and soon was named head of all the YMCA women in Germany, who eventually numbered several hundred. She sailed for home in July 1919 but returned to France to assist in the organization of library work undertaken by the American Committee for Devastated France.[28]

Another young Y volunteer, Faith Jayne Hinckley, wrote about her first duty station in 1917 at Base Camp No. 1, located at the port of St. Nazaire in Brittany, France. She recalled that her hut was "at best not more than a barn, but to secure lumber was a difficult task, and even this structure was built at a cost to the Y of $12,000. No chairs had yet arrived; tables and benches the German prisoners were making; one stove had been promised the following week."[29] But the men who crowded the hut that first day were happily writing letters and seemed to find the accommodations quite wonderful. After all, Miss Hinckley noted, it had

> a roof that did not leak, four walls and a canteen, with the promise of more.
> . . . It was all I had asked for, a chance to create an atmosphere for the men
> landing from America and on their way to the front. All we did that first
> afternoon was to make about 1,200 jam sandwiches, and at 6:30 sharp the
> canteen counter began to creak from the pressure of human force, and step-
> ping to my place at the cigarette counter, I looked into a sea of faces . . . our
> Marines and engineers, God bless them![30]

At Christmastime, an engineer regiment stationed at the port raised money for a Christmas tree for 1,500 French children, a typical U.S. gesture toward the youngsters of the war-torn country. "At noon on Christmas day," Miss Hinckley recalled, "a beautiful, double rainbow crossed the sky, and a silence fell over camp as all gazed in deep wonderment. At 2 o'clock the huge army trucks began to appear in camp, loaded with little French babies in their usual black garb; the band was playing from the platform and a soldier chorus sang the carols, after which each soldier of the regiment led or carried a little child to the tree for his or her gift."[31]

In the summer of 1918 there were twenty-nine Y huts at the French port of St. Nazaire; Miss Hinckley served at many of them, "from the Motor Corps to Infantry, from Naval Station or Aviation Field, and deep into the Government Forest to the Engineers."

That summer and fall, the influenza epidemic struck and spread from the United States around the world. Troop ship convoys carrying hundreds of sick soldiers from the United States steamed into St. Nazaire, and the victims "dropped on all sides of us," Miss Hinckley wrote.

> There were more than 20,000 men in camp. Two nights before I left [transferred to an advance station], 20 died in the puptents, and 500 lay on the floor of our YMCA hut. My heart ached almost beyond endurance, for the new men and the old soldiers of our base. Men had stood in line for hours; we had not closed the canteen except for twenty minutes since 10 o'clock that morning, and all day long new men marched into camp. Men were dropping with the "flu" and the hospitals were filled. We served [coffee and food] until midnight, stepping over the men who were then lying in long rows on their barracks bags.[32]

In the summer of 1918, when the German Imperial Army was again attempting a drive to the west, two unusual women arrived at YMCA headquarters on the Rue d'Aguesseau in Paris: Addie W. Hunton and Kathryn M. Johnson, only the second and third black YMCA women to come to France to serve the thousands of black soldiers on duty overseas. The first black volunteer, Mrs. James L. Curtis, had arrived earlier and been sent to St. Sulpice near the great port of Bordeaux, where thousands of black troops were working as stevedores, unloading supply ships from the United States. Upon arrival, Mrs. Curtis was told that because of the roughness of the men, she would not be allowed to serve them.[33]

Her colleague Addie Hunton noted, "Although she was quickly returned to Paris, the few days she had spent in the camp made a bright spot for the men there in that veritable wilderness of hardships. That she made ice cream and other 'goodies' for them, and best of all, let them open their hearts to her, was never forgotten by the men of that camp." When Mrs. Hunton and Miss Johnson reached Paris, they found Mrs. Curtis "with a group of men secretaries ordered home. It was then that for the first time we questioned the wisdom of our adventure. Surely we had not given up home, friends, and work for such an experience! . . . The fact that prejudice could follow us for three thousand miles across the Atlantic . . . tremendously shocked us."

Miss Johnson was assigned to Brest, another huge port with a large contingent of black stevedores. "But that area, too, seems not to have been keen to the advantages of a colored canteen worker. She was returned to Paris," Mrs. Hunton recalled.

At length, all three women were sent to St. Nazaire, where 7,000 black troops were permanently stationed, serving mainly as stevedores. That southern French port was the site of the largest YMCA hut in France, and the first for black men. There the three women remained for the duration of the war and for the dreary winter that followed it. "Time and again we were lifted up by rumors that other [black] canteen workers were on the way [to France]. But always the rumors proved false. . . . Two hundred thousand colored soldiers and [only] three colored women in France," Mrs. Hunton wrote in frustration. Her colleague Kathryn Johnson recalled great pleasure in working with men of her race through the YMCA, but she found racial prejudice invariably a heartbreaking problem: "The service of the colored welfare workers was more or less clouded at all times with that biting and stinging thing which is ever shadowing us in our own country, and which marked our pathway through all our joyous privilege of giving the best that was within us of labor and devotion."[34]

Although vastly outnumbered, the three black Y secretaries did the best they could. At their hut in St. Nazaire were hot chocolate and cookies, a cheerful reading room, a schoolroom where some 1,100 illiterate soldiers were taught to read and write, and—most memorable—the Sunday evening chat hour. Mrs. Hunton recalled:

> Somehow it came to us that this was a lonely time for the men. Sunday, just after supper—away from home and no special place to go. So we discussed it and began with just informal talks on current topics, apart from the war or the army. We had talks on race leaders, on work after the war, music, art, religion and every conceivable subject. We instituted a question box that was generally opened with fear and trembling, for the questions might be anything from, "When will you make us some fudge?" to "Which is the greatest science?"[35]

The secretaries also found time to write letters for the soldiers, to establish a money order system, to search for lost relatives at home, to do shopping for the men, and—the best morale booster of all—to spend an hour of their time simply listening to men who wanted to tell someone their stories of joy or sorrow. But the black women had far less time than they wanted for simply listening. As Miss Johnson observed, "In a hut of similar size among white soldiers, there would have been at least six women secretaries, and perhaps eight men. Here the only woman had from two to five male associates. Colored workers everywhere were so limited that one person found it necessary to do the work of three or four."[36]

In the first spring of peace, 1919, the YMCA assigned Mrs. Hunton to the YMCA facility at the Meuse-Argonne American Cemetery, located near the town of Romagne, some twenty-three miles northwest of Verdun. That huge collection cemetery was one of eight such sites in Europe where U.S. dead were brought in for permanent burial. Many of the bodies had been hastily interred—sometimes several months earlier—in local church cemeteries or in shallow, temporary graves as combat raged across the area. Officers and men of the Graves Registration Service, many of them assigned from black labor battalions, had the tremendous—and tremendously unpleasant—task of locating the bodies and transporting the remains to the permanent cemeteries.

"Here was a tremendous task for the surviving American soldiers," Mrs. Hunton wrote.

> Whose would be the hands to gather as best they could and place beneath the white crosses of honor the remains of those who had sanctified their spirits through the gift of their lifeblood? It would be a gruesome, repulsive and unhealthful task, requiring weeks of incessant toil during the long heavy days of summer. . . . Strange that when other hands refused the task, swarthy hands received it. We looked upon these soldiers of ours, the splendid Pioneer [black] regiments and the numerous fine labor battalions, as they constructed the cemeteries. . . . We watched them as they toiled day and night, week after week, through drenching rain and parching heat.[37]

Yet those physical hardships were nothing in comparison to the instances of discrimination "that seared their souls like a hot iron, inflicted as they were at a time when these soldiers were rendering the American army and the nation a sacred service. Always in those days there was fear of mutiny or rumors of mutiny. We felt most of the time that we were living close to the edge of a smoldering crater."

Because Romagne was so far from supplies and rations were often scarce and poor, the Y women prepared and served food for the soldiers all day long.

Feeding the men, however, was "but a small task compared with that of keeping [them] in good spirits and reminding them again and again of the glory of the work they had in hand." As Mrs. Hunton remembered, "For weeks at Romagne we watched these men fare forth with the dawn to find the dead on the 480 square miles of the battlefield of the Meuse-Argonne. At eventide we would see them return and reverently remove the boxes from the long lines of trucks and place them on the hillside beside the waiting trenches that other soldiers had been digging all the long busy day."[38]

When the soldiers had completed their grisly task, the two black Y women returned to Paris for reassignment. For ten days they waited, asking continuously that they be permitted to go to Brest, the greatest embarkation port in France. At the embarkation camp, as many as 40,000 black servicemen awaited transportation home, comforted by only one black male Y secretary at a time when Y headquarters in Paris had as many as forty black men and women secretaries eager for reassignment there. When Mrs. Hunton and Miss Johnson finally were permitted to go to Brest, they learned that the head of women's work for that region had tried repeatedly—and unsuccessfully—to have black women assigned to the post. The office in Paris, however, had refused to send them, claiming that the office at Brest did not want black female secretaries. Apparently, many white Y secretaries who sailed overseas had brought their prejudices with them.

By the end of the war, only nineteen black women had gone to France as Y secretaries. They are believed to be the only black women to have served overseas with a service organization.[39]

A major aspect of General Pershing's 1917 charge to the YMCA was to see to the amusement of the troops, as well as to their physical and moral well-being. Such entertainment was never viewed by Y officials as a luxury. On the contrary, one official, Winthrop Ames, observed, "Entertainment has been discovered to be . . . a necessity—as vital as sugar to food."[40]

The significance of entertainment was clear to the YMCA, both in France and at home. It meant relief and recreation, an escape from the strain of the unnatural life of a soldier, and it involved both enjoyment of the talents of others and active participation on the part of the servicemen themselves. To serve those ends, the Y Red Triangle hut—the soldier's home and club, his corner grocery store and church—also became his theater, his movie palace, his source of entertainment.

The Y mobilized the entertainment community and sent more than 800 professional theatrical artists to tour the camps of the AEF in France. These men and women were augmented by some 500 professionals engaged overseas and by 12,800 soldier actors in staged and costumed plays, circuses, and shows.

The Y professionals played instruments, sang, danced, recited, and did special stunts for soldier audiences estimated at an astounding eighty-eight million.

Some of the finest theaters in France were leased, but more often the performers worked in the Y huts on shaky improvised stages, in hangars or railroad repair shops, in hospital wards, and even alongside muddy roads in big shell holes or in the shelter of a few trees—wherever an audience of soldiers could be gathered.[41]

The Y's Entertainment Department advised volunteers before they left for the war zone:

> The fact that you are coming to appear there will have been chalked up a week ahead on the bulletin board outside the hut, and the hut will be packed with boys to welcome you. They will be standing outside the windows as far as they can hear. If you are late, they will wait. You see, it's not only entertainment you'll be bringing them, but entertainment from home, home that's 3,000 miles away. . . .
>
> They want cheerfulness and gaiety and clean laughter and good catchy music, and stirring recitations, and little swift plays—anything that's good of its kind, and well done, and that is "Made in America." You'll never realize how much it will mean to those boys to have you come 3,000 miles to serve them—how much they need you—till you stand before your first audience and get their welcome. We of the theatre can personally help to speed the victory, because . . . in addition to entertainment we can bring the unspoken message that America is with them and behind them every day and every hour.[42]

In addition to live entertainment, the new "moving pictures" were a big attraction overseas. Movie projectors were portable—although temperamental—by this time and were frequently carried by the volunteers on rolling canteens and on trucks, following scheduled tours of appearances. YMCA personnel orchestrated more than 150,000 film showings in France in barns, quarries, dugouts, or any convenient place, preferably dry, that could serve as an auditorium. In the hospitals, the films brought relief during many tedious hours.[43]

By early 1918, entertainers of every sort were donning the YMCA uniform and heading overseas. Everyone who could perform in any way set out to do his or her bit, from a talented young violinist from Tacoma, WA, to the nationally popular vaudeville singer and comedienne Elsie Janis, whose routine included jokes, vocal parodies, high kicks, and somersaults.

The musician from Washington State, Eunice Prossor, was studying in New York when she was picked to join four other young women in a YMCA troupe called "The Hearons Sisters," who in February 1918 sailed for France, the first volunteer group to organize. Thus began a junket that carried them 25,000 miles by truck, train, and cart to fill some 2,000 engagements, including four months in Germany with the U.S. Army of Occupation. "We were first in Paris for nine days, long enough to fill nine engagements," Miss Prossor recalled.[44] "We had been told to give the boys variety, and I nearly had prostration remembering the multifarious things I was to be and do. We all played mandolins, I played solos on the violin, I was part of the background in little sketches, I had to be a gypsy, we were Japanese girls with fans, I played a duet with Charlotte who played the clarinet, and then I was a soloist again. . . . And then I was a wreck." In addition to the many roles and changes of costume Miss Prossor had to worry about were the innumerable props that had to be kept track of and transported from one engagement to the next. These props included "three mandolins and a guitar, a small drum, oriental parasols, floppy hats and knitting bags. We carried all these things in an enormous long box-like affair which was the size of a steamer trunk, and the bane of our existence."

One day fellow troupe member Anna Hearons rushed in with the latest orders: the entertainers were going to the Front. "There was instant commotion. Our one and ever engaging thought had been to get as near as possible to the actual fighting line, where 'things were doing.' So we started for Toul to play for the 26th Division."

Their first concert in the Toul area took place in a tent. "The rain came down in torrents. Then the big guns started up on the Front, and soon we could hardly hear ourselves think. We felt like a minor act in a three-ring circus. That evening we played to 1,200 men at Vertuzy. We had a truck for a stage, a garden for a dressing room, and our audience packed the streets and hung from every available window."

After a show at Hammonville, the women were asked to "play in the gunpit for the boys who couldn't get over to see us, so we started off over the fields, some of the boys carrying the mandolins and others [carrying] the actresses, for the ground was full of shell holes as big as houses." Miss Prossor recalled:

> I added interest to a violin number by getting my bow tangled up in the netting that camouflaged the gun, and Ruth wrote a message on a shell that was to go over that night. But the shell never went over. The gunpit was blown up an hour after we left it, though we heard there were no casualties. If we had been blown sky-high . . . it would have been no more than we deserved. The stage that day was made of boxes of ammunition and the whole thing was decorated with hand grenades.[45]

A more prominent Y trouper, Elsie Janis, the U.S. vaudeville star, was playing the Palace Theater in London in April 1914. Three months later, England
was at war. "In a few days one hundred thousand of England's best had been
spirited away," she wrote. Soon "the wounded were coming home in thousands; the camps were full; and I spent every spare moment I had, and some I
did not have, singing in hospitals and camps."

In April 1917, the United States entered the war. "From that time on I had
but one idea, and that was to get to France and do for our boys what I had done
for the others. For I thought, if the Tommies [British troops] liked me in their
own land and surrounded by their own families, what would our boys feel,
3,000 miles away from home?"[46]

Miss Janis and her mother, who was her constant traveling companion, were
off to France early in 1918 and, upon arrival in Paris, were approached by the
YMCA.

> They had a map of France with dots all over it, showing where the Ameri-
> cans were, and where their circuit [of performances] would take me if I
> would go. At first I was not too keen on being with the YMCA. It sounded
> rather like it might cramp my speed. And I asked them quite frankly if my
> friends could come to the shows whether they were Young Christians or not.
> [Miss Janis always referred affectionately to Y personnel as "Young Chris-
> tians."] They explained that they had only one idea, that was to make the
> boys happy. As we had the same idea, we agreed to start at once.[47]

Miss Janis practiced on the boys in Paris, performing a selection of stories
and songs that ended with "Over There," the soldiers all joining in. "I was on
about 35 minutes that night, and when I finally tore myself away (I did not
want to leave at all!), I went home, sat down and cried from sheer joy! . . . For
a week we went every night to places around Paris where our boys were. One
night to a tractor school, next to some anti-aircraft boys, then out to some poor
engineers who were only an hour from Paris, but not allowed in the city."[48]

Miss Janis, her mother at her side, traveled far and wide in France, entertaining at hundreds of U.S. camps and stations, often "in a plethora of the finest
mud I've ever seen." She performed at U.S. Army Headquarters, Chaumont, at
the camp hospital, "where they had a gang with the mumps. Having had them,
I went in and gave a show. They were so grateful, as they thought they would
not see me." The next day, she "got a note from the boys who were quaran-
tined, saying, 'Dear Miss Janis, we can't get out, but won't you come and sing
one song under our windows? Signed, Scarlet Fever, Mumps, Meningitis, and

other Bugs.' I went, of course. . . . Two hundred and forty American wounded came in yesterday."[49]

At one stop, Miss Janis and her mother saw crowds of U.S. troops headed for the Front. "About 1,500 men were due to entrain at eight, but the general allowed them to come to the show. They had full equipment, tin hats and all. After the show they marched to the train cheering and singing. . . . The general thanked me and said I had put 'pep' enough into them to make them walk right into Germany singing."[50]

On her second tour of the battle area, Miss Janis gave a show to 2,000 men in an old Roman theater at Angers and performed another at a rest camp—"I imagine it is called a rest camp because the mud is so deep that if you once step in it you rest there," she observed.[51]

Hearing that some 2,000 wounded U.S. soldiers had arrived at Neuilly, outside Paris, Miss Janis asked permission to visit the hospital. "They were very courteous, but not too enthusiastic," she wrote. "They probably thought I would be rather too strenuous for a ward full of very badly wounded men. However, we went. Mother took all the things people take to the wounded, and I took the broadest grin I could produce."

Visiting this ward was sobering for Miss Janis. "There was not a man there who did not have one or two limbs in the air, all hung up on what I called gymnasium stuff, with that marvelous drainage system of the more marvelous Dr. Carrel which has saved hundreds of lives in this war. I thought I had seen badly wounded men during my hospital work before, but I have never seen boys 'shot to pieces' like those boys were."

Miss Janis particularly remembered "one boy who was so swathed in bandages that all I could see was one very nice blue eye and the corner of one very strong American mouth." She said to him, "Well, old dear, you certainly got yours, didn't you?," to which he replied, "Yes, I did, but the last time I seen the Germans they were running up a hill."[52]

At AEF headquarters at Chaumont, Miss Janis was invited to meet the commander-in-chief, Gen. John J. Pershing. "I was scared stiff," she recalled.

> Someone suggested that I should sing him a song. . . . I told a story and the lid was off. Mother had to stop me. I was so carried away by that big man's laugh I could have gone on forever. When I had finished, he said, "Elsie, when you first came to France, someone said you were more valuable than a whole regiment. Then someone raised it to a division. But I want to tell you that if you can give our men this sort of happiness, you are worth an Army Corps."[53]

On May 3, 1918, the Army's newspaper, The Stars and Stripes, referred to Elsie Janis as "an oasis of color and vivacity in a dreary desert of frock-coated and white-tied lecturers who have been visited upon us. Therefore, we are for her! . . . She inspires every man with an overwhelming desire to turn cartwheels all the way along the rocky road to Berlin." The newspaper described one of Elsie's appearances:

> She gave the boys a show in a railroad shed that had a stage set at one end. There came a signal to clear the track and with a great toot-tooting and a still greater uproar of men, a locomotive trundled in. On the cow-catcher [on the front of the engine] was Elsie, waving her hand and laughing as if she were having the time of her life, which she probably was. The locomotive made its way to the stage till it was near enough for the agile actress to make it in one jump. She did. With her black velvet tam perched on one side of her head, and her arms held high, she cried: "Are we down-hearted?" They were not, and said as much at the top of their voices.

Then, and always, until she died in 1956, Elsie Janis proudly carried the title "The Sweetheart of the AEF."

When hostilities ceased in November 1918, nearly every one of the two million U.S. soldiers in the AEF wanted to return home at once. But with the limited number of ships available and the unfinished business ahead for the victorious armies, this was impossible. Drills and fatigues soon became monotonous for troops deprived of an enemy and forced to linger on in France, and boredom quickly set in. It was a trying time for everyone. As many men as possible were sent for rest and relaxation to the various leave areas, where the Y secretaries continued their programs. Aix-les-Bains eventually employed a staff of twenty-seven Y women and twenty-three men and was used as a training school for new Y volunteers.

Other Y secretaries trooped into Germany after the Armistice with the U.S. Army of Occupation, setting up entertainments, athletic events, and educational programs to hold the interest and enthusiasm of the men during the long months they waited to leave for home. The fifteen original Y huts in Germany increased to thirty-six as the occupation wore on. The Y also operated a huge bakery and ice cream plant in Coblenz, which turned out quantities of treats for the U.S. troops. The original Y staff across the Rhine numbered thirty-five women but rose eventually to seventy-two.[54]

Most Y women in France passed up the opportunity to head home in 1919 and stood by their huts at the embarkation ports to help the men spruce up for their return to the States, to arrange a shopping service for the departing doughboys, and to provide the programs that countered the tedium of waiting to sail. And the work of the Y continued when the men went aboard the transports bound for New York. Y secretaries sailed with them, bringing all kinds of equipment to fill the tiresome days of the Atlantic crossing.

To alleviate their boredom, troops remaining in France and Germany were encouraged to participate in sports and games, and the large-scale athletics program culminated in the Interallied Games held near Paris in June and July 1919. That remarkable undertaking involved contestants invited by General Pershing from each of the Allied nations. Pershing Stadium, where the games took place, was built mainly by the U.S. Army engineers, with funds donated by the YMCA, who presented the structure to General Pershing. He later presented the stadium to the French people for use in sports events.

After the Armistice, Y personnel also helped many units organize theatrical troupes that traveled throughout the AEF giving performances. Furthermore, the Y contributed largely to education programs in the Army, especially in the founding of the Army University at Beaune, France, attended by some 10,000 soldier-students.

In these and other innovative projects at home and overseas, the YMCA contributed enormously to the war effort: some 26,000 paid Y staff men and women served in 1917–1918, 4,000 huts and tents were established for recreation and religious services, 1,500 canteen and post exchanges were operated, and 1,300 entertainers sent out to perform for the troops.

Reviewing their history, we find that the Y's novel and highly successful entertainment program would be carried on twenty-nine years later during World War II by the United Services Organizations (USO), a body that the YMCA helped create. Other First War contributions were the more than forty cookie and candy factories built and operated in Europe by the YMCA, and the Y also went into the hotel business on a large scale, operating seventy-three such establishments in France alone.

More than 80,000 educational scholarships were given by the YMCA to former servicemen, anticipating the G.I. Bill of the Second World War. The Y's human contributions are equally impressive: six men and two women serving under the Y banner were killed in action, 286 others were wounded, and 319 received citations, including the French Legion of Honor and the Order of the British Empire.[53] Thirteen women secretaries received the Croix de Guerre and many were cited for bravery.[54]

It is clear that the nearly 4,000 women of the YMCA showed the world that they could endure the war's long periods of manual labor, hardship and danger with a spirit and determination that rivalled that of their brothers, the American doughboy soldiers of the Great War. "The women of the Y have proved their right to a permanent place in the work of the social and religious order," said Edward C. Carter, the Y's wartime chief of work for U.S. troops in Europe. "Their development in the short period of their service," he said, "was remarkable."[55]

Notes

1. Following the Flag: A Short History of the YMCA's Work With the Armed Forces (Boston: Boston Armed Services YMCA, 1988), 2–4.

2. The Young Women's Christian Association was another social service organization heavily involved in wartime activities, both in the United States and in the battle zones overseas. The following details were obtained from Helene M. Sillia's History of Women's Overseas Service League (see note 27).

   When the United States entered the Great War in April 1917, the YWCA immediately put its resources at the disposal of the government. Within a month, the YWCA had organized a War Work Council with responsibility for all war emergency activities. The council established several objectives. One was providing social workers for training camp activities to meet the new and increased demands for wartime services to women and girls, including workers in industry and families of servicemen. Another was an intensified program for women war workers, service groups, and recreation programs in Army camps.

   The YWCA's first government project was to open a visitor's hut in the Army camp at Plattsburg, NY, where services were provided for families and women visiting the 5,000 men training there. This endeavor marked the first time that women other than nurses were permitted to work inside U.S. Army camps. Similar hospitality houses, programs, and services were established in other armed forces training centers, in Army hospital camps, and at U.S. ports.

   In industrial centers, YWCA programs were expanded to offer employment bureaus, emergency housing, and Travelers' Aid services for women war workers. The YWCA also worked with foreign-born families during the war years, providing translation, interpretation, and information services for families of enlisted men. The organization also provided multilingual hostesses in military and defense work areas to help war workers and servicemen communicate with their families at home and overseas.

   When the AEF landed in France in 1917, the YWCA extended its war work overseas in cooperation with the U.S. Army. Among its projects were programs for women serving with the AEF, nurses' clubs, hospitality centers, and housing assistance for U.S. and French women. The YWCA later worked to provide aid to war brides of U.S. servicemen and to establish hostess houses for families visiting U.S. military cemeteries overseas.

   Unfortunately, as one source observed (see note 3), "This unostentatious service to the army of women workers—nurses, telephone operators, Red Cross and YMCA workers— with its splendid chain of hostess houses for the men and their visiting relatives and friends . . . has never received the recognition which it merited."

3. Service With Fighting Men: An Account of the Work of the American Young Men's Christian Association in the World War (New York: Association Press, 1924), 130.

4. Following the Flag, 5.

5. Barbara Schroeder, "Women YMCA Secretaries in World War I," Carry On, Women's Overseas Service League manazine (March 1988): 18.

6. Katherine Mayo, "That Damn Y": A Record of Overseas Service (Boston: Houghton Mifflin, 1920), 59.

7. Service With Fighting Men, 61.

8. Day Before Yesterday: The Reminiscences of Mrs. Theodore Roosevelt, Jr. (Garden City, NY: Doubleday, 1959), 85.

9. Archival material on Dr. Marguerite Standish Cockett was provided by Andrea Hinding, archivist, YMCA Archives, University Libraries, University of Minnesota, Minneapolis.

10. Ibid.

11. Ibid.

12. Mayo, 124.

13. Ibid., 137.

14. Her letters were later published anonymously under the title, With the First Division in France: Letters Written by a Y.M.C.A. Canteen Worker While on Active Service in France (n.p., n.d.). This material comes from page 5.

15. Ibid., 9.

16. Ibid., 17.

17. Ibid., 21.

18. Ibid., 29–31.

19. Ibid., 58–59.

20. Ibid., 80.

21. Ibid., 85.

22. Service With Fighting Men, 58.

23. Mayo, 268–269.

24. The Stars and Stripes, Dec. 20, 1918.

25. Schroeder, 19.

26. Day Before Yesterday, 91–94.

27. "YMCA Canteen on Wheels," in A History of Women's Overseas Service League, comp. Helene M. Sillia (Newburgh Heights, OH: Women's Overseas Service League, 1978), 261–262. Copies of this publication are available from Ms. Sillia, 3872 E. 38th St., Newburgh Heights, OH 44105.

28. Ibid.

29. Faith Jayne Hinckley, Forgotten Fires (Lewiston, ME: Lewiston Journal Company, 1923), 17.

30. Ibid.

31. Ibid., 37.

32. Ibid., 52–53.

33. Addie W. Hunton and Kathryn M. Johnson, Two Colored Women With the American Expeditionary Forces (Brooklyn, NY: Brooklyn Eagle Press, 1920), 136–140.

34. Ibid., 23.

35. Ibid., 145.

36. Ibid., 33–34.

37. Ibid., 233–236.

38. Ibid., 24–26.

39. Service With Fighting Men, 619.

40. Ibid.

41. James Evans and Capt. Gardner L. Harding, Entertaining the American Army: The American Stage and Lyceum in the World War (New York: Association Press, 1921), 57–59.

42. Service With Fighting Men, 624.

43. "She Fiddled Her Way Through France," Tacoma Sunday Ledger-News Tribune (Washington), November 7, 1937, World War I Survey Collection, Archives of the U.S. Army Military History Institute, Carlisle Barracks, PA.

44. Ibid.

45. Elsie Janis, The Big Show: My Six Months With the American Expeditionary Forces (New York: Cosmopolitan Book Corporation, 1919), ix–xi.

46. Ibid., 6.

47. Ibid., 8–9.

48. Ibid., 20–22.

49. Ibid., 60.

50. Ibid., 79–82.

51. Ibid., 103.

52. Schroeder, 18.

53. Following the Flag, 5.

54. Service With Fighting Men, 58.

55. Albert C. Dieffenbach, "Woman's Place Is in the World," The Christian Register, Sept, 11, 1919.

This group of early Y volunteers in France includes Dr. Marguerite Cockett, seated left, a U.S. physician who had driven an ambulance for the French Army and served in Serbia with the Red Cross. She was one of two YMCA workers assigned to establish a hut, or canteen, for the first detachment of U.S. troops, 6,000 men, in a small town near Chalons. (Courtesy of YMCA of the USA Archives, University of Minnesota, St. Paul, MN)

In the summer of 1917, Mrs. Theodore Roosevelt, Jr., organized the first YMCA canteen in Paris and designed a uniform for Y women. She also developed much-needed leave centers for U.S. troops. (Courtesy of YMCA of the USA Archives, University of Minnesota, St. Paul, MN)

YMCA volunteers set up kitchens in any kind of shelter they could find, including this ruined house in Varennes-en-Argonne, Meuse, France, where these women were serving men of the Eighty-second Division in October 1918. Pictured here brewing several gallons of hot chocolate are Mary Sweeney, center, and Bernetta Adams Miller, right. Miss Miller, of New York City, was wounded during her duty overseas, and both she and Mary Sweeney were awarded the French Croix de Guerre. (U.S. Army Military History Institute, Carlisle, PA)

A YMCA rolling kitchen attached to the U.S. Third Division. Elizabeth Barker stands in the wagon, preparing the hot chocolate so beloved by the troops. M. A. Nash is working below, breaking kindling wood to stoke their oil-drum stove. The Y divisional forces did their best to follow their troops, despite the scattering of units, traffic blockages, and hazardous weather. (U.S. Army Military History Institute, Carlisle, PA)

The Y took seriously General Pershing's 1917 order to see to the amusement of the troops, and they found that hundreds of Americans, from clowns to opera stars, were eager to go to France under the auspices of the YMCA Entertainment Department. More than 800 professional artists toured the area of the AEF, including this singer and his accompanist, entertaining in the ruins of a fought-over French town. (National Archives photo no. 111–SC–18922)

Gertrude Ely of Philadelphia, far right, and her colleague, Mary Arrowsmith, operated a Y hut near the U.S. hospital at Froissy in France during the first U.S. engagements in the Cantigny sector in May 1918. After their daily work in the canteen, many volunteers worked nights helping in the hospitals, bathing the wounded, dressing wounds, keeping records, and serving wherever they were needed. Both of these women received the French Croix de Guerre for their work in the trenches, dugouts, and hospitals. (Courtesy of YMCA of the USA Archives, University of Minnesota, St. Paul, MN)

Vaudeville star Elsie Janis, seated onstage, had been entertaining troops since she began singing to British wounded in 1914. Here she visits members of the 101st Machine Gun Battalion at Bois de Rehanne, France, in May 1918. Seated, right, next to an officer, is her mother, who always traveled with her. (National Archives photo no. 111–SC–14265)

Some of the grandest spas in France were converted by the YMCA into leave area destinations for U.S. troops. Here, the elegant bar at a hotel in the southeastern port of Nice became the canteen, staffed by Y volunteers, while other vast rooms were used for various activities for the vacationing doughboys. The Y also leased large fields for athletics, and organized sight-seeing tours, theatrical programs, concerts, card tournaments, swimming, and water games for the men, serving hundreds every day. (Courtesy of YMCA of the USA Archives, University of Minnesota, St. Paul, MN)

Addie Hunton, a widow, went to France in 1918 as a YMCA secretary, one of the handful of black women who were permitted to go overseas to serve at camps and ports where more than 150,000 black men were on duty with the AEF. (Courtesy of YMCA of the USA Archives, University of Minnesota, St. Paul, MN)

= 7 =
The Woman Physician in the Great War

They were not called to the colors, but they decided to go anyway.

—Dr. Esther Pohl Lovejoy

In the nineteenth century, a woman who chose medicine as a career was subjected to blatant discrimination at best, scorn and derision at worst. In the early twentieth century, female physicians fared little better. Even in the face of urgent need during the Great War of 1914–1918, the U.S. Army Medical Department refused these women doctors the opportunity to serve in an official capacity alongside their male counterparts. Male doctors and female nurses on duty with the American Expeditionary Forces (AEF) in 1917–1918 were seriously overworked and close to exhaustion in the final months of the war, and they became easy prey for the influenza epidemic that swept the world in the autumn of 1918. Many fell ill, and a number of nurses died. But although the Army was desperate for help, female doctors were permitted only as "contract surgeons," or civilians on hire, a designation that made use of their talents and training but withheld military rank, pay, and benefits. Many women physicians did serve, however, with the French Army and with such social service organizations as the American Fund for French Wounded, the American Committee for Devastated France, the Smith College Relief Unit, and other independent overseas groups.

At home, in June 1917, the newly formed Medical Women's National Association (MWNA), later the American Medical Women's Association (AMWA), gathered in New York for its second meeting, with 300 concerned women present. Among other actions, the convention "adopted a naive resolution calling upon the War Department for a square deal regardless of sex, color, or previous condition of servitude," wrote one of the members, Dr. Esther Pohl Lovejoy.

Dr. Rosalie Slaughter Morton of New York presented an illustrated lecture about the work of women physicians overseas, and MWNA president Dr.

Bertha Van Hoosen named Dr. Morton chairman of the War Service Committee, whose aim was to register female medical workers, raise funds, and develop plans for service in the war zone. The committee adopted the name American Women's Hospitals (AWH) in honor of the exemplary work of the Scottish Women's Hospitals then serving in Europe. The convention also authorized Dr. Lovejoy to go to France on an inspection tour as the official representative of the MWNA, and the group appointed war service committees in various states to organize hospital units to serve overseas.

During the first year of activity, more than 1,000 women physicians registered with AWH; many certified for overseas service with the American Red Cross. The Red Cross also agreed in March 1918 to sponsor AWH dispensaries and hospitals in any country, for civil or military purposes.[1]

In August 1917, Dr. Lovejoy sailed on the *Chicago* with Dr. Alice Barlow Brown, of Winnetka, IL, and other volunteers. "An atmosphere of hope and expectation pervaded the ship," she wrote. "None of us knew just what we were going to do, but we all entertained an inward and outward conviction that we had been appointed to live at this day and age for good and sufficient reasons which would be revealed in due time." When they reached France, Dr. Brown, with a nurse and interpreter, went to serve with the American Fund for French Wounded in the Meurthe-et-Moselle area. Dr. Lovejoy joined the medical staff of the Children's Bureau of the American Red Cross in Paris and was assigned to investigate and report on organizations applying for assistance.

Meanwhile, the AWH concentrated on fund-raising and registration at home, while Dr. Lovejoy continued her survey in Europe. Her report to the Medical Women's meeting in June 1918 coincided with the sailing of the first AWH unit to Europe under the direction of the American Red Cross. Dr. Lovejoy later wrote about the unit's experience: "This [AWH] service has not been a bed of roses. Sometimes it has been a bed of straw in a box car, a rug on the deck of a sailing smack, or a cot in a typhus camp. Our hospitalers have endured discomforts, survived diseases and manifold dangers, but they have lived abundantly. . . . They can never be poor though they die in the almshouse—the place would be enriched by their presence."

Dr. Lovejoy also felt strongly about the position of the U.S. military. "This relief agency [AWH], which was inaugurated while the United States was mobilizing for war, is the outgrowth of the desire of American medical women for their share of the work they were qualified to perform. Our government provided for the enlistment of [female] nurses, but not for women physicians. This was a mistake. It is utterly impossible to leave a large number of well-trained women out of a service in which they belong, for the reason that they won't stay out."

Dr. Lovejoy pointed out that the men of the medical profession were called to military service in 1917, and "the nation stood ready to provide transportation, buildings, medical and hospital supplies, rations, rank, salary, insurance and well-fitting shoes. We were grateful for the opportunity of service and concomitant blessings enjoyed by our professional brothers, and from the standpoint of our disadvantage, we rejoiced in their good fortune." Despite this disadvantage and the fact that "the women of the medical profession were not called to the colors," they "decided to go anyway."

At the inception of the AWH in 1917, as Dr. Lovejoy wrote, "there was light, but no funds. Our workers were all volunteers and paid for the privilege by financing, according to their means, part of the service in which they were engaged. The cost of travel, equipment, supplies, and general overhead was carried in this way." In the weeks and months that followed, the AWH grew, and donations of clothing, surgical instruments, ambulances, and other equipment poured in. "Possibilities for service were opening in different directions, but we were handicapped by lack of funds. In the language of an eager salesman, the AWH was a 'selling proposition,' but our leaders were physicians of the old school and loath to go into the business of getting money in a direct business way." Indeed, during the first year from June 1917 to June 1918, only $24,000 was raised. However, during the following year, a campaign committee led by Dr. Gertrude A. Walker generated $200,000 in support of the AWH.

At the beginning of that second year, in June 1918, the MWNA board chose Dr. Mary M. Crawford of New York City as its chairman. During her term, medical women were sent to serve in different parts of Europe, southwest Asia, and northeast Africa; the MWNA extended its cooperative work with other organizations; and AWH work was established in France and undertaken in the Balkans.

AWH No. 1 opened in the village of Neufmoutiers in the Seine-et-Marne area of France in July 1918 under the direction of Dr. Barbara Hunt of Bangor, ME. Dr. Lovejoy wrote:

> A building was assigned for this purpose by the French Sixth Army, with the understanding that the hospital should be available for both civil and military cases. This was the first hospital conducted and financed entirely by our committee.
>
> I should like to say that it ran like clockwork from the beginning, but this would not be the truth. As a matter of fact, it ran like most of the hospitals in the war zone, in a very uncertain fashion. But it stayed in the field, gaining strength as time went by. Within a few months, as the Germans evacuated territory, our hospital moved joyously toward the north, where the need was greater and the facilities for work much better.[2]

During the summer of 1918, the medical women at AWH No. 1 wrote home about the renewed German offensive at Chateau Thierry and about the nightly raids on Paris, only twenty miles away. One of the doctors reported:

> In the midst of this excitement, our hospital building was prepared for use as quickly as possible. . . . The Allied counter drive, destined to end the war, was begun July 18. For several days before this, the gray-blue and khaki-clad soldiers had been disappearing from the district, and within a week our commanding officer ordered building repairs and preparations discontinued.
>
> The Army had moved back into the Aisne [area] and our refugees were returning to their homes. A new location in the devastated region was to be assigned for our hospital, and in the meantime two physicians, with nurses, were to proceed at once to Meaux to assist in the treatment of wounded French soldiers arriving by ambulance from the Front.[3]

While they waited for a new site, AWH No. 1 opened dispensaries and a dental service at Neufmoutiers and made daily visits by ambulance to villages in the Aisne, holding consultations and bringing back the sick to the hospital. In September they moved to the village of Luzancy-sur-Marne, fifteen miles from Chateau Thierry. One of the doctors reported:

> Our hospital was installed in the Luzancy Chateau, which had been in almost constant use as a hospital since the beginning of the war, first by the Germans, then by the French, and last by our own Americans. This was a dear old place, with a frontage on the bank of the Marne.
>
> While the general clean-up was in progress [trying] to make a ravishing but infected old chateau look like a clean new hospital, 13 dispensaries were established in outlying districts to meet the immediate need [of the residents] for medical assistance. The passage of troops, and the occupation of villages by large numbers of soldiers in the spring and summer of 1918, had resulted in a scarcity of food and a very unsanitary state of affairs.
>
> The returning refugees were in run-down physical condition. The stage was set for epidemics. Diphtheria and scarlet fever appeared. These diseases were soon controlled, but typhoid and influenza, spreading over the district, reached the proportions of a disaster.

Hundreds of French civilians were sick, and the district was practically without medical attention except for the workers of AWH No. 1, assisted by two women doctors serving with the American Committee for Devastated France. Dr. Lovejoy described the situation. "During the typhoid epidemic, which lasted three months, our medical staff became emergency health officers. Double shod with supplementary sabots [wooden shoes], they shuffled through barnyard filth from one hovel to another. Streets and courtyards were cleaned, decaying debris dug out of holes and corners, and these disease-breeding spots liberally sprinkled with disinfectants." Nearly the entire population of the infected area was given anti-typhoid inoculations, and this disease was finally on the decline when the influenza epidemic flared up. Dr. Lovejoy reported:

> Calls came from every direction. The cars and ambulances of the AWH were running day and night, and before the end of this epidemic we were caring for the sick in more than a hundred villages. These poor people were ill prepared for such [an epidemic] visitation. Twice during the war they had been driven from their homes, and for four years had lived from hand to mouth in strange places. In the fall of 1918 they had crept back behind the advancing American and French armies and had taken refuge under any sort of shelter they could find near their ruined homes. Stricken with influenza in these cold damp places, many of them developed pneumonia and died.

Pleas for help poured in to the AWH. "Time after time the ambulances of the American Women's Hospitals were stopped on the highway by officials of different districts asking for help, and letters making similar requests were received daily. One of the letters was addressed to Monsieur le Directeur de l'Hopital Militaire de Luzancy. This officer manifestly did not know that our work was conducted by women, but when help is needed in such emergencies, sex is immaterial."

Meanwhile, other branches of the American Women's Hospitals' service were developing, as described in letters from the staff:

> Dr. Manwaring came in late last night, tired but contented, with 65 patients in a radius of 30 miles to her credit. From the opposite direction, Dr. Fraser and Miss Drummond appeared. They had been sent, several days before, to arrange for a hospital at La Ferte-Milon, and returned with tales of shell holes in their damp, fireless bedrooms, but [they were] happy and enthusiastic regarding the outlook. The hospital building is being repaired, and a dispensary service to outlying villages is already being operated from that center.
>
> Our dispensary under Dr. Mary MacLachlan at Luzancy grows and grows. On Sunday, the place looked absolutely affluent. In addition to the usual crowd, which in spite of weakness from sickness, walks impossible distances, there were five conveyances lined up with patients from ever so far away. Yes, we work on Sundays! It is wicked, but there is no chance to go to church anyway, and as a choice of sins, under the circumstances, it would be more sinful to rest.

The work of the Luzancy unit proved so satisfactory, in fact, that the American Red Cross sent for six more units of the same kind in October 1918. "This was a big order," said Dr. Lovejoy, "but hundreds of well qualified medical women, registered from the different states, were anxious for service, and it was merely a matter of selection. The first two groups, the Chicago and California units, were organized and ready to sail when the Armistice was signed."

Luzancy Hospital easily converted its military area to civilian relief after the war ended, and with the return of more refugees, the work increased enormously. Among the many services offered by the U.S. women doctors, possibly the most thrilling to the French peasant refugee was the dental service. "It will be a joy forever in France," wrote Dr. Lovejoy, "at least as long as our fillings last. The fair fame of American dentists in European capitals antedated the World War by several decades, [but] only the rich and powerful had employed American dentists for years. Doctors, midwives and undertakers were recognized necessities, but dentists were luxuries, and American dentists could be afforded only by the opulent."

AWH No. 1 had three dentists on the staff: Dr. Kate A. Doherty, Dr. DeLan Kinney, and Dr. Edna Ward. "They were all too popular for their own good," said Dr. Lovejoy. "When the day's work was done there was always somebody begging for attention, which was never refused."

Dr. Kinney tended countless patients who, in many instances, had lived a lifetime without a toothbrush. She worked tirelessly and skillfully among the ragged residents of the devastated villages of the Marne, and her "pulling clinics" were followed by other sessions devoted to repairs. Chairs were brought out for the patients and placed in the shade of the big plane tree near the hospital. During the winter following the war, Dr. Kinney devoted all her time to the sixteen villages of the Picardy region that were under the care of the Smith College Relief Unit.[4]

Dr. Ward had given up her practice in Cincinnati to enlist with the AWH unit in 1918. She did general hospital work at Luzancy for several months until she noticed the need for dental care among the thousands of war orphans whose teeth had not been inspected for six years. The Ohio dentist accepted the challenge, and with her own supply truck, driven by an English girl, she covered large areas of France and Belgium, bringing relief to hundreds of neglected children.

Early in 1919, Dr. Ward's most important overseas service began when she started work with the outlying battle-scarred towns in the Aisne area. She took the time to learn French in night school, and by the middle of 1919, she had established five dental centers for refugee children in the district. Small booklets on the care of teeth were printed in French and distributed by the American women, and Dr. Ward brought in another dentist, Dr. Nellie Goodman of Cincinnati, to help with the work. Years later she was still receiving letters from French youngsters to whom she had distributed toothbrushes.[5]

American Women's Hospital No. 2 was established at La Ferte-Milon, Department of the Aisne, under Dr. Ethel V. Fraser of Denver, CO. Dr. Lovejoy reported on that development:

> This small hospital had a big motor dispensary route. With the help of one nurse, an ambulance and chauffeuse [woman driver], Dr. Fraser cared for the sick in 48 villages, taking medical cases to her own hospital and sending the surgical cases to Luzancy for operation.
>
> Here is a characteristic message [from Dr. Fraser]: "Tell Dr. Fairbanks that I have a grand Pandora Box for her, with appendices, gall bladders, hernias, tumors and a million, more or less, tonsils and adenoids needing operations, in my villages."[6]

Dr. Charlotte Fairbanks of St. Johnsbury, VT, was the chief surgeon, and for her, "the entire district, surgically considered, was one grand Pandora Box, eventually totalling 852 cases. . . . She was operating from morning until night on all kinds of chronic surgical cases, which had accumulated during the four years when it was impossible for a poor civilian to have the care of a surgeon in that part of France."[7]

In February 1919, AWH No. 1 prepared to move to a location in the "badlands" along the Aisne, where wartime destruction had been greater and the need for their services had become correspondingly more demanding. But it was not easy to slip away from Luzancy without appropriate French ceremony. The hospital announced that no patients would be received after the end of March, and the mayor of the town replied that a special day of thanksgiving would be observed on Sunday, March 30, to honor AWH personnel. Dr. Lovejoy recalled the day:

> There are great days in the lives of all human beings and communities. . . . March 30, 1919, was a great day for the members of the staff of Hospital No. 1, and the entire population of friends and patients they had known so intimately during a period of tribulation. Citizenship in the town of Luzancy was officially conferred upon the staff . . . and all were accorded Médailles de la Reconaissance Française. Speeches were made, the school children sang the "Marseillaise," and American Women's Hospital No. 1 had taken official leave of Luzancy.[8]

Meanwhile, other American women physicians had found different ways to be of service in the Great War. Typical of these was Dr. Anne Tjomsland, one of the first women to intern at Bellevue Hospital in New York City. Born in Norway, Dr. Tjomsland received her early education in Chicago and Minneapolis. She graduated from Cornell College [later Cornell University] in 1910 and received her medical degree from the Cornell Medical School four years later. Bellevue accepted her as an intern only "after a long and arduous fight, and the taking of an examination," she wrote later. "In those days (1914) it was difficult for any candidate to enter Bellevue as Interne, and we competed with some sixty men candidates."[9]

Dr. Anne Tjomsland and Dr. Geraldine B. Watson "entered Bellevue triumphantly but a little uneasily" in July 1914. During the first six months, "fingers were pointed from all sides" at those first women interns. "They responded to this vulgar pressure by being rigorously circumspect. They smoked no cigarettes in the hospital grounds, received no men callers, and took only emergency phone calls."[10]

But they wasted little time on self-pity and filled their days with observing operations, taking responsibility for their own first cases, and experiencing the thrill of having patients completely trust and depend on them. Eventually, of course, the women doctors of Bellevue were accepted by their male colleagues, and they were soon asked, like the men, to stand the staff a beer every time they brought in a corpse.[11]

It was natural, then, that Dr. Tjomsland should expect to accompany these same men colleagues when they set out to support the AEF in France as Base Hospital No. 1. But because the Army Medical Department did not accept female physicians in 1917, Dr. Tjomsland had to sign on with the Bellevue unit as a contract surgeon—a civilian employee such as the dietitian, X-ray technician, and secretaries also listed on the hospital's roster.[12]

When members of Base Hospital No. 1 arrived at Vichy, France, in March 1918, they took over the two largest luxury hotels in the ancient spa city. The Hotel Carlton was designated the Surgical Department, and the Hotel l'Amirauté became the Medical Department. Dr. Tjomsland served at the Carlton. The hospital staff made up more than 300 beds and set up a ward for the seriously wounded in the Carlton's ornate dining room, with rows of white iron cots lined up beneath the immense crystal chandeliers. Their first patients were ambulatory wounded from a nearby French military hospital; they were happy fellows and made themselves at home.[13]

Two days later, the French soldiers were transferred to make room for a convoy of U.S. wounded. The flood of casualties from the units that had fought at Cantigny, Chateau Thierry, and Belleau Wood were brought over the road to

Vichy in fleets of trucks and ambulances. "From then on, they arrived in waves, rolling up day after day. No sooner had the doctors and nurses read the tags and labels on one case, got him cleaned up and operated on, than another rolled in. Endless rows of clay-colored bodies under khaki army blankets lay still on stretchers in the halls."[14]

One early June morning, Dr. Tjomsland wrote:

> Down in the streets they were—our lads—for the first time in our history straight from the front, loaded atop and inside of huge trucks, yelling till their wounds hurt. . . . It was strange to handle men with the smoke of battle still hanging about them. We often thought of the comparatively clean odor of these men when, later in the year, we received the battle stench from the Argonne.
>
> It was all as new and shiny as death to us: strange to hear them say they had "jumped off" the morning before, strange to hear the reverberation of the barrage, to feel the all-pervading insanity of strife wipe out our best convictions—to live, when all of us had gone mad.[15]

The medical efforts of the hospital staff were vital—and appreciated—but nevertheless, as Dr. Tjomsland noted, "the most effective help was the effortless presence of other patients. They were as ready with banter, cigarettes, the price of a beer or one of the vin sisters [rouge and blanc], as they were with blood for transfusions. . . . There was not much need of discipline; we were learning that when mankind is pushed to extremities, its behavior on the whole is pretty decent."[16]

Late that summer, the Vichy hospital increasingly took on the character of an evacuation hospital, treating only those who would suffer if transferred. "What," Dr. Tjomsland wondered, "would we have done [at home] at Bellevue with 40 or 50 patients coming into one ward as fast as the stretcher bearers could carry them, an equal number having been evacuated a few hours previously?"

The staff's work was made even more difficult because the wards, holding sixty to seventy men apiece, were not easily monitored open spaces; rather, they were hotel rooms opening into a central corridor, with four or five men in each room. Dr. Tjomsland described the emotional toll of caring for these patients:

> Imagine such a ward on a hot summer night, with one nurse and one wardmaster in charge. To the severely ill or wounded, the thought of sleep was far away. They did not sleep—merely dozed. Vague dreams of details unending, of empty canteens and blown-up rations, of dead buddies; sudden

sharp visions of home and mother, of familiar faces and things chasing through their brains; held between a desire to live and the end of suffering, they lay in impassive silence, wailing now and then in their delirium, we who cared for them mute witnesses to their sufferings and patience.[17]

Other U.S. base hospital units began to arrive at Vichy that summer, and ten other spa hotels were converted to hospitals. "By August 1918, Vichy was one of the largest hospital centers in France. The Bellevue unit now occupied space in 18 buildings, able to accommodate five to six thousand wounded and sick."[18]

In September, Dr. Tjomsland noted, "about twenty bundles of rags and blankets had come into the ward from the Argonne. For mere bundles they seemed. It was difficult to conceive that by washing, feeding and giving a bed to those run-down human machines, they would in a few days develop enough steam to again start running, each according to his light." She never forgot "that shadowy army—sixty thousand strong—that passed through our hospital center at Vichy, men to whom we are still cemented past recall by that strange fraternity growing out of having felt a man's blood trickle over your hands."[19] She recalled a quiet, springtime observation of Decoration Day, when the staff remembered those they had lost. "To us who watched the struggle of those young bodies that set like the sun, glowing to the very end, the long rows of white crosses seemed to repeat the faltering postscript we received from one of the mothers: 'I suppose there is no mistake about it being my boy?' "[20]

Another physician who made her way into service during the Great War was Dr. Nellie N. Barsness, born in 1873 to parents who were among the first Norwegian settlers in western Minnesota.[21] She worked as a teacher for several years, saving her money to enter the University of Minnesota Medical School, where she received her medical degree in 1902, becoming one of the first female physicians in the state. "I knew that there was a place for women physicians because there were women and girls who neglected their health," she wrote later. "At that time, some considered being a doctor was a man's job. If my father was a little embarrassed about my choosing a medical career, he lived to be grateful."[22]

Dr. Barsness interned at Luther Hospital in St. Paul, MN, and was admitted to the hospital staff in electrotherapeutics (the use of electric stimulation to obtain muscle contractions). "This was something new, so I went to Chicago to take a course in the subject," she wrote. "X-ray was then used on bones and gradually became used in treatments." When World War I began, many doctors and nurses went into service. Dr. Barsness served with the French Army, first in hospitals and later in clinics. Probably because of the great need to treat victims of poison gas, which often affected the eyes, Dr. Barsness worked at a hospital in Cempuis as an ophthalmologist, even though that was not her specialty.

After the Armistice, she assisted French doctors by conducting clinics in the cities of Nancy and Reims and surrounding small towns, and she was decorated by the French minister of war for her work with casualties under hazardous conditions. Always eager to learn, she went to Paris before leaving for home.

"We visited the clinic where the mutilated soldiers were rehabilitated," she wrote from Paris. This "clinic" was probably the workshop of the U.S. sculptress Anna Coleman Ladd, who made copper masks for French and U.S. soldiers who had suffered disfiguring facial wounds (see Chapter 8). Dr. Barsness recalled:

> As they marched into the dressing room, they looked like other well men, interested in business. Inside the dressing room, each man was taken over by a doctor, who took off one piece after another [of the copper mask] from the face and head, leaving an unbelievable sight. Even the hairs were planted in the mask. We marvel with deep gratitude at this scientific art that can give life again to these innocent victims.[23]

Dr. Mary Merritt Crawford was another female physician who had to forge her own path to service in World War I. Dr. Crawford attracted attention in 1908 as the first female ambulance surgeon at Williamsburg Hospital in Brooklyn, NY. A graduate of Cornell Medical School, she had been hired by Williamsburg because she scored higher than the male applicants in a competitive examination for internships. A crowd always gathered to see her hop aboard the rickety horse-drawn ambulance, she recalled. "I was a sensation," she said. "But you see, there wasn't much going on in the world in those days."[24]

Dr. Crawford had risen to the post of chief surgeon at Williamsburg and had set up a private practice in Brooklyn when war loomed overseas in 1914. She decided to go to France.

> I wrote to three or four places and applied, and wrote to Dr. [Joseph] Blake of the American Ambulance Hospital [near Paris], but to no avail. Then one day my mother saw a newspaper notice that the Countess of Talleyrand, who was [the U.S. heiress] Anna Gould, had sent a thousand dollars to the "New York Sun" to pay the fare of American doctors to come to France. Military doctors were badly needed.
>
> She had asked Dr. Rambeau, who was head of the Pasteur Institute in New York, to select the doctors. I went right over [to see him], and he

passed me. The "Sun" gave me a ticket on the old [ship] *Rochambeau*. They gave me a ticket to return . . . and twenty dollars in gold. Ten dollars to get me from Havre to Paris, and ten dollars to get me from Paris back to Havre. (Also told me not to expect anything more from them.)[25]

Dr. Crawford sailed for France in September 1914, shortly after the war began. She reached Paris after a slow trip, only to be told by Madame Talleyrand that the French didn't need any doctors. "She didn't have anything for me," Dr. Crawford recalled. "I was pretty well flattened, you know, because I'd come over there and I didn't have much money, though I had my ticket home. But I wasn't going to go home. I stayed at the Ambulance [Hospital] until I could see what to do. I wrote letters to all the doctors on the staff and waited. I almost signed up to go down to Barcelona and take care of the typhoid epidemic which was going on there, because I was NOT going to go home."

But Dr. Crawford was finally introduced to the famed U.S. surgeon Joseph Blake by his secretary at the hospital. Dr. Crawford asked if she could witness his operations that day and followed him into the surgery. However, the anesthetist wasn't there. Dr. Blake looked around, furious. He was a big man and not used to being kept waiting by interns and young doctors. He turned to Dr. Crawford and barked, "Can you give ether?"

Dr. Crawford could and did. "I gave four anesthetics, one right after the other for him that morning. I was just in heaven. That afternoon the medical board was meeting and they had intended to turn me down [but] Blake said that he had taken me on as an anesthetist. Then Dr. DuBouchet, who was the other chief, said he'd take me on as anesthetist in the afternoon. So by nightfall, I had a full-time job." Later, she asked Dr. Blake to put her in charge of detail work for a ward of twenty to forty men. "He gave me a ward, then two, and finally I wound up with four wards, doing the dressings, taking the history of them, and looking after them. I tell you I worked hard."

Unfortunately, she did not do a great deal of surgery, largely due to Dr. Blake's mercurial temperament. One week he told her, "I wish to heaven you could teach these young fellows to work the way you work and do the things that you do." The next week he placed a new male arrival from New York ahead of her. "I, suddenly, having been perfectly independent, found myself being ordered around by this young doctor. . . . I wouldn't take it." When she confronted Dr. Blake about it, he said, "I'll never put a woman over a man," to which she replied, "What kind of a service have you got then?"

Meanwhile, the French had offered Dr. Crawford a job heading up their half of the hospital. Originally, she had refused, not wanting to lose the opportunity to train with Dr. Blake, but after her conversation with him, she accepted the

French offer. "They put me on and I finished up with them," she recalled. She was somewhat disappointed in her new position, however. The French doctor she worked with was "very fussy and thought he must do everything [himself]. . . . I assisted him and that's all. When he found out I was leaving, he did allow me to amputate a couple of legs."

In treating her patients, Dr. Crawford remembered that

> We used a lot of things that nobody uses now. One interesting fact about that service: I saw the beginning of inventions. Giving a man a bath—we had a framework over an ordinary tub with extensions for his arms and legs. We could wash him and pour water on him, but we could keep water away from a part that shouldn't be touched. Dr. [Alexis] Carrel who was over there at Juilly came down and showed us his Carrel solution—irrigating the wound—and I saw the beginning of that. All sorts of contraptions were invented. That's one thing about medicine. A war benefits medicine more than it benefits anybody else. It's terrible, of course, but it does.[26]

As the war raged on in Europe, the United States joined the fray in April 1917. At that time, Dr. Alice Weld Tallant was a professor of obstetrics at the Woman's Medical College of Pennsylvania (now the Medical College of Pennsylvania) in Philadelphia. She promptly took a leave of absence to become a director of the Smith College Relief Unit. That summer, she accompanied the unit to an area along the Somme where they helped the rural population of villages devastated by battle and the retreating German Army.[27] Dr. Tallant, one of the unit's two doctors, worked alongside "women skilled in children's work, carpentry and handicrafts; one was a farmer, one was a high-school teacher; six were trained social service workers, and six qualified as chauffeurs."

The Smith Unit concentrated its efforts in five areas: public health, stores and supplies, farming, transportation, and social service proper, with its three subdivisions of visiting, sewing, and child welfare. Members of the unit had brought with them as much equipment as they could carry: camp beds, blankets, carpenter's tools, food, automobile parts, and clothing for distribution, as well as six portable houses and stoves to heat them. The French Army supplied other barracks and portable cabins, but no heat, electricity, running water, or plumbing.[28]

As they settled in, Dr. Tallant was questioned by a French military doctor about the needs of the American women. She replied that more than anything else, they needed toilet facilities. The officer made a sweeping bow and announced, "Mademoiselle, it will be my greatest pleasure to make you a present of one." The next day he sent a squad of soldiers to dig a latrine.[29]

For the first six months, that unit of eighteen women carried out their aid program from cheerless, muddy headquarters in the ruins of an ancient chateau at Grecourt in the Picardy region seventy-five miles north of Paris. One unit member described the daily grind. "The doctors . . . were the first to begin. A doctor's bag was their main reliance, since boxes of medicines failed to come through. This meager source of supplies was augmented by the kindly cooperation of the military doctors of the region, and later by a generous grant from the American Red Cross."

To make their rounds of approximately 500 patients, the doctors had their transportation allotment, plus emergency service whenever possible. "They also had Tambour, an ancient horse detached from the artillery, a high two-wheeled cart, and a soldier in a brave new uniform, to drive." These were a gift from a town official at Nesle. "But most frequently, [we] will recall our doctors, of a Sunday morning, or perhaps of a bitter afternoon, knapsack on back, starting cheerfully away on foot. Cheer, in fact, was their main stock of medicine. . . . Candy, hair ribbons, and more practical but perhaps not more efficacious, toothbrushes, beguiled the youngsters into habits of cleanliness."[30]

The Smith Unit's dispensary was "officially open six days in the week, and on Sunday was never quite shut." From August to October 1917, more than 500 treatments had been given: minor surgery and treatment of sores, skin diseases, and ailments arising from malnutrition. "There is a great deal of rheumatism," wrote a reporter for the London Daily Mail. "Pneumonia and similar troubles are expected. The people are living on the mud floors of stables, under leaking roofs, lying on board shelves without straw."[31]

In addition to the dispensary service, the Smith doctors made medical rounds weekly to each of the sixteen villages under their care. In three of the villages, there were permanent dispensary quarters. "All medical service, medicines, combs and toothbrushes, and supplementary feeding such as eggs and milk, from our cows, were free, to give the fullest encouragement to healthful living," one of the Smith volunteers wrote home. In spite of the shortage of pumps and fuel everywhere, the results were striking. "One scarcely recognized the clean—though often ragged—children of 1918, as the same as those who had watched so listlessly our arrival six months before."

At the end of her six-month leave of absence, the unit's director, Dr. Tallant was recalled to the Woman's Medical College in Philadelphia. But as soon as the spring term was over, she rushed back to France and caught the last train to the devastated regions. When she found the Grecourt chateau had been retaken by the enemy and its personnel evacuated by the Red Cross, Dr. Tallant joined Anne Morgan's American Committee for Devastated France.[32]

She also offered her services at the American Army Hospital, where 120 patients were awaiting attention, but she was turned down because the U.S. Army did not accept women physicians. Undismayed by her rejection, Dr. Tallant went on to a French Army Hospital, where she was welcomed and helped care for both civilian refugees and the French military wounded. During the battle of Chateau Thierry, she worked for two frantic months in the French receiving ward until the crisis passed.

The French Army authorized the women doctors to wear one stripe so they could give orders. On inspection one day, a French general asked, "The American ladies have one stripe; how long does it take to get two?" "Usually one year," the commanding officer replied. "But," queried the general, "wouldn't you say the ladies have had unusually intensive service?" The U.S. women doctors had the second stripe within an hour.

Dr. Tallant rejoined Anne Morgan's American Committee for Devastated France after the Armistice, in time to cope with the worldwide epidemic of influenza, or "Spanish Grippe," as it was called in France. Of more than 300 flu victims, she and her partner did not lose one patient, which Dr. Tallant attributed to the use of brandy, added to standard prescriptions, to offset the flu's weakening effect on the heart.

Dr. Tallant was awarded France's Croix de Guerre for her service in caring for the wounded under bombardment during the last months of the war. But just as precious to her was a less elaborate medal from the citizens of a small village in Picardy. This special souvenir was engraved as follows: "The inhabitants of Vic-sur-Aisne are grateful." Dr. Tallant, who later became an internationally known gynecologist and obstetrician, returned to Philadelphia after the war and worked for another eighteen years on the staff of the Woman's Medical College. She also served for many years with the Babies Hospital and St. Martha's House in South Philadelphia.[33]

Bellevue Hospital physician Anne Tjomsland continued to practice general medicine and anesthesiology in New York and New Jersey following the Great War. At the outset of the Second World War, she wrote to a friend: "No, I am not in the service; have not even asked, as they would be sure to turn me down; women are not wanted in this present fight, it seems—that is, women doctors. But it leaves all the more for us to do at home. Am working sometimes sixteen hours a day, and there is no end to the work one might do!" She continued to write about medical history and in 1952 produced a translation of the Saga of Hrafn Sveinbjarnson: The Life of an Icelandic Physician of the Thirteenth Century. She died in 1958 at the age of eighty-eight.[34]

After being decorated for her service by the French minister of war, Dr. Nellie Barsness came home to the Midwest late in 1919 but returned to Europe to study in Berlin and Vienna. She enjoyed a long and thriving practice in Minnesota and was honored in 1954 "for meritorious service to the people of her community" for more than fifty years.[35] She died in Minnesota in 1966 at the age of ninety-three.

Dr. Mary Crawford returned home after a year in Paris during the war, but she continued her war work, raising money for France and serving as chairman of the American Women's Hospitals. She never returned to France, but in 1919 she began a pioneering career in industrial medicine by establishing the Medical Department of the Federal Reserve Bank, one of the first such departments in the country.[36]

The program, which she worked on for thirty years, was used as a model for numerous companies across the country. Late in life, Dr. Crawford was asked if she had not been terribly afraid during her wartime hospital work in France. She replied simply that she didn't think she'd been afraid at any time in her life.[37] A devoted Cornell University alumna, Dr. Crawford died in New York City in 1972, aged eighty-eight.

The American Women's Hospitals program, which served in France in 1918, continued to work in Europe into the 1920s. After the Armistice, however, war relief efforts were thrown into disarray. Patriotism and wartime fervor declined rapidly as Americans left Europeans to fend for themselves. In the AWH, committee members resigned, donors withdrew pledges, and even personal friends discontinued support. Still, many founders of the AWH realized that sickness and need did not end when the war ended. Dr. Lovejoy claimed that the "aftermath—local wars, revolutions, famine and forced migrations were worse than the war in some countries."

Dr. Hunt, director of AWH No. 1, declared that "the war has been won; now the peace must be won." Throughout France, Serbia, and the Near East, the AWH met medical emergencies, established public health programs, and provided social welfare services. Typhoid fever, influenza, malaria, and a variety of other diseases literally plagued Europe, and, in many areas, the AWH provided the only medical care in the years immediately following the war. AWH service continues to this day in many parts of the world, but greater emphasis is now placed on helping the needy in the United States.[38]

Despite their flawless record during and after World War I, women physicians still were not welcomed into the military at the onset of World War II—except, once again, as contract surgeons. In 1939–1940, the American Medical Women's Association organized a legislative committee to lobby for the commissioning of women physicians into the Army Medical Corps. Through the efforts of this committee and the help of many national women's organizations, as well as the backing of the American Medical

Association, Congress passed the enabling legislation in April 1943. The bill, effective for the duration of World War II plus six months, authorized a temporary commission in the medical corps to qualified women physicians. Permanent legislation was passed in 1952.[39]

Notes

1. Esther Pohl Lovejoy, Certain Samaritans (New York: Macmillan, 1927), 6–12, and Nancy Hewitt, "The American Women's Hospitals," in the newsletter of the Archives and Special Collections on Women in Medicine, the Medical College of Pennsylvania, Collections 6 (June 1982): 1–2.

2. Ibid., 13–22.

3. Ibid., 14.

4. Ruth Gaines, Ladies of Grecourt: The Smith College Relief Unit in the Somme (New York: E. P. Dutton, 1920), 154.

5. Ibid., 243–244.

6. Lovejoy, 23.

7. Ibid.

8. Ibid., 23–26.

9. Letter written by Dr. Anne Tjomsland, October 3, 1963, the Medical Archives of the New York Hospital–Cornell Medical Center, New York City.

10. John Starr, Hospital City (New York: Crown, 1957), 197.

11. Starr, 197–198.

12. Ibid., 206.

13. Anne Tjomsland, M.D., Bellevue in France: An Anecdotal History of Base Hospital No. 1 (New York: Froben Press, 1941), 59–60.

14. Starr, 206.

15. Tjomsland, Bellevue in France, 75.

16. Ibid., 154–155.

17. Ibid., 76.

18. Starr, 207.

19. Tjomsland, Bellevue in France, 155.

20. Ibid., 232.

21. Biographical material, including a family history, an autobiography, and various articles, on Dr. Nellie N. Barsness was furnished by the Pope County Historical Society, Glenwood, MN.

22. Ibid., autobiography.

23. Ibid.

24. John O'Reilly, "Woman Doctor Retiring at 65, to Go to Work," New York Herald Tribune, February 10, 1949.

25. Interview with Dr. Crawford and her sister, Lucy Shepard Crawford, by Edith M. Fox, Cornell University archivist, Department of Manuscripts and University Archives, Cornell University Libraries, Ithaca, NY, 1962, 13–20.

26. Ibid., 19–20.

27. Deceased Alumni Records, Department of Manuscripts and University Archives, Cornell University Libraries, Ithaca, NY.

28. Reminiscences of Dr. Alice Weld Tallant, from "Individual Experiences Concerning Overseas Life," in A History of Women's Overseas Service League, comp. Helene M. Sillia (Newburgh Heights, OH: 1978), 242. Copies of this publication are available from Ms. Sillia, 3872 E. 38th St., Newburgh Heights, OH 44105.

29. Gaines, 66–67.

30. Reminiscences of Dr. Alice Weld Tallant in Sillia, 242.

31. Gaines, 67–68.

32. London Daily Mail quoted in the alumnae magazine of Smith College, Northampton, MA, the Smith Alumnae Quarterly (November 1917): 28.

33. The American Fund for French Wounded was organized by Anne Morgan, Francophile daughter of millionaire U.S. financier J. P. Morgan, to provide medical supplies to the French military. In March 1918, the organization split into two bodies. The first, bearing the same name as its parent, continued to care for war casualties, and the other, incorporated under the name American Committee for Devastated France, worked with various other organizations to provide relief for French citizens in the badly battered war zones.

34. Reminiscences of Dr. Alice Weld Tallant in Sillia, 243.

35. Dr. Anna Tjomsland papers, Department of Manuscripts and University Archives, Cornell University Libraries, Ithaca, NY.

36. Barsness file.

37. Deceased Alumni Records, Cornell University Libraries, Ithaca, NY.

38. Nancy A. Hewitt, "History of the American Women's Hospitals," in Records of the American Women's Hospitals, 1917–1982: An Inventory (Philadelphia: Medical College of Pennsylvania, 1987), 3.

39. Lt. Col. Clara Raven, MC, USAR, "Achievements of Women in Medicine, Past and Present—Women in the Medical Corps of the Army," Military Medicine 125, no. 2 (February 1960): 108–109.

Dr. Esther Pohl Lovejoy, a charter member of the Medical Women's National Association (later the American Medical Women's Association), who was appointed first head of the American Women's Hospitals. (Courtesy of Special Collections on Women in Medicine, Medical College of Pennsylvania, Philadelphia, PA)

Two young U.S. women physicians who found their own way to serve in the Great War: Dr. Anne (Anna) Tjomsland, right, and Dr. Alice Weld Tallant, left above. Dr. Tjomsland entered Bellevue Hospital in New York City as one of the first women interns in July 1914. She expected to go overseas with her colleagues as American Base Hospital Unit No. 1, but because the Army Medical Department would not accept women physicians, Dr. Tjomsland signed on as a contract surgeon. She served in France from February 1918 until her unit returned home in April 1919. Dr. Tallant also went overseas as a civilian, the director of the Smith College Relief Unit, working to aid the rural French population in sixteen villages in the Somme area. She later worked with the American Committee for Devastated France, served refugee civilians and the French military in a French Army Hospital, and was awarded the French Croix de Guerre. (Tjomsland photo courtesy of Cornell University, Ithaca, NY; Tallant photo courtesy of the Medical College of Pennsylvania)

Dr. Nellie Barsness, shown in her French uniform, was welcomed by the French Army and appointed an ophthalmologist at a hospital for gas victims at Cempuis. After the Armistice, she conducted clinics in the French cities of Nancy and Reims and was decorated by the French for her work under hazardous conditions. (Courtesy of Pope County Historical Society, Glenwood, MN)

While Dr. Esther Pohl Lovejoy investigated possibilities for the American Women's Hospitals in France, the medical women at home concentrated on fund-raising and registration. A massive drive was launched in June 1918, with ambulances and uniformed members, such as the two pictured here, soliciting operating funds for AWH overseas; $200,000 was raised for the work. (Courtesy of the Medical College of Pennsylvania)

= 8 =

Red Cross Volunteers

Henry Dunant, founder of the Red Cross, would have been proud, and even the stern Clara Barton, an early nursing volunteer, would have smiled with satisfaction over the magnificent humanitarian service provided by the American Red Cross before, during, and after World War I. Known the world over as a symbol of compassion, and fast, charitable action during crisis, the Red Cross was established in 1862 when Dunant, a young Swiss businessman who had witnessed terrible carnage on the Solferino battlefield in northern Italy three years before, proposed the formation of a neutral organization devoted to the care of the sick and wounded of armies at war. An international conference of the Red Cross committee convened in Geneva, Switzerland, in 1863, and the Geneva (or Red Cross) Convention was held the following year. This agreement and three subsequent humanitarian treaties for the protection of victims of war have since been signed by 146 governments worldwide.

While Dunant's Red Cross was taking root in Europe, the United States was embroiled in its own Civil War. One of the thousands of relief workers involved was Clara Barton, who helped care for both Union and Confederate wounded through the United States Sanitary Commission. Miss Barton later went to Europe to join relief efforts for both soldiers and civilians during the Franco-Prussian War of 1870–1871. She returned home to organize, with a group of friends, the American Association of the Red Cross in 1881, and a year later, her organization received official sanction from the U.S. government. Its charter called for the Red Cross "to furnish volunteer aid to the sick and wounded of the Armed Forces in time of war, and to act in matters of voluntary relief and in accord with military authorities as a medium of communication between the people of the United States and their Armed Forces."[1]

The new American Red Cross immediately plunged into relief activity following forest fires, floods, and other catastrophes throughout the country, carrying out Miss Barton's plan for organized aid to disaster victims. The indomitable Miss Barton herself was still in action at the age of seventy-six, when she traveled to Cuba to provide nursing care, medical supplies, food, and other necessities for civilians and the military forces during the Spanish-American War of

1898. The Red Cross went into action again in 1906 in the wake of the San Francisco earthquake and fire, successfully mobilizing and administering fast and efficient aid to the stricken city.

Miss Barton retired in 1904 and died in 1912, but her legacy was in capable hands. In 1909 the organization entered the nursing arena when Jane Delano, a pioneer in the field, began developing programs in elementary hygiene and home care of the sick. More important to the First World War effort, which came just a few years later, Miss Delano organized the Red Cross nurse reserve, which provided a huge pool of trained nurses who were registered and ready to serve, both with the Army and Navy abroad and with the Red Cross at home.[2]

When the Great War broke out in August 1914, the American Red Cross had just 107 chapters in the United States. But the wartime demands on the organization, plus the overwhelming desire of U.S. citizens to assist in the European war effort, brought explosive growth. A nationwide network of 3,864 chapters soon developed; nearly a fifth of the total population of the United States became Red Cross members.

With its broad mandate of aid to both civilian and military victims, the Red Cross offered myriad services, both at home and in the battle zones, in the early years of the war. These included home hygiene and care of the sick, nutrition and first aid, care and reconstruction of the wounded and displaced, prisoners' relief, canteen service, and search assistance regarding wounded or missing soldiers.

In September 1914, the American Red Cross chartered a mercy ship and sent it off to help the wounded of all the belligerent nations, regardless of allegiance. From then on, the Red Cross held firm to its stance of neutrality.[3]

As the war continued, the American Red Cross shipped some $1.5 million worth of relief supplies to Europe. About $350,000 worth went to the Central Powers (Germany and her allies). Further, the agency purchased and shipped medical supplies valued at nearly $230,000 to the German and Austrian Red Cross.[4] By 1916, however, when it seemed that relief agencies overseas would be able to cope on their own, the American Red Cross reduced its efforts in Europe and eventually withdrew from neutral activity. But the organization did announce that no one seeking its help would be turned away.

Then, of course, the likelihood of official U.S. involvement in the conflict loomed. In 1916, the U.S. surgeon general asked the Red Cross to organize fifty base hospital units, all of them staffed from Miss Delano's register of 20,000 nurses. Those units later served in Europe as Army hospitals in the war zone and Navy hospitals in France, England, Ireland, and Scotland.

When the United States officially entered the Great War in April 1917, change came almost overnight to the Red Cross. President Woodrow Wilson announced the formation of a war council to run the organization and turn it into an efficient arm of the government. That all-male council made all decisions, and the women who had formerly directed Red Cross activities were relegated to an advisory committee.

As that first year of involvement progressed, the Red Cross took its place as a powerful social force. Millions of volunteers rushed to the aid of overburdened staff as old services expanded and new ones were added, among them motors corps, canteen, and production services. Many of the volunteers served the active military forces as well as the disabled soldiers in veterans' hospitals. Other Red Cross personnel opened institutes for blind and disabled veterans of the war. The Junior Red Cross was formed in 1917 to accommodate all the U.S. schoolchildren who wanted to help with the war effort. Among their other contributions, the thousands of young people cultivated gardens, made bandages, and collected newspapers and scrap metal.

Overseas, the Red Cross nursing service took on new importance, providing a constant stream of trained women for service with the military. As their work spread from the hospitals to civilian areas, Red Cross staff struggled to meet the rehabilitation needs of nations whose internal social structure had been destroyed. Although the Red Cross is now remembered mainly for the work of its nurses, both military and civilian, in the Great War, this organization provided many other social services in the massive relief effort in the war zone: line of communication canteens for French troops before U.S. soldiers arrived in France; huts with resting, writing, and reading rooms, and other amenities for the military; and volunteers with the Red Cross Home Communication Service.

The first Red Cross nurses to sail to France embarked aboard the mercy ship borrowed for sixty days from the Hamburg-America Line and rechristened *The Red Cross*. The ship sailed from New York on September 12, 1914, under command of retired U.S. Navy officers. The departure was exciting. The liner, painted according to international agreement for Red Cross vessels, was beautiful in a fresh coat of white, encircled by a broad red stripe. There was a bright Red Cross on the funnel, and the Red Cross and U.S. flags flew proudly. Miss Delano herself was on hand to see her nurses off.

The liner carried ten units of medical personnel, each group comprising a medical director, two assistants, and eleven nurses headed by a supervising nurse. A double unit was assigned to each of the great powers—France, England, Russia, and Germany[4]—with one unit each to Austria and Hungary.[5]

Heading one unit was Josephine Beatrice Bowman, who had resigned from the Navy so that she could join the Red Cross aboard the mercy ship.[6] She was assigned first to the Haslar Royal Naval Hospital near Portsmouth, England, and later to Paignton, in Devonshire, where U.S. millionaire Paris Singer (of the sewing machine fortune) had loaned his palatial estate for use as a hospital. Lady Randolph Churchill and an organization of U.S. women living in England, the American Women's War Relief Fund, directed the project at Paignton.

Miss Bowman wrote of the spacious accommodations at the mansion, Old-way House, although, she admitted, "it was our deepest regret that we were not a little nearer the front with such a splendidly equipped hospital." At first there was a period of inactivity at Paignton, but in the spring of 1915 large numbers of wounded Canadians were brought in, and the staff was happy to be busy at last. "We had many convalescents and some cases of frozen feet, but we also had a few serious cases," Miss Bowman wrote.

> One Scotch lad came in before Christmas with fifty wounds in his back, his left arm, head and shoulders, bad wounds made by the explosion of a hand grenade. Another lad came to us with a badly fractured femur. He had lain on the battlefield from Tuesday until Friday with nothing to eat or drink, his kit being just out of reach. He did not know how long he had been unconscious, but upon coming to and thinking the British were around, raised himself and called—only to be instantly layed out again by a German bullet thru his shoulder.[7]

She and her colleagues were quite impressed with the "pluck, patience, courage, and cheerfulness" of the British soldiers:

> We realized what caliber they were made of when we heard the terrible conditions they faced to fight for their country. During the winter some stood in water to their knees, others to the waists and arm pits, and one lad who had lost one foot and the toes off the other thru frost bite, said that he saw men frozen in the trenches with their rifles fixed ready to fire. These men were in the scout or outpost trenches, where absolute silence reigned. So in absolute silence, King Winter had taken those lives the Germans could not find.

In October 1915, those early Red Cross "mercy" units were called home, partly for lack of funds, partly because it appeared they had served their purpose. After April 1917, of course, when the United States entered the war, there was a renewed sense of purpose for the American Red Cross, for U.S. soldiers were now involved in the fighting overseas. Hundreds of Miss

Delano's registered nurses shipped out almost at once with base hospital units, and many of them served under incredibly difficult conditions close to the firing lines.

One, Elizabeth Ashe, signed on for duty with a California base hospital in 1917, even though she had exceeded the prescribed age limit. Before she could sail, however, she was urged to help organize the first American Red Cross pediatric unit to be sent to France. "There is a crying need for effective work among children [in France]. France has been at war for nearly four years, and most of the available medical men are doing army duty," wrote Dr. William Palmer Lucas, who became chief of the Red Cross Children's Bureau in France. "In some communities in France, there have been no doctors since the national mobilization in August 1914," he continued. "It may be said that, as a whole, French children are underfed, undernourished, and insufficiently clothed. There is a great need for medical treatment and for the education of mother and child in certain practical rules of child hygiene. The Infant Welfare Unit [later the Children's Bureau] will be prepared to give such immediate relief as it can."[8]

Miss Ashe sailed in July 1917 with a group of U.S. pediatric specialists to study the situation and formulate a plan. As was their usual practice, the Red Cross group proposed to cooperate with French specialists to strengthen and develop existing programs, rather than force their own new ideas on the beleaguered nation. "Special efforts will be made to protect children from tubercular infection which is the gravest medical problem which confronts France," Dr. Lucas wrote. "It kills about 80,000 of her population every year. This means an average of more than 100 a day, more than nine an hour."

Miss Ashe, who served as chief of nursing service for the Children's Bureau through the end of the war, was especially well suited for the bureau's enormous challenges, having founded the Telegraph Hill Neighborhood Association in San Francisco and the Bothin Convalescent Home for Women and Children in Marin County, CA. In France she helped organize a new hospital at Evian-les-Bains, a popular prewar spa on the shores of Lake Geneva. Here the Red Cross was attempting to care for thousands of French citizens who had been deported to Belgium by the Germans five months before and were now being sent back by train, through Switzerland, to Evian.

"We have a big villa there which was a hotel, with modern plumbing and a sort of outdoor pavilion, which will be an ideal place for the sun cure [for tuberculosis]," Miss Ashe wrote to friends at home.

> The hospital and dispensary are to be open both day and night, as the train comes in at night. We will commence with 100 beds. The idea is that we are

to examine the children physically when they come in. Poor little things . . . arrive in such filthy condition that they have to be fumigated before they can be touched. The poor people have taken these long painful journeys three times, first from their village to another French town, then to Belgium, from Belgium here, and now they say, "What next?"

Miss Ashe wrote in October 1917 that she had just met a train filled with 680 Belgian children. "It was the most tragic sight imaginable. Two-thirds of the children were taken from their parents and sent to France to be supported. These children were facing starvation and their mothers parted with them to save them. The children were tired and forlorn after a three days' trip, but shouting at the top of their voices, 'Vive la France!' with joy in their faces at being again in France." After being marched to the spa casino, the children were fed a meal of meat and potatoes. Then, a doctor "examined all these children during the afternoon; any ill children who come in the future will go either to our hospital or to a convalescent home."

The sheer number of refugees was challenging, according to Miss Ashe. "One thousand French people arrive daily at Evian. . . . It is a peculiar task to find lodgings for them, after a night or two at Evian, and then find homes or friends for them all over France. This has been going on since last February. The majority of them are perfectly helpless people, tiny babies carried by young mothers, the sick and feeble of whom there are many ambulance loads."

Miss Ashe and her associates opened their hospital October 28, 1917, with a measles case. "We already find that we are being swamped with children," she wrote. "These poor 'repatries' [repatriating French citizens] seem to have such faith in the Americans that they trust us implicitly." The busy nurse wrote home asking her friends to send "flannelette nightgowns, all sizes to 10 years; caps for disinfecting heads, just a mob cap made of gingham, pink probably, with good quality elastic in it. It is very necessary. Do get someone busy making these. We also need bloomers for all ages up to 12 years; rompers, aprons, high neck, long sleeves, NOT black; woolen stockings if possible, for winter; sweaters, dark colors to pull over the head, with sleeves, and woolen dresses."

After a week at Evian, Miss Ashe was dispatched to Lyon, where the Red Cross was setting up a convalescent home for children in a magnificent chateau that had been bequeathed by a wealthy woman for that purpose. "You never saw such a place," Miss Ashe exclaimed. It had "56 rooms, besides the lodge and a central heating system. The house is full of wonderful old carved furniture, tapestries, etc. I shall select several big rooms and store them pro tem." Miss Ashe and Florence Holzmann, business manager for the Children's

Bureau in the Lyon zone, worked out a "good feasible plan for the house . . . really a palace." Although it was magnificent, "nothing could be more unsuitable than it is for a children's home." Still, the relief workers could fit twenty-seven beds in the dining room alone.

A few weeks later, Miss Ashe devised a children's hospital from the German Consulate at Lyon, an ornate stone mansion boasting an emperor's suite in green and gray, with an adjoining bathroom done in gray onyx veined with green. An American writer for The Ladies Home Journal, Gladys Moon Jones, later described the scene:

> The valuable books in the library were boarded up and officially sealed. The room became the infants' ward, where war babies, some of them enemy fathered, found the sun and an altruistic love. The boudoir of the former mistress of the palace was used as a nurses' dressing station. . . . Upstairs the gorgeous suites are the children's wards. So the elaborate mansion with the sunny terrace became a 115-bed hospital known as the Hospital Holtzmann. The inspiriting legend, "Croix Rouge Americaine," was written over the door, and three times a week numbers of French tonsils were extracted by American doctors and nurses in the Kaiser's very own bathroom.[9]

A major problem at the mansion was that every effort to start the heating system failed. No one could understand why the furnace didn't heat but only filled the place with smoke. At last someone thought to examine the chimneys, and the mystery was solved. It was found that the previous French caretaker had expressed his loyalty to his former German employer by cementing up all the chimneys.

Gladys Moon Jones further reported that the Americans in Lyon did more than provide emergency medical attention to the French children. "They also tried to bring to the townspeople the American methods of public health. The greatest effort in this direction was the Baby Show. Invitations were issued to the citizens to attend this demonstration in the large Industrial Fair Building on the Place Bellecour." The exhibit was a huge success, drawing more than 177,000 people, an average of 9,000 a day. Perhaps the greatest attraction was the Glass House. "Inside of this, an American nurse bathed a real French baby every two hours. There was always a crowd pressed against the Glass House, waiting for the next baby proferred by some mother for the purpose. The French mothers, so afraid of 'le courant d'air' [fresh air] gradually became accustomed to the idea of taking off all the baby's clothes to bathe it."

Miss Ashe continued her work in other areas of France, establishing a maternity hospital and a child-care center for the children of women munitions workers at Toul, as well as clinics and various other facilities in the backwaters of the war. By mid-December 1917, she was able to write:

> I think we have accomplished in our bureau a great deal in the short time since it was organized, just four months. We have four hospitals and twelve dispensaries with about 15 doctors and 100 nurses and aides at work, besides the Paris office, which investigates and passes on the claims of every children's society in France, orphan asylum, creches, etc. I am afraid this sounds boastful, but you can have no idea of the terribly discouraging times we have; the nurses nearly go mad with the difficulties. For instance, Dr. Baldwin at Nesle in the war zone has been running three dispensaries and a hospital for two months without gauze, alcohol, or night gowns.

By February 1918, Miss Ashe reported that she had sent for seventy-five more nurses for Red Cross Children's Bureau work and would soon need more, for she was expecting to open hospital dispensaries in five other cities. In addition, her hospitals would be expected to care for 10,000 refugees from Nancy. "I have great difficulty in providing nurses," she wrote.

The difficulties would worsen. Late in May, when the American Expeditionary Forces (AEF) launched their first major combat operation along the Western Front, the shortage of hospital facilities and nurses became alarming. The Red Cross had to reassign many of the children's nurses to care for wounded U.S. troops, and several homes and hospitals full of infants and youngsters had to be evacuated so those facilities could be made available to the military.

Miss Ashe was able to retain some of her children's nurses, but as she had written earlier, "I am afraid my heart and thoughts are more with our men these days than with the poor pitiful French babies, although my work is for them." That spring, Big Bertha, the huge German railway gun, was shelling Paris as the enemy pressed toward the city. "Our work is suffering terribly by it," Miss Ashe wrote. "Yesterday the Military Affairs sent in a call for twenty nurses. Fortunately most of my nurses are available."

She herself was finally drawn into the military emergency. "I have been really nursing at last," she wrote on June 12.

> I have been going to the American Ambulance [Hospital] at Neuilly, near Paris, every day helping out. When our Marines went so suddenly into the fight at Chateau Thierry, our hospitals weren't prepared for the large number of wounded that suddenly and unexpectedly arrived. It was terrible. The hospital at Neuilly almost overnight increased from 600 to 1,500 beds. The nurses were routed out from their beds at eleven p.m. one night, and the

wounded from the operating room brought right in [and tucked into in the same beds].

After seeing conditions at Neuilly, Miss Ashe asked for a "vacation" from her Children's Bureau work and spent that time nursing U.S. wounded. "It was a week of horror," she wrote, "but thankfulness, too, that I have the training which enables me to relieve a little of this suffering." She was thankful, too, for the dedication of her nurses. "The adaptability of these nurses to war needs has been a surprise to everyone. . . . We feel very proud of them and very happy that, in the time of need, the Children's Bureau was able to make such vital contributions to the care of our wounded."

The children of France continued to command the devotion of Miss Ashe through the final months of the war and into the peace following the Armistice. She sailed for home in the summer of 1919, one day after she had enjoyed a ringside seat at the Place de la Concorde for the glorious July 14 victory celebration and parade in Paris.

Red Cross nursing played a vital role in World War I, yet it was but one phase of the vast and sweeping Red Cross war effort. Early on, the U.S. government and the military, under Gen. John J. Pershing, had assigned specific overseas wartime duties to certain of the large U.S. social service organizations who were eager to do their part. The largest group, the YMCA, was given the task of entertaining the troops in the military camps and later was assigned to provide canteens—in effect, huge post exchanges—for the troops. At the same time, the Red Cross was asked to take on canteen work at the hospitals, railroad junctions, and ports of debarkation and embarkation, as well as in the cities of France.

While waiting for U.S. forces to arrive, the Red Cross staff established model canteens for the French Army along the lines of communication (LOC) that connected the French base sections with the Front. When the AEF did land, the bulk of the Red Cross work naturally shifted in that direction. But countless U.S. women volunteers had gained experience serving in the LOC canteens that had supplied rations to literally millions of French soldiers.[10]

At permanent base establishments, the canteen staff sometimes maintained more extensive operations. For example, at the Issoudun Flying Field, the staff provided a special diet service for the patients of the camp hospital, an officers' mess, a mending shop where soldiers' uniforms were renovated and mended, and a laundry and shower-bath system for the camp. Sometimes the LOC canteens also boasted an infirmary, several rest-rooms with toilet facilities, and barracks where the men might sleep for a few hours, take a shower, and have a meal. Twenty-two of those frontline canteens were located where they could serve evacuation hospitals, as well as troops going up to the trenches and coming back on relief.

Usually those establishments were staffed by canteen women, who went in trucks to villages that were often only the bleak, ruined memory of a town. There they found, if possible, a house that still boasted a roof, where they could improvise a counter and feed coffee, doughnuts, sandwiches, and anything else they could lay hands on, to truck and ambulance drivers, dispatch runners, and passing troops of all types.

The "outpost" canteen closer to the Front than the LOC, served small comforts, newspapers, and magazines to troops in supporting trenches, to first-aid dressing stations, and to troops in transit. Each outpost, staffed entirely by men, was centered around a tent-warehouse located as near to the Front as artillery fire permitted.

In addition to these overseas canteens, the Red Cross operated countless railroad canteens in the United States, located in any convenient and accessible building in the railroad yards. Possibly as many as 55,000 U.S. women donated their time to those facilities, meeting troop trains and serving refreshments of all kinds. They also dispensed magazines, newspapers, and sometimes box lunches or complete meals offered in a cafeteria line.[11]

The base canteen at Vichy, France, was typical of the overseas canteen. There in the ancient spa town, several U.S. hospital units were located, along with some fifty Red Cross personnel. Volunteers had transformed a casino into a "hut" with a canteen, dance hall, reading and writing room, commissary department, library, theater, sewing room, and a diet kitchen. During the month of October 1918, the Red Cross in Vichy estimated that it had distributed (without charge) 78,278 packages of tobacco, 7,480 tubes of toothpaste, 7,650 toothbrushes, 3,650 combs, 3,460 so-called comfort bags (small cloth bags filled with treats and necessities), 2,850 packages of chewing gum, 1,650 cakes of soap, 1,245 bars of chocolate, and 1,200 sticks of shaving soap. Other gifts for the troops included pencils, matches, shaving brushes, cards, washcloths, sweaters, razor blades, checkers and other games, thread, pipe cleaners, drinking cups, gloves, canes, socks, pajamas, and underwear.[12]

Base Hospital No. 20, from the University of Pennsylvania, recorded details of a festive Thanksgiving dinner at Vichy in 1918, right after the Armistice. "The Red Cross furnished the turkeys for the party, which included the entire American force [in the area]. This required 1,300 kilos of dressed turkeys and 600 kilos of chicken, costing 12,800 francs." Later, decorations were furnished by the Red Cross for Christmas trees in every ward of the various hospitals manned by Base 20, and each soldier received a pair of socks containing candy, oranges, nuts, cigarettes, handkerchiefs, cookies, matches and Red Cross Christmas cards. Another part of the [Red Cross] work consisted in the women personnel meeting all trains, greeting the incoming patients with a smile, and presenting chocolate and tobacco with that touch of sympathy which only a woman can give. Then, too, when the soldiers were discharged from the hospital and sent back to duty, the Red Cross representatives accompanied them to the train to say good-by and distribute tobacco and other little necessary comforts.[13]

Base Hospital No. 46, from Portland, OR, reported in its history that when a wounded man was brought in from the field, he had usually lost all his personal effects somewhere between the dugout and the hospital and arrived minus all necessities and comforts. Fortunately, the Red Cross was on hand to put things right:

> After a good sleep in a real bed [the soldier] begins to think of the toilet articles he misses; a Red Cross "ditty bag" containing the elementary necessities is ready. If he is able to look at the papers he finds one at hand each morning. When he wants to write a letter home he finds Red Cross stationery in the ward. During his convalescence there are games and puzzles to lighten the dragging hours, and when he gets up he is given a Red Cross convalescent suit and maybe a Red Cross sweater. As soon as he is able to get out he finds his way to the Red Cross Recreation Hut, with its canteen, piano, billiard table and movies.[14]

Many years after the war, Army nurse Charlotte Grace Chilson described the canteen at the French hospital where she was stationed:

> I recall the little woman in our hospital Red Cross canteen, "Mother Stude," as the boys called her. I have forgotten how many hundreds of gallons of cocoa she made each day and every boy who could hobble was invited. He could have one or ten cups, according to his capacity, so long as he didn't waste any. Our [Red Cross] hut was an old building in the hospital back yard, painted and remodeled. Bright curtains were hung, pretty shades for the lights, and baskets of flowers made the place hark of home, and every boy adored "Mother Stude." It wasn't only the cocoa which made them love her. She just loved them all so much that they just couldn't help adore her.

Miss Chilson remembered the concrete and intangible services of the Red Cross as invaluable, both for nurses and soldiers. After a convoy of wounded came in, as soon as possible, Red Cross bags containing "everything he needed for comfort was found for the boy from the Red Cross stores. A young lady came in with pencil and paper ready to write letters for those who didn't feel like writing, and those girls seemed always ready to do some little thing which we [nurses] wanted to do but couldn't find the time for."[15]

The men of Evacuation Ambulance Company 7 also remembered Red Cross workers fondly:

> All through our trials, all through the dark days of the war, the Red Cross was with us always. At the first aid station, at the field hospitals, wherever our ambulances took us, we would find the little chocolate wagon, and there was always a cup of hot chocolate, a cookie and a cigarette for us. They moved with the army. There was always a smile and a cheery word for us. They were with us all hours of the day and night. We began to depend upon them, they acted as mother and comforter to the soldier boy. Their labors never ceased. . . . We do not know what we would have done without them.[16]

In early 1917, a young U.S. expatriate living in Paris joined the Red Cross, and in October she was assigned as a canteener to the newly organized aviation camp at Issoudun. After the war, she wrote anonymously about her experiences.[17]

> At Issoudun, we have a little canteen about six meters wide and twenty meters long, in which we cook, eat, feed soldiers, congregate, show the cinema, house the piano, etc. The air is so thick I could chop it with a hatchet any time.
>
> We live in a little wooden building exactly the same size—sometimes one to a room and sometimes two to a room. The walls are one thickness of very thin wood and there is no form of heat except a stove that will not draw. It is also supplied with briquets, which are no longer coal, but only black earth.

The weather was not only cold, but muddy, she wrote. "I went to the quartermaster's storehouse and bought a pair of shoes. They call them hobnail shoes. They weigh like lead but are said to be mud proof. Several of the girls wear rubber boots. We have named Issoudun the muddiest hole in France. The work here is very hard. I dress up to go to bed. One must keep warm somehow."

Keeping up with the inflow of cadets undoubtedly helped. "A great gang of Aviation Cadets arrived today. . . . Some of them came in after their evening mess. We had motion pictures for them. They ate us out of sandwiches and drank up all the tea, coffee and cocoa. They are the hungriest people I ever saw." In November, there was more rain and more mud. "Also more cadets. They are into everything. They also shovel cinders for the making of roads. The cadets are building barracks and roads. Some of them have taken up cooking." This was no doubt a relief to the cooks in the canteen kitchen.

In mid-December, heavy snow and bitter cold came to Issoudun. The anonymous relief worker recalled the funeral of one patient. "At the funeral when the order to play was given, the band blew into their horns but they were frozen up so only squeaks came out. And all the while the body was being lowered into the grave. Someone suggested a non-freezing attachment."

At Christmas she wrote, "I am awfully weary. We have no mud for once. . . . The ground is frozen so hard that the graves in the graveyard must be dug by blasting. The German prisoners do this blasting. When the cadets hear it they shout, 'Bravo!' and drink toasts to the next one to go west [be killed]. The cadets are irresponsible." Belated Christmas presents did not arrive until after the turn of the new year, and many of them were destroyed in transit.

> The pathetic part of the 1917 Christmas was the great number of smashed packages that arrived from the States, full of the most extraordinary hand-knitted sweaters and socks—socks with points on the toes and heels—socks that never saw a soldier's foot. Some packages contained broken cameras, others dried-out fruit cakes. One lad received a baked chicken dipped in paraffin to preserve it from deterioration. The paraffin did preserve the chicken from deterioration but not from decomposition. When the package was opened, someone suggested a gas mask.

During the long, cold winter, music boosted the morale of the air cadets. "The post band began to flourish. Some new instruments came from the never-never land of all good things, namely the Red Cross at Paris, and the boys began to play on pitch." Music, however, could not counter the tedium of being grounded. "The cadets were low. They wanted to fly. Many of them are employed at Headquarters; others are cooks; some are doing odd jobs at the flying field. The remainder stand guard." The cadets eventually did get to fly, of course, and this particular Red Cross canteener was dismissed from the service because of a conspicuous love affair.

Closer to the line of battle than Issoudun, a young American woman, Doris Kellogg, was assigned for several months in 1918 to Orry on the Oise, a camp near Chantilly for "permissionaires" (French soldiers on leave). The men returning to the Front from their furloughs would stop here on the way back to their regiments. "We serve them three meals a day," she explained, "and all day long, hot coffee, chocolate, sandwiches, hard-boiled eggs and bread. We girls do all the work excepting the actual cooking and dish washing. We make salad, serve the food, cut the bread (this is a real job, too, hundreds of pieces a day), etc., etc., etc."[18]

In July 1918, however, her duties became far more urgent. "Tonight was the most unforgettable experience of all," she wrote.

> The wounded are pouring in here [Chantilly] by scores and we heard that they needed food over at the huge tent evacuation hospital and that there were many Americans there.
>
> We got out our camion [truck], loaded it with a crate of tobacco, hot chocolate, bread and eggs, and ran over there. I cannot begin to express the condition of things in those tents. They are swamped with wounded and are without hope of doing anything for the men except what is utterly essential.
>
> We took off our coats and pitched in. I gave water to boys who were writhing in pain, fed men who had not eaten for two and three days, and tried my best to make the poor devils a little bit comfortable on their stretchers that will probably be their beds for a day or so more. . . . Most of them could not rally enough to even think, and after giving them some water we just let them sleep. As we came out to the auto, the ambulances were still piling in, and the full moon gave enough light to help along the work of unloading.
>
> They say we [the U.S. troops] are two and a half miles from Soissons and that it must fall.

Later in July, this Red Cross canteen girl wrote to her family about the sad funerals of the wounded who had died in the hospitals nearby. "We follow the hearses a long way through the forest road to a new cemetery that has been cleared this last week. . . . I tell you, since I've seen our Star Spangled Banner draping those coffins, the flag has had a new meaning for me."

Nearly as numerous as the hundreds of canteen volunteers were the Red Cross searchers, another important cog in the gigantic Red Cross machine. The term searchers was borrowed from the British forces, who used this title for men assigned to obtain information among their troops about those missing in action.

The visitors and searchers branch of the Red Cross Hospital and Home Communication Service began operation in March 1918. A completely new development in the history of war work, the searchers service eventually extended to all hospitals in the AEF. The plan was to provide, through the work of U.S. women volunteers in the hospitals in France, a connecting link between the families at home and their men in hospitals overseas, to send out from the hospitals some news of the men being cared for in France. This would spare their families the suspense of waiting indefinitely for news. When a soldier died in hospital, the service provided what information censorship permitted about his illness, death, and place of burial. Searchers also attempted to learn from comrades in hospital whatever they might know of the fate of men reported killed or missing in action. Often a searcher's investigation proved that a man reported dead had survived instead, or that a soldier was dead who had been reported missing.[19] In addition, the Home Communication Service, of which the searchers were a part, also photographed the graves of U.S. soldiers buried in France and sent the pictures home to their families. More than 170,000 such photographs were taken.[20]

The nurses, especially, were enthusiastic about the work of the searcher. Constantly busy attending to patients' physical needs, they welcomed additional support that ministered to the patients' personal needs.

Early on, searchers discovered that the men were very anxious about their families at home, worrying about unpaid allotments or other difficulties. In these instances, the searcher would obtain information on the particular case and refer the matter to the man's hometown Red Cross chapter. The searcher's assurance to the wounded doughboy—"Somebody in your Red Cross at home will go to see your family and make sure they have everything they need"— brought visible relief to many a worried soldier.

A thousand other small services were on the searcher's agenda. She spent many hours writing letters for the wounded who were unable to do so. One young searcher, Eleanor Barnes, described the experience. "After giving the address of the Miss or Mrs. Somebody, the dictator would usually grunt, grope for words, flounder about, perhaps writhe a bit in pain . . . grope for words some more, and then he would dismiss the task with, 'Oh, just tell her I'm alright. You know, fix it up so she won't worry.' Always some 'she' to be considered."[21]

The searcher, also known as a "hospital visitor," frequently brought to the hospital wards the magazines and stationery and chocolate, fruit, and other treats so enjoyed by the wounded soldier, and she wrote "telegrams and cables and letters and reports that were necessary in ever-increasing numbers as the hospitals were filled to capacity with the tragic aftermath of [the U.S. battles at] Belleau Wood and Chateau Thierry and Saint Mihiel."

One of the searchers, Evadne M. Laptad, recalled the waning days of the war, when she served at Base Hospital No. 36 at the old French resort town of Vittel. "Supplies from Paris, renewed with amazing regularity and generosity, considering the transportation difficulties, afforded such things as comfort bags—was ever anything more worthy of its name than the comfort bag of blessed memory?—and toilet articles, chewing gum, chocolate, and cigarettes."[22] In addition, "a special fund provided flowers for the ward and for the burial services of men who died; it paid, too, for nightcaps [head coverings] for patients who, in an overcrowded building, were lying on cots in draughty halls; and for the sharpening of dulled surgical instruments in some of the operating rooms."

Miss Laptad remembered that as time went on,

> the task of writing a letter from the hospital for each man who could not write for himself, became so great that, instead, a report giving each man's condition and, if possible, a brief message to his family, was sent in to the Paris office, where a letter embodying this information was written to each man's next of kin. This meant for us a great extension of our service, as such reports could be made concerning a hundred men in the time it would have taken to write twenty letters.

Cables were sent in particularly distressing cases, often as many as 250 a day dispatched to the United States from the Paris Red Cross headquarters.

Miss Laptad's memories of 1918 included the Marines who were brought to the hospital early that spring, "almost a whole company of them, all gassed; the Tommies who thronged one whole hospital building after Soissons; the hundreds and hundreds of doughboys who came in from the Argonne; the trainload of captured American wounded sent down by the Germans after the Armistice from their hospital at Trier." She remembered the wounded soldiers, how they "laughed and joked and did little kindnesses to those worse off than they, the little Chapel, the cemetery on the hill-top, the 'off-duty' nurses making cake or candy or something else that would cheer their patients like a glimpse of home, the gay little Christmas trees in the wards."

The work of the searchers continued after the Armistice in November 1918, for there remained a list of approximately 10,000 missing men to track down and nearly as many inquiries to answer from families in the States who had been told only that a husband, brother, or son was killed in action. The Red Cross searchers kept working on these lists and were able to issue reports on 6,200 of the men in question before all searching in France ended in June 1919.[23] These search reports contained information about the grave of the fallen soldier and often a brief account of any worthy or heroic action attending the death, as well as, on occasion, the last words or the expressed desires of the dying man. These were recorded not only for their historical significance but also as a consolation to the bereaved families.

While the searchers were working on their many duties throughout France, another American woman, under the aegis of the Red Cross, was able to help

Allied wounded in a way that could not possibly have been imagined before 1914. She was Anna Coleman Ladd, whose husband, Dr. Maynard Ladd of Harvard Medical School, had gone overseas in 1917 to take charge of the work of the Red Cross Children's Bureau in the Meurthe-et-Moselle Department of France. Mrs. Ladd, a well-known U.S. sculptor, had become interested in the work of Capt. Derwent Wood, an English pioneer in the treatment of facially disfigured wounded men, who was making "portrait masks" for those cases who were beyond the further help of the plastic surgeon.[24]

There were many of these unfortunates. An American doctor Capt. Bertram M. Bernheim wrote:

> One thing depressed me very much in Paris—I saw many face wounds, most awful in character. Much wonderful plastic work has been done on them, and the results are brilliantly horrible, because, as one surgeon says, "No case is favorable." Lower jaws are remade out of bone grafts taken from the leg, and chins are made from the neck and cheek. The men are all cheerful and happy, probably because they came off with their lives.[25]

Mrs. Ladd took up where the plastic surgeons left off. In 1917, she wrote to Captain Wood, who sent her the details of his procedures. She then applied to the American Red Cross for assistance in setting up a studio in Paris for the benefit of the French "mutilés," or disfigured men. Because the U.S. government forbade travel to Europe for women who had relatives overseas, and Mrs. Ladd's husband was on duty in France, she had difficulties in obtaining permission to proceed to Paris. However, determined to go, she finally enlisted in a British ambulance unit that would take her to the war zone.

She landed at Bordeaux in December 1917 and went at once to visit the Val de Grace Hospital in Paris, where the sight of the terrible cases of disfigurement suffered by French soldiers inspired her to resign from the ambulance unit and begin work on the portrait masks. Within a month she had opened the American Red Cross Studio for Portrait Masks in Paris. She then spent several months pursuing experimental work at the studio as well as in various French hospitals.[26]

In the spring of 1918, Mrs. Ladd received the first of the heroic French soldiers in her Left Bank studio.

> On rainy afternoons, they would linger around the little stove, smoking and singing, the blind playing dominoes, the others, cards, or drinking chocolate, with all the gaiety and "sainte blague" [gallows humor] of their kind. A French nurse would come in, guiding a young soldier who, when his bandage was removed—revealing the place where a face once had been—

would eagerly enter into explanations or criticisms of the modelled reconstruction on the cast, feeling the planes with the sensitive fingers of the
blind.[27]

The process of creating a portrait mask began with a plaster cast of the
mutilated face. On this cast was modelled the missing portion—nose, jaw,
cheek, eye, forehead, ear—if possible guided by photographs taken before the
mutilation. From the plaster model, a thin copper mask was made by electro-
plate and lined with silver. It was adjusted very carefully to fit the disfigured
face, then painted with a hard enamel paint (originally, oil paint had been
used, but it was found to chip off easily). The men could smoke through the
half-opened modelled lips and tug at the mustache of real hair that had been
securely fastened to the mask.

The mask could be held in place in a number of ingenious ways. If it was a
jaw, it was adjusted by means of a wire that fit around the ears and was covered with rubber tubing. A nose, eye, or ear was fastened on by means of a
pair of spectacles. At first the masks covered the entire face, but these were
found to be too hot and heavy to wear and so were reduced greatly in size and
thickness.

As time went on, the studio reported that the masks were indispensable in
cases where the lower jaw was entirely gone.

> These cases salivate constantly and by putting fresh gauze in the mask, the
> "mutilé" is always clean and tidy. They can also smoke when they are wear-
> ing their masks. . . . Those who have lost their noses can breathe much more
> freely with a mask than with a bandage and are much more comfortable.
> Wounds in the forehead leave the brain exposed very near the surface and
> the mask is a great protection against a possible blow, which might be fatal.
> Also, these cases suffer very much from heat, cold and noise, and the mask
> protects them from these irritations.

The psychological impacts of those severe facial wounds especially
inspired Mrs. Ladd's work. "People get used to seeing men with arms and
legs missing, but they never get used to an abnormal face. And so these men
are the object of aversion to almost everyone. A man who is repulsive to look
at cannot get a job which will bring him in contact with the general public,
and so it is much harder for these men, who have already given so much, to
earn their living."

Not surprisingly, the disfigured soldiers had serious problems with self-
esteem. "Men with mutilated faces are very sensitive. They all have little
pocket mirrors which they take out on all occasions, furtively examining their

appearance to see just how badly they really DO look," the studio reported. Through its work, the studio was able to give the men not only a new face, but a new sense of hope. "One man who came to us had been wounded more than two years before and had never been home, as he did not want his mother to see how badly he looked. Of all his face there was only one eye left. After 50 operations on his face, he came to us. We made him a mask with which he was very much pleased. He has been home now and told me the other day that he is going to be married." Many patients later wrote to the studio, telling of new jobs and new homes, "since the women they loved were no longer afraid to live with them. Years later they would write of little poilus who had been born to them."

By early November 1918, Mrs. Ladd reported that she had received 120 requests for masks from the French and had worked on five for U.S. soldiers. "Sixty masks have already been completed; and the letters of gratitude from the soldiers and their families hurt, they are so grateful. My men with new faces were presented to the French Surgical Society twice; and, I heard (I refused to appear, as it is the work, not the artist, I wanted presented) they received votes of thanks from the 60 surgeons present." In December, with the war ended and her volunteer year completed, Mrs. Ladd returned to Boston, leaving the studio in the hands of two French sculptors and a U.S. woman, Mary Louise Brent, who had served with the American Fund for French Wounded throughout the war.

Just before the Armistice, the worldwide influenza epidemic, which killed more Americans than did military action, gave the Red Cross another chance to prove that it was ready for service in any disaster. At home, some 15,000 nurses, dietitians, and others were recruited and sent to care for flu patients in military camps, hospitals, coalfields, munitions plants, and shipyards, where they remained until the epidemic finally subsided in the spring of 1919. Tent cities were set up to ease the overloaded hospitals, and workers around the country produced more than 371 million relief articles (clothing and surgical dressings) in the twenty months ending February 28, 1919.

Throughout the war, the Red Cross Bureau of Prisoners' Relief, located at Bern, Switzerland, had looked after some 3,700 U.S. soldiers who had been prisoners of Germany. In addition to providing food, clothing, and comfort items, Red Cross volunteers also delivered mail from home. Probably 90 percent of the parcels sent to those prisoners actually did reach their destination. The bureau also included the Division of Allied Prisoners, through which Italian and French prisoners were helped in special cases.

After the Armistice, other Red Cross personnel were scattered from the British Isles to Siberia's far reaches, and they remained on duty as the troops began returning home. In 1919, Red Cross men and women continued to staff the massive relief programs for refugees and other victims of World War I. An estimated 3,953 Red Cross workers served in these social programs during the Great War period. Of these, 2,503 were women, and each believed, as one volunteer explained, that "American women sent us to France to take their place for a little while, and we did the best we could."[28]

Notes

1. "A Brief History: The American Red Cross," pamphlet, ARC 626, revised November 1980.

2. In an interview printed in The Red Cross Magazine, August 1918, Miss Delano explained her view of the Red Cross nursing service. When asked by the interviewer what would happen to the hospitals at home if all Red Cross nurses were deployed to France to care for U.S. troops overseas, she replied, "We don't expect every nurse to go abroad." Rather, she envisioned a tremendously important task for those who remained at home. "She will have not only to maintain our lines against the inroads of disease common in peace time, but also against all the evils war brings in its train—high prices and reduced food among the poor, congestion around the new mushrooming industrial plants, all the dislocation of war, in fact, with its threat of epidemics and weakening of health safeguards." Indeed, she continued, "We want just as many trained nurses to enter the Red Cross service for that work as for the work abroad with the Army and Navy Nurse Corps. We must distribute our nursing army to the best advantage."

3. Patrick F. Gilbo, The American Red Cross, the First Century: A Pictorial History (New York: Harper and Row, 1981), 55. Unless otherwise noted, details of the history and development of the Red Cross organization were obtained from Gilbo or from the book cited in note 4.

4. The Armies of Mercy: Harper's Pictorial Library of the World War, vol. 7 (New York: Harper and Bros., 1920), 46.

5. Portia Kernodle, The Red Cross Nurse in Action (New York: Harper Bros., 1949), 96.

6. Miss Bowman was reappointed a U.S. Navy nurse when she returned from overseas in 1915. After the war, she was ordered to the newly commissioned Navy hospital ship *USS Relief*, on which she was one of the first women to serve. She was appointed superintendent of the Navy Nurse Corps in 1922 and served until her retirement in January 1935.

7. J. Beatrice Bowman, "Des Moines Woman Writes of Life as English War Nurse," Des Moines Capital (Iowa), July 16, 1915.

8. As quoted in Intimate Letters From France and Extracts From the Diary of Elizabeth Ashe, 1917–1919 (San Francisco: Bruce Brough Press, 1931), 5–6. All subsequent passages quoting Miss Ashe and Dr. Lucas are from this book. Dr. Lucas, who headed the Child Welfare Unit, was professor of pediatrics at the University of California and the originator of the Save a Belgian Baby movement.

9. Gladys Moon Jones, "Women of the A.E.F.: The American Red Cross and Refugee Children at Lyons," Ladies Home Journal (May 1929).

10. Edward Hungerford, With the Doughboy in France: A Few Chapters of an American Effort (New York: Macmillan, 1920), 105.

11. Sarah Elizabeth Pickett, The American National Red Cross: Its Origin, Purposes, and Service (New York: Century, 1924), 73–77.

12. Anne Tjomsland, M.D., Bellevue in France: An Anecdotal History of Base Hospital No. 1 (New York: Froben Press, 1941), 221–225.

13. History of Base Hospital No. 20, organized at the University of Pennsylvania (Philadelphia: E. A. Wright, 1920), 167–169.

14. Maj. Otis B. Wight, ed., On Active Service With Base Hospital 46, U.S.A., Mar. 20, 1918 to May 25, 1919 (Portland, OR: U.S. Army Medical Corps, n.d.), 138–139.

15. Reminiscence of Charlotte Grace Chilson, Army Nurse Corps, World War I Survey by Hermine Scholz, 1986, U.S. Army Military History Institute, Carlisle Barracks, PA, 5.

16. G. W. Glazier, ed., Evacuation Ambulance Co. 7 (n.p., n.d.).

17. Anonymous, One Woman's War (New York: Macaulay, 1930), 210–235.

18. Doris Kellogg, Canteening Under Two Flags: Letters of Doris Kellogg (East Aurora, NY: The Roycrofters, 1920), 70–115.

19. History of Base Hospital 36, organized by the Detroit College of Medicine and Surgery in April 1917 (n.p., n.d.), 183–184.

20. Gilbo, 81.

21. Helene M. Sillia, comp., A History of Women's Overseas Service League (Newburgh Heights, OH: Women's Overseas Service League, 1978), 237. Copies of this publication are available from Ms. Sillia, 3872 E. 38th St., Newburgh Heights, OH 44105.

22. History of Base Hospital 36 (Evadne Laptad report), 184–185.

23. Gangplank News (published at the embarkation camp at St. Nazaire, France), June 25, 1919, final edition.

24. Records of The American Red Cross, 1917–1934, File 942.52, "Studio of Portrait Masks," 1917–1920, National Archives, Washington, DC.

25. Capt. Bertram M. Bernheim, MCUSA, Passed as Censored (Philadelphia: J. B. Lippincott, 1918), 23.

26. Sillia, 239–240.

27. See note 24.

28. Armies of Mercy, 60.

The first U.S. nurses to go overseas during World War I were these aboard the mercy ship *Red Cross*, waving goodbye as the ship moved down the East River, heading for France, in September 1914. (Bowman Collection, Naval Historical Center, Washington Navy Yard, Washington, DC)

Hundreds of Red Cross canteens for servicemen sprang up all over the United States and throughout the overseas war zone in 1917–1918. Typical of the friendly service is this canteen at Toul, France, with Mary Vail Andress of Sparta, NY, in charge. Miss Andress was awarded the Distinguished Service Medal in May 1919 for her service in Toul, where, under her supervision, "this work grew from the ministering to soldiers passing through in hospital trains to an undertaking of extensive proportions which aided and cheered thousands of men in the service," according to the medal citation. (Library of Congress, Red Cross Photo Archives)

Among the many volunteer services supplied on the home front was the Red Cross Motor Corps, organized in the District of Columbia in April 1917. These women were often trained in motor mechanics, first aid, sanitary home care, and litter drills, and they performed a number of duties, including carrying bandage materials and supplies, collecting salvage, and transporting visitors. The corps grew to a peak number of 12,000 in the summer of 1918. (Library of Congress, Red Cross Photo Archives)

Overseas, hundreds of the nurses recruited and registered by the Red Cross were serving with Army base hospitals some miles from the Front. Other hundreds worked in evacuation hospitals, casualty clearing stations, and field hospitals closer to the battle zone. Here a Red Cross nurse of the 126th Field Hospital irrigates the eyes of gassed soldiers from the Eighty-second and Sixty-ninth Divisions, north of Royaumiex, France. After such treatment, affected doughboys were relieved to find that they were not permanently blind. (Signal Corps Photo no. 22015, Library of Congress, Red Cross Photo Archives)

U.S. women worked overseas in a number of other volunteer social service organizations, often sponsored or aided by the Red Cross. Here Anna Rochester of the Smith College Relief Unit ministers to the wounded amidst the tents of AEF Evacuation Hospitals Nos. 6 and 7 at Souilly, on the Meuse, France. Such volunteers served hot soup and coffee, assisted with medications and bandages, and generally made themselves useful to the nurses and corpsmen of the hospitals. The men pictured were wounded less than a month before the end of the war, in October 1918. (National Archives photo no. 111–SC–30555)

The "patron saint" of U.S. nurses in World War I was Jane A. Delano, superintendent of the Army Nurse Corps in 1909, and in 1912 director of the Red Cross Nursing Service. She is shown here, left, just before she died at Savenay Hospital Center in France in April 1919, struck down by mastoiditis and complications of the flu epidemic. Buried overseas, she was later reinterred with military honors at Arlington National Cemetery in Washington, D.C. (Library of Congress, Red Cross Photo Archives)

Anna Coleman Ladd, pictured at her studio in Paris, France, with an assistant, left, and a disfigured French soldier. Mrs. Ladd, a well-known U.S. sculptor, studied the British technique of making portrait masks for facially disfigured wounded and opened a studio for the work, sponsored by the American Red Cross, in January 1918. (Photo no. USZ62–90459, Library of Congress, Red Cross Photo Archives)

"Before" and "after" photographs of Mrs. Ladd's mutilated French customers
(continued next page)

"Before" and "after" photographs of Mrs. Ladd's mutilated French customers (continued from previous page)

= 9 =

The Salvation Army

"I want to send my Army to France," said the Salvation Army's U.S. commander Evangeline Booth to Gen. John J. Pershing, who headed the American Expeditionary Forces (AEF) overseas. It was spring 1917, and the United States had just entered the European conflict."I have an army in France," Pershing replied. "But not MY army," Evangeline Booth shot back.[1] And thus the Salvation Army became one of the devoted social service organizations working with U.S. troops during the First World War.

By the time the vanguard of Pershing's two-million-man force arrived in France in June 1917, Commander Booth had been busy organizing her own army. She was, after all, the imperious daughter of the fiery father of the Salvation Army, William Booth, who took his stand in 1865 in front of London's Blind Beggar saloon to proclaim the simple message of salvation to the city's outcast masses.[2] Earlier in the war, she had been eager to aid wounded soldiers and civilians throughout the battle zone. She appealed to the public through newspaper articles and pleas in the Salvation Army publication The War Cry asking for contributions of old linen. Enlisting volunteers to help, Salvationists cut and rolled the linen into bandanges, sterilized and packed them into bales, and shipped them overseas. In New York City, Commander Booth herself supervised the Old Linen Campaign.

By December 1914, thousands of pounds of bandages had been shipped. Volunteers could not handle all the material that poured into collection depots, so the Salvation Army appealed for funds to hire the unemployed to help with the processing. Evangeline Booth urged, "Pity all you like, but for God's sake, give!" It was a rallying cry that would serve her well over the following years.

She and her forces were ready when President Woodrow Wilson declared war against Germany on April 6, 1917. Although she deplored all war except the war waged against sin, Commander Booth announced in a War Cry editorial, "The Salvationist stands ready, trained in all necessary qualifications in every phase of humanitarian work, and to the last man will stand by the President for the execution of his orders." She moved decisively to offer service to U.S. soldiers in every area. Summoning a Salvation Army national war council, which created a national war board, she also appointed national, territorial, and provincial war secretaries. The entire Salvation Army organization was quickly mobilized for war service.

Soon Evangeline Booth's army had set up service centers, also known as huts or hostels, outside of, but adjacent to, military camps in the United States. There they established canteens, recreation and meeting rooms, and libraries for servicemen. Religious services were available on Sundays. Moreover, the Salvation Army provided facilities for servicemen in seventeen naval and military clubs, thirty-three rest and recreation rooms, and numerous railway station canteens.

But Commander Booth wanted to do more. "American boys are going to France," she said. "We must go with them." Given General Pershing's sanction, she chose Salvationist lieutenant colonel William S. Barker to proceed overseas and investigate how the Salvation Army could best serve U.S. troops in the war zone. She knew her man: Barker was a fearless and persistent officer. "If you want to see Barker at his best, you must put him face to face with a stone wall and tell him to get through it," she said. "No matter what the cost or toil, hated or loved, he'd get there."[3]

Barker sailed for Europe in June 1917. A cordial Pershing put a sidecar at Barker's disposal and suggested he go out to the camps, look the field over, and report to him on his findings. Barker knew that the advance guard of the AEF had landed in France, and other troops were arriving almost daily. They were not being sent immediately to the Front but were billeted in small French villages where they were learning more than they wanted to know about French rain and mud.

The mud was more like Portland cement than anything else, they decided. It coated their clothes and hair, slid down their necks, into their shoes, and sometimes even into their hip boots. Troops who had expected to be fighting great battles found themselves drilling in mud from morning to night. Many of the young soldiers were away from home for the first time, and an epidemic of depression and homesickness spread through the U.S. encampments. In view of that unhappy situation, officers of the First Division welcomed Salvation Army help in boosting the morale of U.S. soldiers far from home.

Back in the United States, meanwhile, Evangeline Booth had been praying for a door to open that would officially allow her Salvationists to serve in France. Firmly believing that her prayers would be answered, she borrowed $25,000 to finance the establishment of overseas work, and later she requested another $100,000 from Salvation Army International Headquarters. Though some of her staff worried about incurring such a debt, she responded, "It is only a question of our getting to work in France, and the American public will see that we have all the money we want."

As soon as General Pershing authorized the Salvation Army to begin its work with the AEF, Barker cabled General Booth to send over some "lassies" (the popular name for women Salvationists). She determined to send only the very best of these to France. "I felt it was better to fall short in quantity than to run the risk of falling short in quality," she declared. "Quality is its own multiplication table. Quality without quantity will spread, whereas quantity without quality will shrink."

The first group of Salvationists to sail for France included a married couple, three single women, and five single men. Carefully screened and handpicked by the commander, the men were younger or older than the U.S. Army's enlistment age; the women were all more than twenty-five years old, chosen as "spiritually mature." They embarked on the *Espagne* on August 13, 1917. As she bid them goodbye at the dock, Commander Booth announced:

> These officers are not going on any pleasure excursion; they are not going out of any sensational curiosity to see how things look, or test how it feels to be at the Front. They go authorized by a specific commission, with their Commander's confidence that they are fitted to accomplish the specific work inscribed upon that commission. Anyone failing will be shot! It is quite enough for us to pay their expenses to be a success—we could not contemplate paying them to be a failure.

Further, she told her troops, "You are going overseas to serve Christ. You must forget yourselves, be examples of His love, be willing to endure hardship, to lay down your lives, if need be, for His sake."

The commander gave a personal charge to every group that went to France. One of the early lassies, later a Salvation Army colonel, Florence Turkington, recalled that she never forgot the challenge to her own group:

> As she [Commander Booth] spoke, although I am very short, I felt myself getting taller and taller. She made us realize our great responsibility. She finally said, "I promise you nothing. I don't know what you will go into; it may be life, it may be death; it may be sickness, it may be loss—I promise you nothing."
>
> But it made us feel tall to know that such a great woman had faith in us. We determined we would never let her down, no matter how much work or danger was involved. She could be warm and gentle on the one hand, but she could also be stern and demanding. She demanded the best from everyone.

The ten-day voyage of that first party in August 1917 was reportedly no pleasure cruise. At sea, they passed the time studying French, practicing their band instruments, and thinking of home. One of the women, Capt. Ethel Renton, wrote in her diary that seasickness and boredom were prevalent, as was the fear of submarine attack. On the seventh day of the trip, the *Espagne* entered the war zone, where the group soon spotted an empty life raft and considerable floating wreckage on the water. The sight produced "rather a strange feeling. . . . Makes you wonder from whence they came. We are all getting anxious."[4] But the Salvationists arrrived safely at the French port of Bordeaux on August 21 and went straight on to Paris to be fitted out with uniforms.

Pershing had given them all the rank of military privates and ordered that they should wear the regulation khaki uniforms, with skirts for the women and the addition of red epaulets and the red Salvation Army shield on the hats.[5] The lassies later added coverall canvas apron to protect their uniforms from cooking splashes.

This first group next visited Le Havre to observe the work of the English Salvation Army. "We saw a regiment of soldiers on their way to the trenches," Captain Renton recorded. "They tried to smile, but on the whole looked sad. Don't feel as if I could ever get accustomed to sights of this sort."

The Salvationists shortly made their first purchase of equipment, a portable tent measuring 25 feet by 100 feet, which was shipped to Demange, where they planned to begin work with the U.S. Army's First Division, headquartered at Gondrecourt southwest of Verdun. The Salvationists also undertook the purchase of a large touring car, not an easy matter in wartime France. Such a transaction was a lengthy business of official government sanction, long delay, red tape, and amazing good luck. Colonel Barker and his party must have had the luck, plus blessings from above, for their patience was rewarded by a huge limousine that served as the entire Salvation Army transportation fleet in August 1917.

Heartlessly overdriven and overworked, that great solid auto was a true all-purpose vehicle for the Salvationists; for many weeks, it even served as an office and bedroom for the industrious Colonel Barker. The sturdy limo carried all of the Salvationists to and from their stations and hauled all of the supplies inside, on its roof, on its fenders, and later also on a trailer. It was often seen tearing along the road at forty miles an hour, loaded with supplies, several passengers clinging to its fenders, and a pile of lumber or trunks trailering behind.

In this same fine vehicle, the female Salvationists finally arrived at Demange late in August, eager to begin their service. One of them later recalled that it rained in Demange every day for three months. Captain Renton wrote that the first hut was almost completed when they arrived, but there was no place for them to sleep. "The men are sleeping in tents with no floors, but still seem happy under the circumstances." The women slept inside the hut, which at the time had no doors, "but one thinks nothing of such details." The weather was so damp and cold they had to sleep in their clothes. "The life was a hard one for the girls. They nearly froze during the days, and at nights they usually shivered themselves to sleep, only sleeping when sheer exhaustion overcame them. There were no baths at all. Even soldiers were at times seen weeping with cold and misery."

When completed, the first Salvation Army hut measured 150 feet by 40 feet, with ten windows on each side. A canteen ran across the back, with shelves for supplies, and tables were arranged in the middle of the room so the soldiers could read, write letters, and play games. Four rooms were built in the back as sleeping quarters, and U.S. Army tents were set up behind the hut to serve as dining rooms. Captain Renton wrote, "We eat Army rations, same as the soldiers. Food good, but no dainties . . . and of course no desserts."

In October she recorded, "Went with Colonel to Bar-le-duc in the afternoon. Succeeded in renting six pianos at $6.00 a month. While signing the contracts we heard a siren warning the people of another air attack. The people in this town live in constant fear. Colonel was thinking of settling here for H.Q., but has changed his mind. People are all moving out; push carts are to be seen everywhere with furniture."

The last entry in Captain Renton's diary noted that her group wished to accompany the Twentieth Infantry, which was moving on to three other towns. The infantry major had requested that the Salvationists go along, she wrote, because he had found there was never such a feeling of contentment in the camps before the Salvationists arrived.

As it turned out, Ethel Renton was transferred to Paris, where she spent the next two years as secretary to Colonel Barker, the hardworking director of the Salvation Army's war work with the AEF. Miss Renton was later cited by Gen. Charles P. Summerall of the First Division for "most exceptional service to the Army in successfully managing the executive office of the Salvation Army in France for a period of two years, and organizing and supervising a remarkably fine hospital service in the city of Paris."[6]

Another of the lassies in the first overseas group was Capt. Geneva E. Ladd, whose mother had instructed her to wear heavy horn-rimmed glasses to disguise her blonde good looks when she was with the troops. She later recalled how the Salvationists prepared countless cookies, candies, and pies for the homesick soldiers during those first few weeks overseas. A deserted French apple orchard provided a bonanza of tasty pies at one camp, but these treats soon took second place to the famous Salvation Army doughnut.

Ensign Helen Purviance, a young, newly commissioned Salvationist from Indiana who went to France with the first contingent, is generally credited with introducing the popular doughnut to the troops. According to most accounts, that homemade treat first appeared on the Salvation Army menu in September 1917, when Helen Purviance was working in a rain-soaked, dripping tent of a hut at the French town of Montiers-sur-Saulx, southwest of Demange. She was sharing duty that day with Ensign Margaret Sheldon, a former Salvationist "slum sister" who had worked at a Salvation Army home for unwed mothers in Chicago before the war.

"We decided to cook up something special for our troops, a First Division ammunition train," Helen Purviance later recounted.[7]

> We had been fixing them hot chocolate and fudge, but I felt we should give them some nutrition. I went to the commissary and got what I could: flour, lard, sugar, baking powder, vanilla and canned condensed milk. Margaret and I talked about making pancakes but ruled them out because plates would be needed, and we had no butter or molasses [to serve with them]. At first we made the dough, rolled it out with a wine bottle, cut it in strips, twisted them and made crullers.

These were fried seven at a time in a small frying pan over a tiny, potbellied stove.

Legend has it that the women later decided to try to cut the crullers into doughnut shape and were probably the first to attempt that delicacy. Helen Purviance went to a French blacksmith and somehow instructed him to make a crude doughnut cutter from a milk can and a shaving-soap tube. According to other popular legends, the most ingenious, but also the heaviest, cutter ever used by the lassies was a seven-pound shell casing fitted inside with a one-pound shell casing.

"It seemed like doughnuts would be quicker and easier to make, and might remind the boys of home a little bit," Helen Purviance concluded. The doughnuts were a smashing success. "We made 150 that first day," she said, "and the first soldier in line, a buck private from Alabama, tasted one and said, 'Gee, if this is war, let 'er continue.' " The lassies were soon turning out thousands of doughnuts a day for their devoted customers in the AEF, and although other social service organizations overseas served the popular treats, the troops always referred to the Salvation Army women with great affection as "doughnut girls."

Word soon filtered from U.S. camp to camp that the Salvationists were a good sort, that they sold their goods at cost, and that a fellow could even buy on credit when he was broke. When he requested "jawbone" (the soldier's term for credit) at a Salvation Army canteen, he was asked how much debt he had already incurred. If the amount owed was large, he was cautioned not to go too deeply into his next paycheck. But the Salvationists proudly recorded that no soldier was ever refused anything within reason. Often a hut would have many thousands of francs in unpaid debts by the end of a month. But although no accounts were kept and there was no check against them, soldiers always seemed to square their debts on payday, and the canteens lost very little.

In addition to home cooking, the various huts offered a wide variety of supplies at cost to the troops. One of the lassies, Violet McAllister, wrote in her diary in April 1918:

> We opened up our canteen at ten o'clock and all day long we stood at the counter dealing out candy, nuts, blanched almonds, cookies, figs, eggs, jam, and most everything one could think of. We didn't finish until ten p.m. and believe me, we were never more tired in our lives. Our income for the first day is 2,309 francs, which they tell me is the largest first day anyone has ever had. . . . The next day the hut took in 2,500.95 francs, making an income for the two days of about $1,000 in American money. . . . Col. Barker merely tries to make the cost.[8]

Those early doughnut girls, Margaret Sheldon and Helen Purviance, were destined to put in long months of service to the troops before the war ended in November 1918. Ensign Sheldon wrote frequently from France to her friend Elizabeth M. Slinger at the Salvation Army Rescue Home in Los Angeles.[9] In October 1917, her letter was sent from

> a part of France that is very old, and is about 200 years behind the times, but with it all it is a grand place. . . . For breakfast you must have your coffee in a bowl, and your bread in a big hunk. You get no butter with it; that is all one ever gets for breakfast, but we certainly did enjoy it. . . . I will be glad of anything you would send, some jam, candy or chewing gum, or papers to read, something that one can cheer the boys with. They are not going to have an easy time of it, as it is very cold here and not many comforts.

In November, Ensign Sheldon wrote that winter's snow had begun. "I am sitting in a room without any fire, and no place to make one. The only light I have is a candle. Today I made 22 pies, 300 doughnuts, 700 cups of coffee. We have a French stove, the oven holds one pie, and you can imagine the work, and only wood to burn."

The following month, she confided in her friend about her financial situation. "About our salaries, we get our first Outfit, and board, but any extras we want we must buy, and my salary is the same ($4.00), but it is terrible how things wear out. I have worn out two pairs of shoes already, and lost so many of my clothes. You see, they wash them down by the river, and they drop them, sometimes you are the unlucky one." As winter set in, financial hardships were accompanied by physical hardships. "If you could send me some cough drops and something for colds, as so many of the boys have colds. . . . I have had a terrible time with my feet, but they are getting better now. It was a very bad case of trench feet, they were red and itchy and all swollen up, the blisters break and they are awfully sore." Still, she felt the effort was worth it. "The boys are so glad to get the things I make. We sell all at cost of flour and sugar. The wood is given and so is my time and strength; the coffee is sold. We sell a pint of coffee with sugar and canned milk in it, and a quarter of a pie for ten cents."

In April 1918, Ensign Sheldon wrote again. "I am not allowed to give any names of villages [where I am stationed]. But I suppose you have seen by the papers what we are doing, and when you know that I am with the First Division, and follow the boys, you can about guess. . . . I am proud to be attached to this Division, they are the bravest of the brave." In addition to canteen duty, her work with these soldiers included religious meetings. At these services, the men were never pressed for conversions or declarations of faith (nor were such protestations a condition of Salvationist service). "We have two meetings a week and about 300 men attend. We have fine times and the men do enjoy the singing. . . . We make about 2500 doughnuts, 60 cupcakes, and 50 pies, and 300 gallons of cocoa a day. . . . I expect to be on the move soon again, and if I go WEST [soldier slang for death], it's as a Soldier I am and proud to be one."

After a brief respite in Paris, Ensign Sheldon was transferred yet again. "You will be surprised to hear that I was one of the girls who went to the Front," she wrote. This was not uncommon. The women who came to France with the various social service groups often became very much a part of the military units they served, and although they were not officially attached to these units, the unit commanders frequently requested their continued presence as the troops moved about behind the lines or advanced to the Front. From their forward position, Margaret Sheldon wrote, "Our Hut, or barn, was about five kilometers from the third-line trenches. I saw much and heard much. . . . I made doughnuts and every night the Runners would take them up to the men, and if you could see the scraps of paper with the words of thanks, you would feel it payed [sic]. There is a joy in doing something for others, if it is only serving a cup of cocoa."

Within the week, the Salvation Army group moved once more, Ensign Sheldon's tenth move since coming to France the previous September. It was still snowing on April 19, 1918, when she wrote to her friend, describing life on the march. "The men are on a three-days march, to the Front. We have a Hut, the tent is brown and has a white inner lining, and we have tables and benches that fold, so you see in about three hours after landing, all is ready for business. The phonograph is the entertainer, and with it some books and plenty of writing paper complete our hut."

In mid-June she was with a group in the woods,

> well under cover from the Huns. At our last place he found us, and made it rather hot for us and killed some of our best men and eight of the officers in the company. We had to leave there and each night we slept in the Hotel Commons—that's the name the boys have given the war trucks. It got rather risky to sleep in the trucks, as the trees were too scarce and Fritzie could see the truck, so we slept on the ground beside a hay stack, and the birds would call us in the morning.
>
> We slept in dress, as the boys call it, with our shoes and hats off. We slept like that for three weeks, and there was a heavy raid every night. The Major of the train got us fixed up in a house that was forsaken, but some of the beds are there, and it's quite comfy after sleeping on the ground rolled in a blanket.

Eventually, the hardships and stress began to take their toll.

> We hear the long-range guns whistling, and see the mud fly, and see many of the buildings break and go to smash. . . . We have not had one good night's sleep for a long time. . . . If one could only forget the suffering and the many lives that are being sacrificed. . . . I wish you could send me some books, or some papers, how glad I would be. The few books we have are almost worn out by being used so much. I wish you could send me some songs. It would be fine. . . . Sometimes I long to be where I could rest my head for just one short hour. But the desire soon leaves me when I see the boys come in. . . . The older men are getting tired out, and the young boys are beginning to look old.

As Ensign Sheldon explained to her friend, danger was never far behind. "When we were on the other front, our hut was about half a mile from the Front and a big shell hit within ten yards of it, but it did not go off. If it had, we would all have been finished." In July Miss Sheldon observed, "We don't like sunny days and moonlight nights—it makes too much fun for the Germans.

Some of the boys just came in out of the trenches. They are like wild men, poor boys, they look fifty years old."

On July 15, 1918, the German Army attempted to expand the Marne Salient and encircle Reims, driving across the river and into mixed French and U.S. units. From July 18 through the end of August, U.S. divisions, including the First, joined in attacks to drive the Germans back from the Marne to the Vesle, reducing the salient and removing the threat to Paris. During that time, Margaret Sheldon told her friend, her band of Salvationists were on the alert again because

> the Division is moving. At least, what is left of it. My, the last drive nearly finished us. . . . First we were four days at the dressing station, 90 hours of steady work, giving the boys drinks and fruit and all the cheer that one can give at a time like that. It was an awful sight to see them come in trucks and ambulances, just loaded, and the blood running thro' the floor, and thro' it all the boys had a brave smile, bless them. It was the worst battle yet, and the Germans realize by now that the Yanks are all here, with grit and nerve and guns, too. . . . Some of the boys are terribly wounded, and their suffering is hell. One almost goes wild when you see them, and there is so little you can do.

Miss Sheldon wrote about sleeping in a cave, "but we didn't get much sleep. The cooties [body lice] kept us awake." As she had several times before, she asked her friend to "send some phonograph records and books or anything for the boys. I would like some records that are lively and cheerful. Ours are about all worn out, as they go from 7 p.m. until midnight sometimes, but the boys get so much pleasure out of them. . . . If you send me money I will get fruit for the boys in the hospital. They like it and it's good for them. It is very scarce and very expensive."

Later in July, Margaret Sheldon wrote that she and her boys had seen some "real hard times. The fighting has been hard, but I believe the victory will soon come now. We girls were allowed to help at dressing station No. 3. . . . The suffering was awful, but no braver boys could be found anywhere. We gave them drinks and kept the flies off them, as they are the worst pests in France. It seemed so little, what we could do."

By August, Margaret Sheldon reported that she and her Salvation Army crew were in Domrémy, the town where Joan of Arc spent her childhood. "We are still trying to get the Huns. Every night they try to get us, but so far God has taken care of us all. It would be a treat to get just one good night's rest, but when it is all over, then I can."

One day in September, Miss Sheldon wrote about turning out 1,500 dough-nuts in three hours. "I made them and one of the boys fried them, and we fed every outfit that is represented in the Division. We served lemonade and drinks free, and they did enjoy it in this terrible hot weather."

Long lines often formed at the door to a Salvation Army hut when the lassies were serving refreshments. One observer wrote that when the men lined up for doughnuts or pies, there often would be a separate group of doughboys "hover-ing near the line, but not part of it, looking on hungrily. After a while, a lassie would announce: 'All of the men who have already had pie, please step out of line and all who want coffee and pie, but have no money, please line up.' "[10]

Later in September, Margaret Sheldon wrote from a village where German troops had lived just seven days earlier.

> They were driven out by our own boys, at the cost of many brave lads. . . . I pray God to bless each heartbroken Mother. It is Hell, and worse. Let me tell you in one week we disposed of seven tons of Canteen supplies, beside about 20,000 doughnuts, and hundreds of gallons of coffee. . . . Our house is only half here, the rest is blown to rubbish, the roof is almost gone, and the walls are all full of holes. But we have a little room [where] the boys come in, and talk and sing; the other room they write and read in, and at night we sleep in it. Sometimes there are about 600 men where there is only room for 300. But it is the [Salvation] Army and that means home to the soldier.
>
> For three weeks here we never undressed. We had gas shells hitting us, and high explosive shells throwing the dirt all over us, but not one of us got a scratch. . . . I can't tell you all I would like to. It is all too sad.

After the Armistice on November 11, Sheldon, her colleagues, and the troops moved on to the town of Cornay, where she was stationed in an ancient chateau. "It is a sad sight to see the hills all peppered with holes where the men crawled in like groundhogs," she wrote. "The saddest thing is the graves all marked with crosses." Christmas, however, was a joyous occasion.

> We had a large Christmas tree for the boys, and plenty of holly and mistle-toe, and it all came from the Argonne Forest, where so many Americans lost their lives. The tree was put up in the church. The roof had been blown off, but the boys put a canvas over it for us. We had a treat for everyone. They got chocolate, lemon candies, oranges, cocoa and cake. We had a program for them and we all had a wonderful time. Only God knows how hard we tried to give the boys some Christmas joy.

The troops were able to give that joy right back. "They gave us the biggest surprise, when they gave both of us a hand pocketbook, and a fountain pen, and a box of writing paper, and a lovely umbrella. Then they made a great speech. I just sat there and cried. Can you imagine a good Christmas in a shell-torn village? Yes, and the best Christmas I ever had and the best I ever expect to have."

Ensign Sheldon followed the First Division as the troops moved into Germany with the U.S. Army of Occupation. On January 20, 1919, her crew took over the large dance hall and the basement kitchen of the Gasthof Rheingold in Coblenz, and she was billeted in a comfortable room in a villa with a German family. "Just think of being able to sleep between sheets again," she wrote. "What a treat. But we can say with Paul, 'We can content in whatsoever place we are in because we are working for Him.' " After three months, she finally found a bit of time for herself when she was granted a brief leave at Nice in southern France. "At present my needs are new nerves," she wrote. Ensign Sheldon sailed for home in June 1919.

Of all who served overseas, including chaplains, no Salvationists were killed by enemy action, although a few were gassed. Most suffered from extreme fatigue, unhygienic conditions, parasites, and nervous exhaustion. Only one died in the service, Maj. Stanley Barnes, who succumbed to pneumonia in 1918.

Though Commander Booth carefully chose the Salvation Army's doughnut girls, none received any formal instructions for wartime service; they had, however, been taught in Salvationist training schools what Evangeline Booth called "the service of humanity." The lassies in Europe simply served as their Salvationist sisters at home had served before them: by doing every useful, kindly thing that came to hand.[11] They darned socks, sewed on buttons and chevrons, mended uniforms, wrote letters, extended credit, acted as bankers, did whatever needed to be done. They joked and talked, and mostly they listened. And many times they sobbed quietly as "their boys," wounded, were carried back from the Front, or worse, never returned.

The Salvationist women sang a lot, and preached and prayed sometimes, too, although their primary purpose was not to "save souls." They were charged by their commander in "that much greater art, the art of dealing ably with human life in all its varying conditions and phases. It is in this art that we seek by a most careful culture and training to perfect our officers," she said.[12] Armed with that art, the lassies somehow had the knack of fitting in, in any situation. U.S. doughboys sometimes wondered at how the Salvationist women had become so popular, and they were told, "You have to remember, they've always been popular with the homeless. Now, we're the homeless."[13]

The Salvation Army's role in France was "a natural," according to Commander Booth. "It must not be forgotten that The Salvation Army, wherever it is established in 61 countries, has been trained to endure hardship and privation, to deal with the miseries and wants of unfortunates. . . . Our workers, skilled and experienced in practical relief work, and long since consecrated to God and His service, are the 'little mothers' of the battlefield."

One of the most popular Salvation Army services in those pre-allotment days was its money transfer system. The U.S. soldier often had more money than he could spend in the war zone, but there was no way to send it home, even if his family was in need of financial help. To help with this problem, Salvationists often forwarded the soldier's funds by money order to New York, from there to the corps officer nearest the soldier's home, and thence to the appropriate family. Often cases of need were discovered through these visits, and other Salvation Army services could then be made available to help families in distress. The money transfer plan also worked in reverse on occasions when friends at home sent money to soldiers overseas.

As the war went on, the Salvation lassies sought out and tidied up the hasty wartime graves of the U.S. dead, decorating them with small U.S. flags and French wildflowers. On Decoration Day 1918, each grave in the Treveray area received a tin-can vase of flowers, along with a U.S. flag sent personally to France by Commander Evangeline Booth.[14]

Throughout the years of U.S. participation in the Great War, there were, of course, other social service agencies at work overseas. The Salvation Army cooperated with all of these; there was no open competition and there was much collaboration. On one occasion when a Salvation Army canteen ran out of supplies while a long line of soldiers waited to be served, a YMCA truck drove up, pulled in beside the Salvationist vehicle, and continued serving where the doughnut girls had left off.

In July 1918, a U.S. canteen worker with the Y wrote from an AEF engineering camp at Abainville, France:

> There is a Salvation Army hut here, the first one I have seen. . . . The staff comprises one man and two women; they are pleasant people, "real home folks." Two or three times a week—for supplies are hard to obtain—they make pie or cake or doughnuts. On these nights, passing the hut on our way back from mess, one sees a long line stretching down the road, waiting patiently for the chance to get a piece of pie "like Mother used to make."
>
> Our relationships are cordial. We help each other out in the matter of change. They come to our hut for sweet chocolate and movies; we go to them, when our consciences will permit, for doughnuts. I only wish that one of their huts could be in every camp in France.[15]

Legends abound concerning Salvation Army service in France. It was often recorded that the "sweet, clear voices of the lassies" inspired the troops who longed for home. One famous report was sent by Lt. Col. Fred Fitzpatrick to his wife in Salina, Kansas.[16] "I am not a poet or very sentimental," he wrote,

> but I saw a scene last night in Neuvilly that I want to tell you about. Picture a church about the size of ours at home, with all the north wall out except a supporting column in the middle, holes in all the other walls, all the windows gone, the floor covered with debris of wreckage.
>
> Over the altar [is] a beautiful picture of Christ ascending to heaven; beneath the picture [is] the office of the field hospital, some wounded on stretchers in the northeast corner. . . . About one fourth of the way from the west end of the north wall, a fire had been built, around which were three Salvation Army lassies (God bless them), among about two hundred men. . . These were the men who had been facing death a thousand times an hour for the past three days, who had not had a wash or a chance to take off their shoes and had been lying in mud in shell holes—men who looked as though they were chilled to the bone.
>
> Men on their way to the Front, knowing all the hardships and dangers which were ahead of them, but who were worried only about the delay in traffic. Doctors who had been working for three days and nights without rest; men off ammunition and ration trucks who had been at the wheel so long that they had forgotten whether it was three days and nights, or four; the wounded on their stretchers enjoying a smoke.
>
> As I stepped in the doorway, there were the feminine voices singing— singing the good old tunes we all know so well, and not a sound in the church, but as an accompaniment the distant booming of big guns, the rattle of small arms, the whirr [sic] of air craft, the passing of the ever-present column of ration and ammunition trucks going up to the Front, and the wounded coming back. . . . There was that crowd of men giving absolute undivided attention to those good brave girls who were not making a [religious] meeting of it. It was just a meeting that grew, men who in their minds were back with mother and sister. The girls sang the good old songs and then one of them offered a prayer, in which all those men joined in spirit. . . Every man in that building that night was in the very presence of God. It was not a religious meeting; it was a meeting full of religion.

Two of those lassies singing in the ruined church that night were sisters Alice and Violet McAllister, who had been helping with the wounded at a First Division field hospital at Morte Fontaine on the Soissons front. The third Salvationist woman at the church was Eva Springer, a widow and Army missionary who had given up her sabbatical leave to work in France.[17]

At the end of September 1918, the McAllister sisters had found themselves marooned in the ruined village of Neuvilly when their infantry unit moved forward into the first phase of the U.S. Army's attack in the Meuse-Argonne sector. Trying to find transport to their field hospital at Cheppy to the north, Alice wrote:

> The roads were clogged with traffic. Ambulances and ammunition trucks had preference over everything else, of course. We simply crawled along and many times were completely stalled. In the late afternoon we found ourselves at a standstill near a small village. We decided to leave our truck and driver, and walk into town. There seemed to be a lot of activity around the church, so we went in and found it was being used as an evacuation center for the wounded. We told the officer in charge we would be glad to help if there was anything we could do.

The willing sisters were directed to a new Thirty-fifth Division field hospital that had been set up in a field outside the village. There they spent the night working with the hundreds of wounded. As Alice recalled,

> They had come so fast there was scarcely time to get the tents up. All they could do was to dress their wounds, wrap them in a blanket and lay them on the ground to await ambulances to take them away. . . . It was their first time in battle and they were badly shot up. A young wounded officer in one of the tents kept crying out, "My poor boys, they are all shot to pieces." This was slow work and it was bitterly cold. Our fingers got so numb that one of the soldiers cut the side out of a 25-pound lard can and filled it with lighted candles. It gave out a surprising heat and we were able to stop occasionally to warm our hands.

Back in the village the next day, the McAllisters tried to catch up on their sleep in the ruins of the church. While they were settling in, "some soldiers came to ask us if we would sing for them," Alice wrote later. "Of course we would, and we got our guitars from the truck. In the meantime they had built a fire on the stone floor of the old church and placed some boxes beside it for us to sit on." And thus ensued the meeting described by Lieutenant Colonel Fitzpatrick. Alice described the scene. "We tried to fill every [song] request. . . . We sang on and on, and the soldiers crowded around us. Someone asked my sister to sing 'Mother Macree,' and her beautiful voice rang out through the old church and surely thrilled every listener. When she finished, she suggested that we all join together in praying the Lord's Prayer. Reverently the heads were bowed and we all prayed together."

The Salvation Army forces overseas were never large. At no time were there more than 500 Salvationists on active duty, and relatively few of those who served were women.[18] Because Salvationists were not subject to the Government restriction preventing married women from going overseas when her husband was serving in the war zone, a number of Salvationist women did accompany their husbands. One of those was Louise Holbrook. Her group was stationed with the U.S. First Division, traveling with these troops wherever they went, often dangerously close to the action. When the division was cited for braving 180 days under fire, the Salvationist workers were cited along with them. In a memoir she wrote for the Salvation Army archives[19] Mrs. Holbrook described her experiences.

> At one small place we had for a hut a bare shelter, [a large piece of] corrugated iron on four poles. We placed tables outside and gave the men a place to write. We scattered magazines around and set an old door on logs for a counter. We had candy, chocolate bars, and "limonade," which was a very weak lime and lemon combination. . . . In the evening I would get out my guitar and start strumming. Someone would call for "Moonlight on the Wabash," then another would ask for "K-K-K-Katy" and another for "Tipperary." They would sing and sing, and before they knew it, they would be led into [old family favorites], "The Roll is Called Up Yonder" and "Nearer, My God, to Thee." I would repeat the 23rd Psalm, or they would ask for the 91st Psalm. Sometimes they asked for that every evening. There is such comfort in those blessed words, "He that dwelleth in the secret place of the Most High shall abide under the shadow of the Almighty."

In addition to ministering to the soldiers' spirits, Mrs. Holbrook also provided more tangible sustenance—the ubiquitous doughnut. "At this place I was making doughnuts every day. . . . One day I had made over 3,200 and had been at it from dawn. I mixed my dough in a big dishpan, lifted it out onto the table, filled the pan with lard, heated it, and fried the doughnuts. Then repeated the whole performance."

When the Argonne drive started, the troops and Salvationists were transferred to the Neuvilly area. "For more than a week we were on the road. We traveled all day and part of the night, standing in the back of an Army truck, or sitting on the floor, never knowing where we would spend the night, sleeping in such places as a tent, an attic, an old stable, in No Man's Land in the open, in a very beautiful French chateau."

On occasion the Salvation lassies and other U.S. women volunteers bunked in with families in the small towns of the war zones. One Salvationist remembered an elderly Frenchwoman with whom she was billeted for a time. "She lived in one of the stricken villages near the Vosges Mountains, and her home had been struck by shells several times. But all through the war this elderly citizen refused to leave the house where she had lived from earliest childhood. 'It is not the guns, nor the bombs which can frighten me,' she told her young American friend. 'But I am very much afraid of the submarines.' "[20]

The evening of September 30, 1918, found Salvationist Louise Holbrook close to the front lines in the Meuse-Argonne sector.

> We drew up at a fence in Neuvilly, and soldiers carried us over the wet and soggy field where a field hospital had been set up [the same facility where the McAllister sisters were volunteering]. And we began nursing the men who had been shell-shocked in the Argonne takeoff. They were located in tents pitched on the ground—no floors, no cots, no stove; with the first cold spell of the winter coming in on us. The mattresses were bed ticks, without straw, and there were so many wounded that there were not enough beds. We put two ticks together and put three men crosswise, and that way two blankets would cover three men.

Many of these soldiers had been in the service less than a month when they were wounded in the Meuse-Argonne that day.

> They were weary and cold and nervous, and during the night the Boche started shelling the adjacent field. The men would start up and commence to shake, and then we would go around and talk to them. I used to say to them, "There's nothing to be afraid of." They would say, "Yes, but those shells," and I would say, "Now you listen here, this is my third big engagement and I tell you everything's all right." It wasn't all right and it wasn't pleasant. All we could do was to give them hot chocolate, and listen to their stories. One of the doctors said, "Let them talk; it will do them a lot of good." So all night they talked and talked, and we just listened.
>
> It was a very cold night. In my diary I find this: "It is cold and muddy, and Violet [McAllister] is trying to warm her feet by the light of two candles." And a little later that same night, "We have no stove, only three candles inside a tin box, and we keep reasonably warm by spells. We heat cocoa and warm our feet there."

The following day, the division was moved to Cheppy-en-Argonne, where they found themselves in a U.S. field hospital or casualty clearing station in a cave that the Germans had fixed up and abandoned. As Mrs. Holbrook recalled, "I was assigned to the shock and fracture ward. There were no other women at the hospital besides the four Salvation Army women." At this point in the campaign, U.S. Army nurses were in short supply and vastly overworked. "My job was to wash [the soldiers'] faces and clean them up a bit and help give them the anti-tetanus serum which was standard for every wound. Then if they were able and could be moved, we sent them on to the distributing centers." Here the wounded would be assigned to specialty or base hospitals behind the lines.

> In our ward, we also set broken bones and treated the men for shock. We had no regular hours for work. We simply kept going until we dropped in our tracks, then slept until we could work again. We put through 7,500 men in ten days. There was a brighter side to it all, though. Such as the bald-headed German who, when he sat up on his stretcher, was found to be wearing nothing but his cap. When we asked him, "How come?" He answered [that he was wearing the cap because] he was afraid of catching cold.

Louise Holbrook had vivid memories of the day when German shells crept closer and closer to their dugout shelter. "The third shell landed on top of the entrance, but did no harm. We were helping with the stretchers, evacuating the men into the dugout. The last man was inside the dugout when we heard the next shell coming. We all made for the door of the hill—jammed the door—and the shell got there first." Mrs. Holbrook was buried to the waist, and Alice McAllister's helmet was dented. "I suspect [she] had a headache the rest of the day." They spent the remainder of the day holed up in the hill. "I am telling this in the first person," Mrs. Holbrook wrote, "but I am not really sure if it happened to me or to Violet [MacAllister]. Our lives were so intermingled and so unnatural that I cannot quite remember."

The McAllister sisters had good reason to remember their trip from Neuvilly to Cheppy. Alice wrote:

> We were getting very worried for we knew our First Division would be going into battle and we wanted so much to get to our hospital. We met a Signal Corps boy we knew and he was going up to the Front by back roads with a two-wheel reel cart carrying telephone cable. If we thought we could stand the rough trip, he would be glad to take us along. We didn't need a second invitation. To say it was rough would be putting it mildly! We bumped out of one shell hole into another. Once there was a hole so big and so deep that we drove down into it and a man with a team of mules pulled us out on the other side.[21]

When the sisters arrived at Cheppy, they found large tents where injured soldiers rested after having their wounds dressed. In front of one of the entrances to the dugout, there was also a stone room used as a dressing station for the casualties. "Here my sister worked," Alice recalled, "helping with tetanus shots and marking a big purple T on each forehead to signify that tetanus had been given. I worked out in the tents, washing faces and hands, giving drinks of water, etc."

Being so close to the Front, the McAllisters saw many casualties and were themselves almost among them. "The fighting in this part of the Argonne Forest was bitter," Alice McAllister recalled. "The Germans were strongly entrenched and the terrain presented great difficulties. The wounded came in thick and fast. We worked from five in the morning until sometimes two or three the next morning! The wounds were dreadful and many did not live. One day as I worked in a tent, there was a dreadful explosion. A big shell landed right in front of our tents!" It was the first of three to land close by, showering great rocks and shattered debris and mud. By some stroke of fortune, no one was hurt. " 'Men, you have just seen a miracle,' exclaimed one of the doctors. 'I believe God has spared us because of these girls who are with us.' "

Although they escaped the German shells, the McAllister sisters were crushed by the "sad news" in October 1918 that they had been chosen to return to the States to work on the U.S. government's United War Work campaign, which raised funds for all U.S. welfare organizations.

> We were horrified at the idea of leaving our work in the hospital, especially now when it seemed the end of the war was in sight. We pleaded in vain to stay. . . . Our uniforms were a mess, but we were assured that new ones awaited us in Paris. The doctors came to our rescue with bottles of ether and tried to clean the blood off our uniforms, and at the same time telling us how much they would miss us. They hoped we would get the job over with and come back as soon as possible. We said a sorrowful goodbye and were driven away toward Paris.

Ensign Helen Purviance, who was credited with introducing the Salvation Army doughnut, also was chosen to return to the States to work in the fundraising campaign.

Back home, these three weary Salvationists in their crisp new uniforms were widely interviewed and quoted in the press, to their intense embarrassment. They made countless personal appearances and speaking engagements along the East Coast, in New York and Washington, DC, and their celebrated commander, Evangeline Booth, even appeared with them on several occasions. At length they were rewarded for this strenuous schedule with a tenday leave, after which they set about pestering headquarters with requests to return to France.

"But it was not to be yet," Alice McAllister wrote. "Christmas time was drawing near and we had heard that troop ships were on their way home. The Commander [Evangeline Booth] wanted us to stay and be on the docks to greet the soldiers as they arrived." On a bitterly cold morning the day after Christmas, the three lassies went down to the port of Hoboken, NJ, and stood on the end of the pier to wave to the troops coming in on the transports. "When they saw our uniforms, such a shout went up from that ship that it fairly shook the pier! They kept it up until we were a little embarrassed." The McAllister sisters and Helen Purviance handed out current newspapers to the debarking soldiers and gave each a telegraph blank so he could send a message home without charge to announce his safe arrival.

In February 1919, the McAllister sisters were reassigned to France and served at the port of St. Nazaire and at Brest's Camp Pontenazen, a tent city accommodating some 90,000 men awaiting transport home.[22] The McAllisters sailed for home in September 1919 on the *Agamemnon*. They were among the last group of Americans to leave France.

Another lassie, Capt. Della Rapson, who was stationed at the Gondrecourt hut near Toul, served an astonishing amount of food to hungry doughboys in the final months of the war. In mid-August 1918, one diary entry notes a "pie record day" on which she and her colleagues served 316 apple pies, "which is the highest amount so far."[23] On September 7, as the U.S. Army was readying for the St. Mihiel drive, she recalled that her group had been advised to be ready to move. "We are to go to a dressing station near the front line. . . . We served rolls and coffee to the 95th Division as they passed our hut. They never will forget it—neither will I. They had been traveling 48 hours and were so tired. Miss Billings and I made 3,120 batter rolls." Later, the Twenty-seventh Division came through as the first phase of the U.S. attack began in the Meuse-Argonne. On October 2, Della Rapson reported her crew made 2,000 doughnuts and suffered through a blast of "sneezing gas," forcing them to don gas masks. The dedicated Salvationists, however, continued their work, making cocoa for the dressing station and hundreds of doughnuts to send to the Front.

On November 11, Miss Rapson noted that it was her birthday. "And also Victory Day. In the afternoon news came that the Armistice was signed. Everybody turned out for a spontaneous parade: American, French, Italians—men, women and children. Flags everywhere. . . . The French women threw flowers at the U.S. boys." For Thanksgiving several weeks later, the crew wanted to make pumpkin pie but had no pumpkin. Instead, they made 1,200 doughnuts, "rolled with a Spalding baseball bat." For dinner, there was a can of salmon, can of corn, coffee, bread, and can of peaches for dessert.

The troops moved out the next day, leaving only the forty men who were working on the roads. But several officers soon appeared and asked the Salvationist crew to prepare for the Twenty-first Artillery of the Fifth Brigade, who would be passing through; fifteen hundred men would be stopping overnight. December 2 proved to be a busy day. Della Rapson recalled, "We made 2,000 doughnuts and at 5 p.m. we began serving them with hot coffee. Finished up at 9 p.m. My, what a sight it was to see these boys marching by all day in battle formation into Germany, the Stars and Stripes flying at the head of the march."

Salvation Army war work in France did not end with the Armistice on November 11. Hospital visitation and nursing service continued, and Salvationists administered in all the old ways to the thousands of troops gathered in staging camps waiting to be shipped home. Salvation Army workers operated huts and resting rooms in the demobilization camps, sent thousands of "safe arrival" telegrams for the troops, and—as always—served coffee and doughnuts to waiting soldiers everywhere.[24]

Shortly after the Armistice, on Christmas Day 1918, Lt. Col. Henry H. Denhardt, commander of the Third Corps Artillery Park at Cornay, France, wrote to Colonel Barker, director of war work for the Salvation Army in France. His request reflected typical AEF affection for the Salvationist women:

> It is with much regret that I have just learned from Miss Sheldon of your order recalling her and Miss Swanson. . . . In view of the fact that your Organization is at present located in Cornay and is quite some distance from any similar Organization, I would ask that you kindly allow them to remain with this Unit until such time as the Unit is recalled from this area or is sent forward with the Army of Occupation.
>
> In the latter event, I would be very much pleased to have them accompany us. There are at present some fifteen hundred men in the Organization in addition to the men of other units who also visit The Salvation Army on every opportunity they have.
>
> The services rendered by them have been invaluable to this Organization in keeping up the morale of the men, and their loss at this time would be keenly felt by all.[25]

Considering such requests, the Salvation Army thoughtfully decided that instead of releasing its personnel for return to the United States, it would begin operations with the U.S. Service of Supply in France. In December 1918, Salvationists obtained from the government twenty large aviation hangars, which they placed at the embarkation ports of Brest, St. Nazaire, and Bordeaux.

The allotment for St. Nazaire arrived on location in February 1919. The buildings went up in about ten days and were completed just in time to provide a venue for a show troupe that had arrived to entertain the men. Improvements in the hangar/auditorium were made as time went on, so that eventually the Salvationist crew could boast, "We have one of the finest theaters in France."

In a smaller building, they provided a canteen, reading and writing room, a large kitchen, and living rooms for the personnel. "Since its opening March 1, 1919, we have endeavored to serve the permanent and transient troops with home cooking daily, a feature of our work which has endeared itself to every American doughboy. Our kitchen has put out 259,913 doughnuts, 4,132 pies, 4,790 cakes, and 7,669 gallons of cocoa in the twelve weeks of its existence. In money orders, 659,900 francs have been transmitted to the States for soldiers."[26]

After the war, an official U.S. government publication observed:

> The welfare associations working with our overseas forces . . . have in great measure ameliorated the material welfare of our combatants, mitigated the sufferings of the victims of war, and maintained high morale near the Front. And they have accomplished the great result of shortening the distance between the soldier and his home. . . . The fame of the doughnuts made by the Salvation Army lassies at the Front will outlive all the hungry doughboys who ate them, but The Salvation Army in France . . . did much more than bake doughnuts.

Official figures indicate approximately 250 Salvationists—132 men and 109 women—were sent to France. The Salvation Army "maintained 77 motor ambulances, conducted 87 hotels for soldiers and sailors, maintained 199 huts and rest rooms for religious and social gatherings and for dispensing comfort to soldiers and sailors, and distributed 100,000 parcels of food and clothing."[27]

Their service was summed up with much more sentiment by the following verse in the doughboys' own newspaper, *The Stars and Stripes*:[28]

Tin hat for a halo;
Ah, she wears it well,
Making pies for homesick lads,
Sure is beating hell . . . .

"Home is where the heart is,"
True, the poet sang,
But "Home is where the pie is,"
To the Yankee gang.

Commander Evangeline Booth's "gallant little Army" also was memorialized in a number of popular songs, among them "Good-Bye Sally, Good Luck to You," by Sgt. Sam Habelow, published by Habelow and Chief Yeoman George Jeffrey in 1919. The cover pictures Helen Purviance at the door of a hut in the battle zone, and its lyrics spell out the affection of the U.S. soldier for the faithful doughnut girls.

> Many times when things look'd blue,
> You stood by and helped us thru.
> Good-bye Sally, Good luck to you.[29]

Salvationists sailing for the States in 1919 carried home memories of their own. As Capt. Mary Bishop boarded a ship at Brest, a band on the pier played "Homeward Bound, What a Wonderful, Wonderful Sound." "I was near to tears," she recalled, "and I thought they must be homesick too." But when she arrived in New York in July 1919, Mary Bishop "felt strange, not at home at all. My heart was still back there."[30]

Returning home, the Salvationists faced a new era as the veteran doughboys spread the word of the Salvation Army's warm, understanding service, their unquestioning kindness, their prayers, their songs, their pies and doughnuts. By 1919 the soldier tributes had become a flood, and the home-front public's approbation quickly took on a practical form as a stream of contributions replaced the grudging trickle of coins that had long supported the organization. The Salvation Army was amazed to find their fund-raising campaigns oversubscribed following the Armistice, and sums that would have dazzled them in 1915 came to be expected and routine. The days were over when bonnetted lassies had to stand on street corners begging for coins to support their work.

Commander Evangeline Cory Booth, who sent the Salvation Army to France in 1917, was awarded the Distinguished Service Medal by U.S. President Woodrow Wilson in 1919. She continued to preside actively over her troops during the peacetime years and was elected the Salvation Army's fourth general in November 1934, the first woman to hold that office. She retired from duty in 1939 and in July 1950, died at her home in Hartsdale, NY, or "was promoted to glory," as the Salvationists say when a comrade passes on. Surely, after a lifetime of devoted service that touched the lives of many thousands of people, Evangeline Booth was indeed "promoted."

Notes

1. Margaret Troutt, The General Was a Lady: The Story of Evangeline Booth (Nashville, TN: A. J. Holman, 1980), 154.

2. It has been said that the Salvation Army came into its own during World War I. Previously, it was often viewed as a narrow, puritanical sect, its somberly uniformed band members standing on street corners playing hymns and passing around a tambourine to collect coins for their work with the less fortunate. Often the earnest Salvationists were the butt of snickering and crude jokes as they went about their business of saving souls.

    It was not generally known that the Salvation Army was founded by William Booth in 1865 as The Christian Mission; its name changed in 1878 to The Salvation Army. It was an international organization with branches in sixty-three countries and colonies, with 21,000 officers and workers. These Salvationists had been serving together for more than fifty years before the Great War broke out in Europe. Thus, in effect, The Salvation Army was doing for the troops overseas only what it had been doing for the needy everywhere since its inception.

    The Salvation Army was—and is—a religious establishment, but as U.S. commander Evangeline Booth explained during the Great War, its religious philosophy "placed Christ in deeds." A U.S. senator explained the Salvation Army's secret of success as "their complete abandonment to their cause, the service of the man." To the Salvationists, this meant all services to all men, regardless of creed.

    There was no holier-than-thou patronizing attitude in the Salvation Army's service overseas, "just a good old Salvation Army–Bowery Mission welcome," as one reporter put it. A U.S. Army officer wrote fervently, "I wish every American who has stood on street corners in America and sneered at the work of the Salvation Army could see what they are doing for the boys in France."

3. Troutt, 152–157.

4. Throughout this chapter, quotations from Captain Renton's diary are found in an article by Judith Johnson, archivist, Salvation Army Eastern Territory Archives and Research Center, "Amid the Carnage of World War I: A Page From the Past," Good News (Eastern Territory newsletter) (October 1987). This quote comes from page 10.

5. Evangeline Booth and Grace Livingston Hill, The War Romance of the Salvation Army (Philadelphia: J. B. Lippincott, 1919), 44. Unless otherwise indicated, quotations in this chapter are from Booth and Hill.

6. Renton diary.

7. Interview with Helen Purviance by Jeff Testerman, St. Petersburg Times (Florida), November 21, 1981.

8. Scrapbook of photographs and war memoirs compiled by Capt. Violet McAllister and her sister, Lt. Alice McAllister, Salvation Army Western Territorial Museum and Archives, Rancho Palos Verdes, CA.

9. Letters from Adjutant Margaret Sheldon, Salvation Army worker with the AEF in France, to Elizabeth M. Slinger of the Salvation Army Los Angeles Rescue Home, September 1917 to April 1919, Salvation Army Western Territorial Museum and Archives, Rancho Palos Verdes, CA.

10. Sallie Chesham, Born to Battle: The Salvation Army in America (Chicago: Rand McNally, 1965), 159.

11. Dr. Ed McKinley, Marching to Glory: The History of the Salvation Army in the United States of America, 1880–1980 (San Francisco: Harper and Row, 1980), 123.

12. Booth and Hill, 13.

13. Chesham, 161

14. Ibid., 160–162.

15. Uncensored Letters of a Canteen Girl (New York: Henry Holt, 1920), 134.

16. Letter from Lt. Col. Fred Fitzpatrick to his wife in Salina, KA, Salvation Army Western Territorial Museum and Archives, Rancho Palos Verdes, CA.

17. McAllister scrapbook.

18. Chesham, 160.

19. Mrs. Maj. L. B. (Louise) Holbrook, "World War I," unpublished memoirs, Salvation Army Western Territorial Museum and Archives, Rancho Palos Verdes, CA.

20. Booth and Hill.

21. McAllister scrapbook.

22. Gangplank News (published at the embarkation camp at St. Nazaire, France), June 25, 1919, final edition.

23. Excerpts from the diary of Della Rapson (Ringle), Salvation Army Western Territorial Museum and Archives, Rancho Palos Verdes, CA.

24. McKinley, 128.

25. Letter from Lt. Col. Henry H. Denhardt, Headquarters, Third Corps Artillery Park, Cornay, France, to Col. William Barker, American Salvation Army, Paris, December 25, 1918, Salvation Army Archives and Research Center, Alexandria, VA.

26. Gangplank News, June 25, 1919.

27. U.S. Official Pictures of the World War, Showing America's Participation (Washington, DC: Pictorial Bureau, 1920), 541.

28. Chesham, 159.

29. Author's collection.

30. Memoirs of Capt. Mary Bishop (Ryan), Salvation Army Archives and Research Center, Alexandria, VA.

Gen. Evangeline Cory Booth, U.S. commander of the Salvation
Army, was the imperious and gifted daughter of the organization's
founders, William and Catherine Booth, and for thirty years ordered
and charted the work of the organization in the United States. It was
she who suggested to Gen. John J. Pershing that she send her army
to France in 1917. (Courtesy of Salvation Army Western Territorial
Museum, Rancho Palos Verdes, CA)

There was no "patronizing, holier-than-thou, we-know-we-are-doing-a-good work-and-hope-you-doughboys-appreciate-it sort of a welcome, but a good old Salvation Army–Bowery Mission welcome," wrote an overseas correspondent after some months in France. Here Gladys McIntyre, age twenty-two, of Mount Vernon, NY, demonstrates that attitude as she offers a friendly smile, along with a treat, to a soldier of the Twenty-sixth Division at Ansauville, France, in April 1918. Gladys and her sister, Irene, were one of two Salvationist sister teams who served in the war zone. (National Archives photo no. 111–SC–10446)

In the course of their service in France, Salvation Army women became famous and beloved as much for their smiles as for their home cooking. Although other service organizations served the tasty doughnuts to the troops, the Salvation Army gets credit for introducing the treats to the battlefield. Helen Purviance, shown here frying up a batch, is credited with introducing the doughnut as she and a colleague, Margaret Sheldon, searched for something nutritious to serve the soldiers. (Courtesy of Salvation Army Western Territorial Museum, Rancho Palos Verdes, CA)

Doughnuts always came first on the Salvationist menu, and the women soon became known to the troops as "doughnut girls." The busy cook shown here is Signa Saunders of Brainerd, MN, right, who cuts the sweet dough while her colleague minds the boiling grease. The hard-working Salvation Army women also turned out endless thousands of rolls, cookies, cakes, and pies. One, Geneva Ladd Staley, even baked a birthday pie for General Pershing, who told her she had the "power to reach any man's heart," she recalled. (National Archives photo no. 111–SC–25485)

Salvationist women were given no special training for their overseas service. They simply served "by doing every useful, kindly thing that came to hand," said their commander, Evangeline Booth. One hard-working Salvationist, Louise Holbrook, found herself in a position to help at an overtaxed dressing station of the Thirty-fifth Division at Bois de Cheppy on the second day of the Argonne offensive in the fall of 1918. Here she registers a wounded trooper, Harry Spark, hit while advancing with a machine gun company, Twenty-eighth Infantry, First Division. (Courtesy of The Salvation Army National Archives)

After The Fight

Gen. Evangeline Booth's army was never a horde; a mere 132 men and 109 women went overseas as Salvationists. Each had a knack for fitting in, often following their adopted units to the edge of No Man's Land. A devoted sister team, Violet, right, and Alice McAllister, traveled with the First Division in the St. Mihiel campaign, establishing a canteen in the Bavarian-type rustic shelters left behind by the Germans who had occupied the area. They are pictured with "the only stove we had to cook on."(Courtesy of The Salvation Army National Archives)

There was no end to the service the Salvationist women provided for their troops. They were cooks and bakers, bankers and postal clerks, nurses and confidantes. They joked and talked, and mostly they listened. Eva Springer, pictured here, used her sabbatical leave to serve in France, carrying along her sewing machine to stitch up rips and mend uniforms. (Courtesy of The Salvation Army National Archives)

Capt. Violet McAllister, left, with her sister, Lt. Alice McAllister, center, and Louise Holbrook, right, were often in the line of fire.(Courtesy of The Salvation Army National Archives)

This shattered church in the ruins of Neuvilly, close to the Argonne Forest, furnished temporary shelter to U.S. wounded in the last month of the war. The McAllister sisters were stranded here by the traffic jams and entered the church, where the soldiers asked them to sing. "They tried to fill every request," an onlooker reported of the moving experience. (National Archives photo no. 111–SC–24942)

Appendix A

Chemical Warfare and Shell Shock

Poison Gas

Both the German High Command and the Allies used poison gases[1] during the First World War. The Germans introduced the horrifying new weapon on the Western Front—near Ypres in Belgium in April 1915—when they released a green cloud of chlorine gas and routed French territorial and African troops.

By the time the United States entered the war in April 1917, there were five types of poison gas available, classified according to their physiological effects on the human body:

Lachrymators (tear gases)—worked primarily against the eyes, but were an effective way to exhaust the enemy because masks had to be worn just the same, making breathing difficult.

Asphyxiators (phosgene, chloropicrin, and chlorine)—caused fluid to enter the lungs (chemical pneumonia) and ultimately caused suffocation.

Toxic gases—passed through the lungs to the bloodstream as direct poisons but were not as effective as the other agents.

Sternutators (diphenylchlorarsine)—caused sneezing, nausea, and vomiting, forcing the soldier to remove his gas mask. These respiratory irritants composed of fine dust were often mixed with more lethal gases, so that when gas masks were removed, the soldier was exposed to the killing agent.

Vesicant (the infamous mustard gas, named for its odor)—caused blistering.

Mustard gas was the king of war gases, first used by the Germans in July 1917. Its advantage was that it did not rapidly disperse like the other gases. Heavier than air, it settled in hollows, and droplets of nonvaporized gas contaminated the soil and water, causing injuries days—and even weeks—later. This gas soaked through a man's heavy uniform when he sat down to rest or relieve himself. The caustic gas mixed with body moisture and burned the skin, causing terribly irritating, slow-healing blisters, which were actually more painful than damaging. The gas also burned the eyes and respiratory tract.

Mustard gas burns were said to take three to five weeks to heal, and an affected man was practically useless for that length of time. Temporary blindness, lasting from days to weeks, was considered to be the least serious effect.

Contaminated clothing often continued to produce painful blisters when handled later by first-aid and medical personnel.

Casualties from poison gas were an all-too-common problem for nurses and medical staff. Gassed soldiers—their clothes, hair, and skin—all had to be washed with uncontaminated water. Then attendants would spray the soldiers' eyes, nose, and throat with bicarbonate of soda and occasionally treat them with alkaline agents and oxygen. If the gastrointestinal tract was contaminated, as from gas-tainted food or water, olive or castor oil was administered to coat the stomach and bowel.

The physical toll of gas warfare was terrible, but the psychological toll was nearly as significant. Gas attacks devastated endurance and morale on both sides of the conflict. Gas alarms, both real and imagined—horns blaring, warning gongs clanging, men shouting—stressed and fatigued the troops. "Gas fright" was one way in which psychoneurosis manifested itself. When the Germans first used chlorine gas against the French at Ypres, for example, those French troops not asphyxiated on the battlefield panicked and fled, and the Germans thereby achieved a stunning local tactical success. In fact, prevailing military philosophy on both sides held that it was more effective to terrorize or incapacitate the enemy than to kill him outright, because of the manpower and resources required to evacuate, treat, and rehabilitate gas casualties.

U.S. Army Medical Department statistics indicate that 224,089 Americans were wounded and evacuated to medical facilities during the Great War. Of these, 70,552 (31.4 percent) were gas casualties. However, of the gas victims, only 3 to 4 percent died.

Shell Shock

Many soldiers have suffered the common nervous disorder that has been known since World War I as shell shock.[2] The term, coined in military reports for patients who were clearly debilitated yet had suffered no physical wounds, was seized upon as a blanket explanation for all neuropsychiatric disabilities that occurred in the armed forces. Doubtless because the word shell was used, the uninformed public came to believe that the disorder resulted from terror of the noise and danger of high explosives, or the concussion of bursting shells.

Many physicians disliked using the term shell shock because it was not an accepted medical term denoting a specific disorder. They preferred to call the condition "war neurosis." It was considered very similar to the neuroses of civil life, although it was highly colored by the terrifying influences of modern combat: high explosives, liquid fire, tanks, poison gas, aerial bombardment, and daily life among the dead and dying. A U.S. observer, Dr. Thomas W.

Salmon, wrote that "the present war [World War I] is the first in which . . . the functional nervous diseases [shell shock] have constituted a major medico-military problem. As every nation and race engaged is suffering from the symptoms, it is apparent that new conditions of warfare are chiefly responsible for their prevalence."

"Shell shock is about as difficult to explain as the term, 'weeds,' " another doctor observed. The condition was indicated by a wide variety of symptoms, ranging from convulsions, coma, paralyses, deafness, and severe headaches to such emotional reactions as depression (often suicidal), elation, fear, anger, rage, and homicidal tendencies.

One authority explained that many of the neurosis cases in the Army would no doubt have occurred under civil conditions anyway, because there are always individuals who, given the right stress, will develop mental problems. Other cases—and these were the majority—were men with neurotic tendencies who might never have become incapacitated under ordinary conditions and would have been recognized merely as nervous, high-strung, or peculiar. But under the strain of living in huge groups, gathered into an army and sent off from home to fight a war, they developed acute neuroses.

Some recruits became overly distressed to find that in the military, their own individuality had to be abandoned; their personal needs and desires meant nothing to their leaders and colleagues; and their unique personalities had to be sacrificed to the well-being of the group. Often such soldiers were unable to cope with these requirements, and they would break down long before exposure to enemy shell fire. This was probably the most common war neurosis, known as "conversion hysteria."

Another type of breakdown involved simple emotional exhaustion. A soldier might have served nobly and gallantly under great stress for many months, or even years, but as time went on, his personal reserve of resistance and energy were gradually exhausted, and he simply broke down. Today, we call this "burn out."

Basically, shell shock in the Great War was usually not the result of continued exposure to gunfire and the clamor of battle (although these were contributing factors); rather, it was brought on by the need to endure a variety of experiences that the mind was unable to accept. Perhaps Leon Wolff said it best in his book In Flanders Fields: "There were hundreds of cases referred to, often contemptuously, as shell-shock, which in later years would be diagnosed not wholly in terms of reactions to artillery fire, but as serious neuropathic disorders resulting from a total experience beyond their capacity to assimilate."[3]

Notes

1. For this information on the use of poison gases in the Great War, I am indebted to Dr. David M. McCoy, who wrote about the subject in the winter 1990 issue of the World War I journal *Over There*.

2. Information on shell shock was obtained from the following sources: Mary C. Jarrett, "The Home Treatment of Shell Shock," in The Touchstone, pamphlet printed by the Everglades Rod and Gun Club, Palm Beach, FL; Guides to Therapy for Medical Officers, U.S. War Department Technical Manual, March 20, 1942; and Colonel Thomas W. Salmon, MC, and Sergeant Norman Fenton, MD, The Medical Department of the United States Army in the World War, vol. 10, Neuropsychiatry p. 2, 3 (Washington, DC: Government Printing Office, 1929).

3. Leon Wolff, In Flanders Fields (New York: Viking, 1958.

Appendix B
For the Record

Following is a list of all women members of the military and social service organizations who were killed or wounded, died, or were decorated during the World War I period.

Every effort has been made to keep this inventory as complete and accurate as possible. Because of fragmentary records and faulty reports those many years ago, however, omissions may have occurred, and misspellings and other errors are bound to have crept in. We regret these, and we would urge the reader to report them in the interests of accuracy for future historians.

Organizations that provided information:
American Battle Monuments Commission, Washington, DC.
Medical Archives, New York Hospital–Cornell Medical Center.
National Archives, Washington, DC, Naval Records Collection, Naval Reserve Force: Yeomen F.
National Archives, Washington, DC, Records of the Adjutant General's Office.
National Archives, Washington, DC, Records of the Bureau of Medicine and Surgery.
National Archives, Washington, DC, Records of the Surgeon General's Office.
Roosevelt Presidential Library, Hyde Park, NY.
U.S. Army Military History Institute, Carlisle, PA.
Women's Overseas Service League Archives, Liberty Memorial Museum, Kansas City, MO.

Publications that provided information:
The First Enlisted Women, 1917–1918, by Eunice C. Dessez (Philadelphia: Dorrance, 1955).
History of the World War Reconstruction Aides, ed. Laura Brackett Hoppin (Milbrook, NY: W. Tyldsley, 1922).
The Medical Department of the United States Army in the World War, vol. 13, part 2, The Army Nurse Corps, by Julia C. Stimson (Washington, DC: Government Printing Office, 1927).
Pathfinder magazine, Feb. 7, 1931.

Service With Fighting Men: An Account of the Work of the American Young Men's Christian Association in the World War, vol. 2 (New York: Association Press, 1922).

"That Damn Y": A Record of Overseas Service, by Katherine Mayo (Boston: Houghton Mifflin, 1920).

A History of Women's Overseas Service League, by Helene M. Sillia (Newburgh Heights, OH: Women's Overseas Service League, 1978).

Authors/historians who provided information:
Thomas L. Gudmestad, Seattle, WA.
Mark M. Hough, Seattle, WA.
Peter J. Linder, Ellicott City, MD.
Gary A. Mitchell, Rochester, NY.
John P. Mull, Milwaukie, OR.
Wendy Murphy, So. Kent, CT.
Helene M. Sillia, Newburgh Heights, OH.
Raleigh Sutton, Elgin, IL.

U.S. NAVY YEOMEN

Killed
None

Wounded
None

Died

This list is from the National Archives, and records that there were 22 deaths among the Yeomen (F) during the World War. This list gives casualties of those women (USNRF) during the World War and subsequently. A few which have no dates and places-of-death were added from other lists.

Note that the same died after the Armistice, November 11, 1918.

Ash, Frances G., July 1919, 12th Naval District (N.D.)
Ashworth, Sara C., October 1918. 5th N.D.
Barnes, Clara L., February 1919. 4th N.D.
Bartlett, Helen Edith, September 1918. Washington, D.C.
Carroll, Mary Margaret, July 1919. 4th N.D.
Churchill, Melda Beatrice, October 1918. San Francisco, CA
Cody, Sophia Theresa, October 1918. 1st N.D.

Coombs, Grace D., April 1919. Washington, D.C.

Corbett, Catherine L., January 1920. 3rd N.D.

Counihan, Mary Margaret, October 1918. 1st N.D.

DeLong, Lillian Holden, October 1918. 3rd N.D.

Dickey, Margaret V., November 1919. 6th N.D.

Dunn, Edna Genevieve, January 1919. 2nd N.D.

Dwyer, Mary Josephine, May 1919. 3rd N.D.

Elmore, Maude, January 1919. 5th N.D.

Ford, Janet, January 1919. 3rd N.D.

Frazee, Edna May, October 1918. 3rd N.D.

Galvin, Ella May, November 1918. 2nd N.D.

Gunion, Dorothy, November 1918. Washington, D.C.

Gunn, Genevieve Alice, October 1918. 2nd N.D.

Haller, Viola, January 1919. 3rd N.D.

Hart, Rosella C., July 1920. 5th N.D.

Hayes, Bertha Ryan

Jeffrey, Winifred Call, February 1919. Southerly

Kane, Katherine T., February 1920. 4th N.D.

Lawrence, Pauline M., July 1918. Washington, D.C.

Lowry, Mary Gertrude

McArthur, Carrie J., March 1920. 13th N.D.

McGaragle, Frances L., July 1920. 1st N.D.

Miccio, Mary Elizabeth

Mock, Jessie May, January 1919. 12th N.D.

Monahan, Mary Agnes, September 1918. 1st N.D.

Murphy, Beatrice Trever, January 1919. Washington D.C.

Murray, Catherine Cecilia, January 1919. 3rd N.D.

Newman, Belle C., May 1920. 3rd N.D.

Norton, Anne Frazier, October 1918. 1st N.D.

Parsons, Ethel Mildred, October 1918. Washington D.C.

Payne, Ruth Catherine, October 1918. Washington D.C.

Peck, Helene

Perlstein, Marion R., September 1920. 1st N.D.

Petrone, Genevieve Josephine, October 1917. 12th N.D.

Pierce, Blanche Eleanor, October 1918. Washington D.C.

Richardson, Maude, January 1920. 3rd N.D.

Rolls, Grace M., January 1920. Washington D.C.

Schackmann, Marie J., February 1920. Newton, Ill.

Scott, Bertha, February 1919. 5th N.D.

Shaw, Ruth C., July 1919. Portsmouth, Ohio

Sweeney, Cecilia Agnes, October 1918. 2nd N.D.
Sylvester, Lena Mary, September 1918. Cambridge, Mass.
Thrift, Lula May, October 1918. Washington D.C.
Todhunter, Lillie Catherine, October 1918. 12th N.D.
Turner, Louisa Catharine, April 1920. 4th N.D.
Turner, May Adele, June 1917. 4th N.D.
Van Valkenburgh, Henrietta, October 1918. 3rd N.D.
Warren, Stella Grant
Weil, Evelyn Freda, February 1919. 3rd N.D.

Decorated
Gold Medal for Merit "War Service"
(Not an official Navy award, but a personal token of esteem from Capt. W. R. Rush, USN, commandant)
Erd, Daisy Pratt—Boston Navy Yard, March 18, 1918

NAVY NURSES

(Statistics on members of the Navy Nurse Corps will be found on pages 263–265)

WOMEN OF THE U.S. MARINE CORPS

No records have been found on Marine women who were killed or wounded, died, or were decorated during service in World War I.

ARMY NURSES

Killed
Ayers, Edith (Attica, OH, May 20, 1917). Base Hospital No. 12. Accidentally killed by fragments of brass from faulty discharge of gun aboard *USS Mongolia* at sea en route to France.
Wood, Helen Burnet (Evanston, IL, May 20, 1917). Base Hospital No. 12. Died in same accident as Edith Ayers, above.

Wounded
Jeffery, Jane. Red Cross nurse, Red Cross Hospital No. 107.
Severely wounded in air raid, July 15, 1918. Refused to leave her post, continued to serve others.

MacDonald, Beatrice Mary. Head nurse, Base Hospital No. 2. Wounded while on duty with surgical team at British casualty clearing station, Aug. 1917. Lost sight of one eye.

Parmelee, Eva Jean. Base Hospital No. 5. Wounded in air raid on the hospital at Dannes-Camiers, France, Sept. 4, 1917. Remained calm and continued to serve. First Army nurse casualty at a base hospital.

Stambaugh, Isabelle (Philadelphia, PA). Base Hospital No. 10. Wounded while on duty with surgical team at British casualty clearing station, Amiens, March 1918.

Died Overseas

Amundson, Esther (Montevideo, MN, Oct. 1918)

Anderson, Nora E. (St. Hilaire, MN, Jan. 1919)

Athay, Florence L. (New York City, NY, Nov. 1918)

Babcock, Hazel E. (Blanchard, MI, March 1919)

Bailey, Margaret S. (Springfield, MA, Oct. 1918)

Baldwin, Jessie P. (Summerville, PA, Feb. 1919)

Bartlett, Frances E. (Andover, ME, Oct. 1918)

Bellman, Jeannette (Dayton, OH, Nov. 1918)

Berry, Lottie May (Frankton, IN, Dec. 1917)

Breen, Anna M.C. (Brooklyn, NY, Nov. 1918)

Buell, Grace G. (Roanoke, IN, Oct. 1918)

Burke, Mary C. (Chelsea, MA, Oct. 1918)

Cairns, Mary K. (Utica, NY, Sept. 1918)

Campbell, Florence W. (Suffern, NY, Nov. 1918)

Casstevens, Geneva (Beecher City, IL, Oct. 1918)

Christian, Carce (Cornelia, GA)

Christman, Caroline H. (Providence, RI, Oct. 1918)

Copeland, Grace (Lebanon, IN, Oct. 1918)

Courtney, Helena J. (Springfield, OH, Oct. 1918)

Cox, Charlotte A. (Baltimore, MD, Sept. 1918)

Dalton, Ella (Toronto, Ontario, Canada, May 1919)

De Mers, Evelyn Jane (Roxbury, MA, Oct. 1918)

Dent, Katharine (New Orleans, LA, June 1918)

Dingley, Nellie M. (Ashland, WI, Aug. 1918)

Drisko (or Drisco), Alice S. (Seattle, WA, Feb. 1919)

Drummond, Henrietta I. (Pawtucket, RI, Oct., 1918)

Eisfeldt, Thelma (San Francisco, CA, Jan. 1919)

Evans, Maud (Ft. Jones, CA, Feb. 1919)

Fairchild, Helen (Watsontown, PA, Jan. 1918)

Fletcher, Lucy N. (Boston, MA, May 1918)
Flynn, Irene Mercedes (New Haven, CT, July 1918)
Forrest, Eileen L. (Gilmanton, WI, Oct. 1918)
Galliher, Nellie G. (San Francisco, CA, Oct. 1918)
Golden, Katherine V. (Somerville, MA, Feb. 1919)
Graham, Florence Beatrice (Goderich, Ontario, Canada, May 1919)
Greene, Katheryne E. (Philmont, NY, Oct. 1918)
Groves, Elma (Lodi, WI, Oct. 1918)
Hagadorn, Alice (Palmer Falls, NY, May 1919)
Hamilton, Margaret (Minevah, IN, Oct. 1915)
Hardy, Sabra Regina (Golden Valley, ND, Oct. 1918)
Harkey, Tula Lake (New York City, NY, Nov. 1918)
Hatch, Elsie May (Edgewood, IA, Dec. 20, 1918)
Hecht, Felicita W. (Norfolk, VA, Feb. 1919)
Hinton, Florence A. (Decatur, IL, Jan. 1918)
Hoffman, Katherine (Queen City, MO, Sept. 1918)
Homans, Helen (Boston, MA, Nov. 1918)
Ireland, Alice A. (Media, PA, Feb. 1918)
Irwin, Katherine P. (Dayton, OH, June 1918)
Joyce, Kathryne M. (Pittsburgh, PA, Sept. 1918)
Keirn, Margaret Eleanor (Carrollton, MS, Oct. 1918)
Kells, Maud Victoria (Sheffield, MA, Oct. 1918)
Kimball, Florence (Lisbon, ND, Oct. 1918)
Knowles, Miriam E. (Yardley, PA, Nov. 1917)
Koellner, Dorothy E. (Fort Madison, IA, Feb. 1919)
Kulp, Harriet L. (Pottstown, PA, Dec. 1918)
Ledden, Claire A. (Ridgway, PA, May 1919)
Ledford, Ima I. (Hillsboro, OR, Oct. 1918)
Lee, Elizabeth C. (Altaville, CA, Oct. 1918)
Lide, Julia (Shreveport, LA, Feb. 1919)
Lippold, Antoinette W. (Oak Park, IL, Nov. 1918)
Lundholm, Ruth V. (Fruitvale, CA, Oct. 17, 1918)
Lundholm, Viola E. (Fruitvale, CA, Oct. ll, 1918)
Lyon, Gladys Nancy (Buchanan, MI, Dec. 1918)
MacDonald, Elizabeth L. (Lake Geneva, WI, Oct. 1918)
Maescher, Ella (Cincinnati, OH, Nov. 1918)
Malloch, Grace L. (Dorchester, MA, Jan. 1919)
McCord, Crystal E. (Washington, IN, Dec. 1919)
McGurty, Catherine (Jersey City, NJ, March 1919)
McMullen, Anna Marie (Allentown, PA, Oct. 1918)

McWilliam, Elizabeth (Summerville, NJ, Oct. 1918)
Micheau, Grace Bell (Baltimore, MD, Oct. 1918)
Millman, Dorothy Beth (Youngstown, OH, Oct. 1918)
Moeschen, Frances W. (New York City, NY, Sept. 1918)
Murphy, Alice V. (Battle Creek, MI, Oct. 1918)
Murphy, Mary (Manitowoc, WI) N.D.
Murphy, Teresa M. (Penacock, NH, Nov. 1918)
O'Brien, Camille (Atlanta, GA, April 1919)
O'Connor, Carmelite (Chicago, IL, Feb. 1919)
O'Connor, Gertrude (Boston, MA, Feb. 1919)
Orgren, Clara M. (Colorado Springs, CO, Oct. 1918)
Overend, Marion L. (Peterboro, Ontario, Canada, June 1918)
Pepoon, Lucile (Chicago, IL, Nov. 1918)
Ragan, Mabel A. (Detroit, MI, Oct. 1918)
Raithel, Hattie M. (Denver, CO, Nov. 1918)
Rapp, Rosa Mary (Jeffersonville, IN, Oct., 1918)
Reveley, Annie D. (Greensboro, NC, Oct. 1918)
Roberts, Annabel S. (Madison, NJ, Jan. 1918)
Robinson, Genevra (Nampa, ID, Oct. 1918)
Rogers, Alice Cunningham (Brooklyn, NY, March 1919)
Rose, Lucinda L. (Clarksburg, WV, Oct. 1918)
Royer, Norene Mary (Spokane, WA, Sept. 1918)
Schonheit, Charlotte (Detroit, MI, Dec. 1918)
Schreiber, Orma Anna (Alma, WI, Oct. 1918)
Seymour, Nina L. (Middleboro, MA, Oct. 1918)
Symmes, Kathleen E. (Aylmer, Quebec, Canada, Oct. 1918)
Thorkelson, Tilda A. (Seattle, WA, Nov. 1918 in the Philippines)
Thornton, Cornelia E. (Achilles, VA, Sept. 1918)
Trank, Florence M. (Holland, NY, Oct. 1918)
Vietmeier, Ida Henrietta (Los Palos, CA, Jan. 1919)
Volland, Magdalena M. (Buffalo, NY, Sept. 1918)
Walker, Anna A. (Boston, MA, June 1919)
Ward, Nellie J. (W. Philadelphia, PA, July 1918)
Watkins, Gwladys (Shickshinny, PA, Oct. 1918)
Weimann, Elizabeth N. (Haddon Heights, NJ, Nov. 1918)
Welsh, Anne K. (W. Roxbury, MA, April 1919)
Wheeler, Luella M. (S. Burlington, VT, Jan. 1919)
White, Marion H. (W. Philadelphia, PA, Oct. 3, 1919)
Whiteside, Lydia V. (Duluth, MN, Oct. 1918)
Williams, Annie (Fredonia, NY, Oct. 1918)

Worth, Margaret W. (Cresskill, NJ, Oct. 1918)
Yochelson, Esther (Buffalo, NY, Nov. 1918)

ARMY NURSES DIED IN THE U.S.A.

Unless otherwise noted, the cause of death for the following nurses was officially listed as "disease." Ther term "disease" was used by officials to indicate death from influenza (the "flu" epidemic) or an associated illness such as pneumonia, meningitis, mastoiditis, or other infections.

Allen, Phoebe, Pueblo, CO. Oct. 1918, Ft. Slocum, N.Y.
Anderson, Anna, Sharon, PA. Dec. 1918, Camp Jackson, S.C.
Aubert, Lillian, Shreveport, LA, Oct. 1918, Washington, D.C.
Baird, Laura A. Gainsville, FL., Oct. 1918, Camp Merritt, N.J.
Barrett, Josephine G., Bradford, VT, Oct. 1918, Camp Wadsworth, S.C.
Becker, Edith C., Ossian, IA, Dec. 1918, Fort Harrison, IN.
Benson, Nona G., Chicago, IL., May 1918, Camp Custer, MI.
Berry, Lottie May, Frankton, IN., Dec. 1917, Camp Sherman, O.
Bishop, Amy Leona, Viroqua, WI., Oct. 1918, Fort Riley, KA.
Bradfield, Edith, Ridgeway, KA., May 1918, Fort Sill. OK.
Brandon, Hazel, Concord, CA., Oct. 1918, Camp Kearney, CA.
Brock, Monica Plainville, CT., Nov. 1918, Washington, D.C.
Brown, Helen G., New York City, Oct. 1918, New York City.
Brown, Martha A., San Francisco, CA., Feb. 1910, San Francisco, CA.
Brownlee, Flossie Esther, Indiana, Oct. 1918, New York City.
Buck, Lydia M. Strathmore, CA., Dec. 1918, Ft. Logan H. Root, AK.
Buman, Rose, Harlan, IA., Oct. 1918, Camp Pike, Ark.
Burden, Hannah Lora, Inwood, IN., Oct. 1918, Camp Sherman, O.
Burk, Ethel M., Oakland, CA., Oct. 1918, Camp Fremont, CA.
Bushee, Mattie V., Washington, D.C. Oct. 1918, Camp Sherman, O.
Butler, Emma W., Calumet, MI April 1918, Camp Dodge, IA.
Byrne, Louise E., Ardonia, N.Y., Oct. 1918, New York City.
Byron, Patricia Irene, Fort Wayne, IN., March 1918, Camp MacArthur, TX.
Cage, Allicia, Hitta Yuma, MS., Feb. 1920, Fort McHenry, MD.
Camilla, Sister M., birthplace unknown, Nov. 1918, Lafayette, IN.
Carney, LeNor, Maxine, Marion, KA., Nov. 1918.
Cassidy, Eleanor, Reading, PA., Jan. 1919, Camp Merritt, N.J.
Catlin, Fannie R., Adams Center, N.Y., Oct. 1918, Azalea, N.C.
Cattles, Edith J., Lead, S.D., Oct. 1918, Fort Douglas, Utah.
Cavitt, Ora E., Salem, OR., Oct. 1918, Camp Lewis, WA.

Cecil, Katherine W. (St. Louis, MO., April 1918).

Chandler, Florence E., Dunlap, KA., Oct. 1918, Fort Riley, KA.

Christensen, Mabel C., Carpio, N.D., Oct. 1918, Camp Lewis, WA.

Clements, Anna G., New York City, Jan. 1919, Biltmore, N.C.

Clifford, Kathryn C., Tuscarora, PA., Oct. 1918, Camp Upton, N.Y.

Collins, Theresa V., Scranton, PA., Oct. 1918, Camp Dixon, N.J.

Connelly, Katherine R. Canandaigua, N.Y., Oct. 1918, Camp Gordon, GA.

Connolly, Katherine K., Trenton, N.J., Aug. 1918, Ellis Island, N.Y.

Coover, Etta P., Colby, KA., Oct. 1918, Fort Riley, KA.

Cosgrove, Anna M., Eau Claire, WI., June 1919, New York City.

Coulter, Grace, Livonia, IN., Sept. 1920, Louisville, KY.

Cummings, May H., No. St. Paul, MN., Oct. 1918, Fort Sam Houston, TX.

Cupp, Lillian E., Trout Run, PA., Oct. 1918, Camp Gordon, GA.

Davis, Cora B., Tampa, FL., Oct. 1918, Camp Gordon, GA.

Dodson, Kate, Casa Blanca, TX., Jan. 1919, Camp Travis, TX.

Donovan, Helen F., Bar Harbor, ME., Sept. 1918, Camp Dix, N.J.

Dwyer, Helen E., New York City, March 1921, New York, N.Y.

Eastman, Lizzie F., Mattapoisett, MA. Oct. 1918, Camp Mills, N.Y.

Emery, Mary Frances, Winthrope, ME., May 1919, Fort McHenry, MD.

Ericjson, Alma M., Jarosco, CO., Oct. 1918, Ft. Logan, CO.

Erickson, Fannie M., Whitehall, MI., Oct. 1918, Camp Sherman, O.

Falkinburg, Grace M., Flushing, N.Y., Oct. 1918, Camp Lee, VA.

Farney, Ruth B., Larned, KA., Oct. 1918, Fort Sam Houston, TX.

Ficken, Magdalene, West Brighton, N.Y., Oct. 1918, New York, N.Y.

Fischer, Catherine M., Wilkes-Barre, PA., Oct. 1918, Camp Dix, N.J.

Foldese, Anna C., Mankato, MN., Nov 1918, Camp Dodge, IA.

Foster, Hazel, A., Bucks Hill, CT., Oct. 1918, Camp Mills, N.Y.

Franklin, Emma M., Glendale, CA., Oct. 1918, Camp Cody, N.M.

French, Mathilda H., Brooklyn, N.Y., Feb. 1918, Fort Sam Houston, TX.

Furgerson, Ada M., Spring Valley, N.Y., Oct. 1918, Fort Ontario, N.Y.

Furr, Alma M., Austin, TX., Aug. 1918, Camp Shelby, MS.

Gardner, Bertha (July 1917)

Gibney, Anna P., Scranton, PA., June 1919, Cape May, N.J.

Girvin, Esther M., Naponset, IL., Oct. 1918, Camp Jackson, S.C.

Good, Mattie V., Washington, D.C., Sept. 1918, Washington.

Gore, Ora M., Chicago, IL., March 1918, Camp Travis, TX.

Gorman, Beatrice, Hastings-on-Hudson, N.Y., Oct. 1918, Fort Sam Houston, TX.

Goshorn, Ethel May, Bellwood, PA., Nov. 1918, Camp Gordon, GA.

Graham, Mary Jane, Bristol, TN., Oct. 1919, Fox Hill, N.Y.

Grimes, Margaret R., McDonald, PA., Oct. 1918, Camp Lee, VA.

Hankinson, Florence G., Grand Rapids, MI., Oct. 1918, Camp Custer, MI.

Hanley, Edna L., Oakland, CA., Nov. 1918, New York, N.Y.

Healy, Mary, Buffalo, N.Y., Oct. 1918, Camp Upton, N.Y.

Heath, Olive, F., Kernville, CA., Feb. 1919, Washington, D.C.

Henderson, Cornelia A., Newburgh, N.Y., Oct. 1918, New York, N.Y.

Hertzog, Meda L., Allentown, PA., Jan. 1919, Camp McClellan, AL.

Hill, Elina W., San Antonio, TX., Jan. 1919, San Francisco, CA.

Hollenback, Lottie R., Olathe, KA., Jan. 1918, Fort Riley, KA.

Hurley, Nell, Los Angeles, CA., Oct. 1918, Camp Bowie, TX.

Jennings, Lucy E., New Richmond, O., Sept. 1918, Camp Sherman, O.

Jones, Mamie, Pontotoc, TX., Dec. 1918, Camp Logan, TX.

Kemper, Anna E., Akron, O., Sept. 1918.

Kirksterp, Daisy, Brooklyn, N.Y., Oct. 1918, Hoboken, N.J.

Klinefelter, Ina E., Diamond, MO., Oct. 1918, New York, N.Y.

Knapp, Estella A., Bradford, PA., Oct. 1918, Fort McHenry, MD.

\Kuhlman, Margaret, Toledo, O., Oct. 1918, Camp Sherman, O.

Langdon, Lillian M., Plymouth,, PA., Sept. 1918, Edgewood Arsenal, MD.

Larsen, Anna E., Escanaba, MI., Oct. 1918, Camp Sherman, O.

Larsen, Effie A., Minneapolis, MN., Dec. 1918, Camp Dodge, IA.

Lausche, Dessie M., Brighton, IL., Oct. 1918, Fort Bayard, N.M.

Leach, Ethel Ozella, Fairmont, IN., Oct. 1918, Edgewood Arsenal, MD.

Le Claire, Florence, Indianapolis, IN., Oct. 1918, Camp Devens, MA.

Lewis, M. Romaine, Scranton, PA., Oct. 1918, Camp Jackson, S.C.

Lindell, Ebba C., Georgetown, TX., Oct. 1918, Camp Beauregarde, LA.

Linehan, Kathryn M., Tomah, WI., Oct. 1918, Camp Taylor, KY.

Linn, Lois, Springfield, O., Oct. 1918, Camp Sherman, O.

Lowe, Grace M., Sweedsboro, N.J., Oct. 1918, Fort McPherson, GA.

MacKay, Lillian, Philadelphia, PA., Dec. 1918, Edgewood Arsenal, MD.

Mackintosh, Jessie J., San Francisco, CA., Oct. 1918, Camp Eustis, VA.

Maher, Anna M., Poughkeepsie, N.Y., Oct. 1918, Camp Upton, N.Y.

Mariner, Jessie B., Patten, ME., Oct. 1918, Camp Hancock, GA.

Marshall, Harlan, St. Louis, MO., May 1919, St. Louis, MO.

McDermott, Penelope, Brooklyn, N.Y., Oct. 1918, Fort Logan, CO.

McDowell, Jessie R., Port Arthus, TX., Oct., 1918, Camp McArthur, TX.

McGrath, Laura C., Willoughby, O., Oct. 1918, Camp Grant, IL.

McGuire, Catherine J., New London, CT., Oct. 1918, Camp Lee, VA.

McIntosh, Jennie, Laconia, N.H., Oct. 1918, Rock Island Arsenal, IL.

McMahon, Mary I., Ironton, O., Oct. 1918, Camp Jackson, S.C.

McNerny, Elizabeth M., DuBois, PA., Oct. 1918, Camp Dix, N.J.

Metcalf, Elizabeth M., Darva, PA., Oct. 1918, Fort McPherson, GA.

Miller, Cecilia E., Chicago, IL., Oct. 1918, Camp Sherman, O.

Minick, Mary Elizabeth, Chambersburg, PA., Oct. 1918, Camp Devens, MA.

Moakley, Helen A., New Haven, CT., Aug. 1918, Fort Bliss, TX.

Morrison, Sophia Ellen, Feb. 1919.

Morton, Hazel P., Phoenix, AR., Oct. 1918, Camp Cody, N.M.

Moss, Marie A., Govanstown, MD., Oct. 1918, Camp Meade, MD.

Munn, Maude A., Philadelphia, PA., Dec. 1918, Camp Mills, N.Y.

Murphy, Anne M., Germantown, PA., Sept. 1918, Camp Lee, VA.

Newkirk, Hattie N., Detroit, MI., April 1918, Camp Beauregard, LA.

Nohr, Agnes Josephine.

Noring, Ella M., West Liberty, IA., Oct. 1918, Camp Merritt, N.J.

Norton, Anna M., New York City, Oct. 1918, Camp Mills, N.Y.

Norton, Mary. Jersey City, N.J., Sept. 1918, Camp Jackson, S.C.

O'Connor, Mary E., Watertown, MA., Oct. 1918, Azalea, N.C.

Ophaug, Helga J., Chicago, IL., July 1918, accident, Fort Sheridan, IL.

Owens, L. May, Greenwood, DE., Oct. 1918, Camp Lee, VA.

Parr, Margaret I., Royal Oak, MI., Oct. 1918, Camp Grant, IL.

Parry, Aurora E., Columbus, O., Oct. 1918, Camp Taylor, KY.

Parsons, Mildred, Basehor, KA., Oct. 1918, Camp Stuart, VA.

Pennington, Pearle W., Presque Isle, ME., June 1918, Camp Jackson, S.C.

Perkins, Etta M., Morgantown, N.C., Oct. 1918, Camp Meade, MD.

Petrie, Evelyn V., Portsmouth, N.H., May 1918, accident, Fort Oglethorpe, GA.

Phillips, Meryl G., Bloomsburg, PA., May 1918, New York, N.Y.

Poo, Frances, Evanston, IL., Oct. 1918, Fort Ontario, N.Y.

Poole, Pearl, Dec. 1918.

Price, Cornelia L., Arlington, MD., Oct. 1918, Camp McClellan, AL.

Quigley, Pauline A., Cedar Rapids, IA., Oct. 1918, Camp Custer, MI.

Reed, Inez E., Oakland, CA., March 1919, accident, Fort Riley, KA.

Ridgers, Teresa E., Cupertino, CA., Oct. 1918, March Field, CA.

Rowell, Katherine, Dec. 1918.

Russ, Freda, Newman, CA., Oct. 1918, Camp Fremont, CA.

Ruth, Flora Margaret, Indianapolis, IN., Oct. 1918, Camp Pike, AK.

Sage, Helen G., Chicago Heights, IL., Oct. 1918, Camp Taylor, KY.

Sanders, Stella E., Nesbit, PA., Oct. 1918, Camp Sevier, S.C.

Sargent, Helen M., Lincoln, NE., Oct. 1918, Fort Slocum, N.Y.

Sauer, Clara H., Roscoe, MN., Nov. 1918, Camp Dodge, IA.

Scheirer, Mary J., Reading, PA., Oct. 1918, Ellis Island, N.Y.

Schurman, Olive, Baltimore, MD., Oct. 1918, Camp Meade, MD.

Seavey, Ruth, Dixon, IL., Oct. 1918, Camp Taylor, KY.

Seiler, Barbara, Council Bluffs, IA., Oct. 1918, Camp Dodge, IA.

Shepard, Hettie L., Joplin, MO., June 1919, accident, Camp Pike, AK.

Shirley, Anna K., San Antonio, TX., Nov. 1918, Fort Sam Houston, TX.

Small, Blanche M., Boston, MA., Jan. 1918, Camp Lee, VA.

Sobey, Helen, Cleveland, O., March 1919, Washington, D.C.

Stanford, Lena.

Stenstad, Julia, Kasson, MN., Nov. 1918, Fort Snelling, MN.

Stowe, Ullie M., Bridgeport, CT., Sept. 1918, Camp Dix, N.J.

Sullivan, Margaret, Framingham, MA., Sept. 1918, Camp Devens, MA.

Sullivan, Mae H., Trenton, N.J., Oct. 1918, Cape May, N.J.

Tanquist, Emily S., Mankato, MN., Oct. 1918, Camp Merritt, N.J.

Taylor, Eva, Steubenville, O., Feb. 1919, Camp Sherman, O.

Templin, Naomi, Redfield, S.D., Oct. 1918, Fort Sheridan, IL.

Thomas, Mary, San Diego, CA., Oct. 1918, Camp Cody, N.M.

Thorsen, Emma J., Arlington, WA., Nov. 1918, Camp Dodge, IA.

Thompkins, Agnes M., Milwaukee, WI., Jan. 1920, Fort Sheridan, IL.

Travis, Goldie N., Bay City, MI., Oct. 1918, Fort Snelling, MN.

Turner, Phyllis N., Wayne, PA., Sept. 1918, New York, N.Y.

Vanderburgh, Emma, New York City, May 1921, Fort Leavenworth, KA.

Viberg, Judith S., Clearfield, PA., Oct. 1918, Camp Lee, VA.

Walch, Caroline R., Norman, OK., Oct. 1918, Camp Travis, TX.

Ward, Lillian, Bellows Falls, VT., Oct. 1918, Camp Greene, N.C.

Weinger, Alberta I., Sawyer, KN., 1918, Fort Riley, KN.

Wellman, Maybelle, Redlands, CA., Oct. 1918, New York, N.Y.

Wells, Matilda E., Trenton, N.J., Oct. 1918, Camp Eustis, VA.

Welsh, G. May, Portland, OR., Jan. 1919, Vancouver Barracks, WA.

Wessel, Dorothy H., Beardstown, IL., June 1919, Springfield, IL.

West, Anna Belle, Centreville, MA., Oct. 1919, Washington, D.C.

Wiggins, Daisy E., Douglas, WY., Oct. 1918, Camp Cody, N.M.

Woodfin-Cecil, Mrs. Katherine, St. Louis, MO., April 1918, Camp Wheeler, GA.

Wright, Mayme L., Gaylord, MI., Oct. 1918, Camp Grant, IL.

Young, Alice M., Wheeling, W.V., Oct. 1918, Camp Sevier, S.C.

Young, Florence M., Ridgway, PA., Oct. 1918, Camp Devens, MA.

Young, Rose A., Winnsboro, S.C., Nov. 1917, Camp Shelby, MS.

Decorated

Distinguished Service Cross

Jeffery, Jane. English Red Cross nurse serving with American Red Cross Hospital No. 107. Severely wounded during air raid but refused to leave her post and continued to serve others.

MacDonald, Beatrice M. (New York City, NY). Base Hospital No. 2. Wounded during air raid at casualty clearing station, Belgium, Aug. 17, 1917. Lost sight of right eye.

McClelland, Helen Grace (Fredericktown, OH). Base Hospital No. 10, organized at Philadelphia, PA. On duty with a surgical team at a British casualty clearing station, Aug. 17, 1917. Cared for a wounded nurse comrade, Beatrice M. MacDonald, during air raid.

Parmelee, Eva Jean. Base Hospital No. 5. Wounded in air raid Sept. 4, 1917. Continued to serve throughout the emergency.

Stambaugh, Isabelle (Philadelphia, PA). Base Hospital No. 10.

Seriously wounded in air raid while at work in operating room with surgical team at British casualty clearing station, Amiens, March 21, 1918.

Distinguished Service Medal

Aubert, Lillian, asst. superintendent, Army Nurse Corps

Brennan, Cecelia, chief nurse, Toul Hospital Center

Brown, Katharine, chief nurse

Burns, Sophy Mary, chief nurse, Base Hospital No. 16

Cameron, Reba G., chief nurse, Plattsburg Barracks and Hampton, VA

Coughlin, Edna M., Base Hospital No. 22, member of an emergency medical team caring for nontransportable wounded of six divisions in an advanced area under fire of shells and aerial bombs

Delano, Jane A., director, Department of Nursing, ARC

Flash, Alice H., chief nurse, Mesves-Bulcy Hospital Center

Goodrich, Annie W., first dean, Army School of Nursing

Howard, Carrie L., chief nurse, Hoboken, NJ, port of embarkation

Leonard, Grace E., asst. director, AEF nursing service

MacDonald, Beatrice Mary, chief nurse, Presbyterian Hospital Unit

McClelland, Helen Grace, Base Hospital No. 10

Milliken, Sayres Louise, chief nurse, Camp Sevier, SC, and asst. supt., Army Nurse Corps

Molloy, Jane G., chief nurse, Camp Devens, MA

Mury, Edith A., asst. superintendent, ANC

Poston, Adele S., chief nurse (psychiatric unit), Base Hospital No. 117

Rhodes, Marie B., chief, Nurses' Equipment Bureau, Military Department, American Red Cross, Paris, France

Rulon, Blanche S., chief nurse, Base Hospital No. 27 and asst. to the director of nursing service, AEF

Ryan, Lillian J., chief nurse, base hospital, Camp Merritt, NJ

Sheehan, Mary E., chief nurse, Vichy Hospital Center, France

Shelton, Neena, asst. to director of nursing service, AEF

Sinnott, Catherine Glynn, chief nurse, nurses' concentration camp, Savenay, France

Stimson, Julia C., director of nursing service, AEF

Sweet, Ethel E., chief nurse, nurses' mobilization stations, New York City, NY

Thompson, Dora E., superintendent, ANC

Vandervort, Lynnette L., chief nurse, Mars Hospital Center, France, and chief nurse, nurses' embarkation center, Vannes, France

Florence Nightingale Medal
Hay, Helen Scott, contract nurse, general supervisor of the 1914 Red Cross Mercy Ship, and senior supervisor of nursing units in Kiev, Russia
Meirs, Linda E.
Patterson, Florence M., member of Red Cross Commission to Romania
Stimson, Julia C., director of nursing service, AEF

French Croix de Guerre (bronze star)
Connelly, Beth Clara
Cornwall, Bertha
Ferguson, Ida
Gibson, Matilda M.
Horn, Mathilda H.
Hovey, Ruth
Johnson, Lillian
Lister, Hannah
MacDonald, Beatrice Mary
McManigill, Ella J.
McNulty, Carolyn H.
Meirs, Linda K.
Perry, Jennie E.
Richardson, Agnes Hope
Rignel, Blanche S.
Sahol, Elina P.
Sharpe, Annie M.

Smith, Alice O.
Taylor, Phoebe F.
Thompson, Sara R.
Todd, Louise M.
Vaugniaux, Emily

French Croix de Guerre (gilt star)
Jorgensen, Sigrid M., Evacuation Hospital No. 4
Nye, Sylvene A.
Radcliff, Lillian E.
Turner, Lila B., Evacuation Hospital No. 4
French Croix de Guerre
Broussard, Eunice
Fish, Janet
Morton, Ruth

Recommended for Croix de Guerre
Durr, Mildred E.
Engvall, Sarah C.
Griffen, Cora
McClure, Jean
Purdy, Louise
Wentland, May

French Médaille d'Honneur
Baker, Aurel
Beers, Amy
Broaddus, Emma
Carothers, Dora C.
Cormier, Bernadette
Diamond, Mary A.
Driver, A. Madge
Francis, Mary L.
Gardner, Agnes J.
Jeffrey, Lucy W.
Kehoe, Frances M.
Krans, Ella Mary
Lombard, Arabella A.

French Médaille d'Honneur des Épidémies

Aaron, Marjorie
Arnold, Elizabeth
Baker, Bessie
Bedell, Ruth E.
Borg, Ida A.
Bowen, Mary M.
Brendel, Myrtle L.
Camblos, Jacqueline
Cassidy, Rose A.
Clarke, Susanne
Cloherty, Marie E.
Corning, Alice
DeLozier, Mary M.
Dingley, Nellie M.
Fisher, Magdalen C.
Gavin, Mary
Gough, Gussie
Graves, Abigail B.
Hadsell, Edith L.
Hagadorn, Alice
Hanchette, Lou
Hartwell, Jennie V.
Henry, Ethel
Hill, Ada
Hopkins, Anna B.
Horner, Blanche
Izen, Clara J.
James, Agnes F.
Johnson, Jane H.
Knapp, Grace
Lauridsen, Karen M.
Loughran, Nellie
MacGregor, Flora
Martin, Florence J.
Mauffray, Helena
McAuliffe, Julia
McCauley, Alice
McGee, Mary G.
McGrandel, Robena M.

McKernan, Inea G.
Monroe, Edith
Morrison, Edna M.
Olsen, Lydia J.
Patmore, Amy F.
Perry, Edith V.
Phillips, Laurie L.
Radcliff, Lillian E.
Reid, Agnes W.
Reid, Elizabeth D.
Ricker, Frances E.
Robertson, Ruth I.
Roche, Katherine P.
Rothwell, Martha D.
Ryan, Lulu
Strub, Ann
Taft, Nora
Tomlinson, Alva
Warwick, Bessie Mae
Watkins, Jeanette J.
Watson, Isabel
Wilkins, Maud M.
Worley, Pearl M.

French Médaille de la Reconnaisance Française
Cornwall, Bertha
de Cairos, May (for reconstruction of France, 1924)
Ferguson, Ida (for bravery under fire)
Hall, Carrie M.
Jarves, Elsie Deming
Stimson, Julia C.
Van Horn, Mabel E.

Belgian Médaille de la Reine Élisabeth
Cromwell, R. Lee, chief nurse, Base Hospital No. 90

British Military Medal
MacDonald, Beatrice Mary, chief nurse, Presbyterian Hospital Unit
Parmelee, Eva Jean, Base Hospital No. 5

British Royal Red Cross Medal, First Class
Allen, Grace E.
Allison, Grace E., Lakeside Unit
Butler, Rose Kate, Harvard Unit
Christie, Janet B., Presbyterian Unit
Claiborne, Estelle Deane, St. Louis Unit
Dunlop, Margaret Alice, Philadelphia Unit
Folckener, Elizabeth M., Lakeside Unit
Fraser, Katherine Margaret, Harvard Unit
Hacey, Malinde I., asst. chief nurse, ANC
Hall, Carrie Mary, Harvard Unit
Jardine, Georgina Mary, Harvard Unit
McClelland, Helen Grace, Philadelphia Unit
McLaughlin, Emily A., chief nurse, ANC
Parsons, Marion G.
Phillips, Lawrie L., chief nurse, ANC
Scott, Eleanor, matron, U.S. Women's War Hospital, Paignton, England
Smith, Robina, Harvard Unit
Spencer, Ruth Helen, Chicago Unit
Stimson, Julia C., director of nursing service, AEF
Taylor, Mance, St. Louis Unit
Urch, Daisy D., Chicago Unit

British Royal Red Cross Medal, Second Class
Arvin, Mary W., ANC
Ascah, Nora Marjorie, Harvard Unit
Balen, Anna M., Presbyterian Unit
Berry, Nettie Josephine, No. 10 General Hospital
Briggs, Helen May, Lakeside Unit
Burcham, Daisy, ANC
Burky, Florence M., Philadelphia Unit
Carruthers, Isabelle E., Chicago Unit
Carson, Anne Lougheed, St. Louis Unit
Connelly, Betty Clara, ANC
Cuppaidge, Constance A., asst. chief nurse
Ebbs, Helen Jane, Harvard Unit
Elwood, Bessie Lydia, No. 3 Stationary Hospital
Engel, Austa White, Lakeside Unit

Evans, Isabel Wakeman, No. 8 General Hospital
Ferguson, Edna Allison, No. 5 General Hospital
Frederick, LaRue, ANC
Gerhard, Eve, asst. chief nurse
Gerrard, Gertrude Mary, Harvard Unit
Gould, Elspeth Anna, asst. chief nurse
Harold, Mary R., Presbyterian Unit
Hayes, Myrtle Elizabeth, No. 5 General Hospital
Hill, Ada, asst. chief nurse
Kennedy, Mary E., No. 6 General Hospital
Lesper, Minnie A., asst. chief nurse
Lewis, Lydia, No. 11 Stationary Hospital
Lewis, Mary Elizabeth, No. 11 Stationary Hospital
Lyon, Elizabeth C., Chicago Unit
MacDonald, Beatrice Mary, ANC
MacNeal, Jane Crawford, Philadelphia Unit
McCloskey, Louise Helenne, Harvard Unit
McGillivray, Edith, No. 6 General Hospital
McKee, Inez, ANC
McKnight, Lillian Sarah, No. 3 Stationary Hospital
McLannan, Vera, No. 8 General Hospital
Miller, Elsie B., ANC
Miller, Lena Branson, Chicago Unit
Morton, Ruth, St. Louis Unit
Nicholson, Ann Estelle, No. 6 General Hospital
O'Brien, Agnes Veronica, No. 6 General Hospital
Parmelee, Eva Jean, ANC
Peterson, Hanna Sophia, Harvard Unit
Petterson, Hanna F., ANC
Powers, Margaret Alberta, Chicago Unit
Rignel, Jennie L., ANC
Roche, Mary Jane, ANC
Sands, Tyldesley L., ANC
Sarafini, Olive E., St. Louis Unit
Schmitt, Dolly Belle, ANC
Schorfield, Minnie, No. 3 Stationary Hospital
Shepherd, Ada Louise Bascom, Harvard Unit
Stambaugh, Isabelle, Philadelphia Unit
Stephenson, Mary E., ANC
Stouffer, Barbara Ellen, ANC

Walkinshaw, Arvilla, Lakeside Unit
Wallace, Olive L., ANC
Wiseman, Katherine Julia, Harvard Unit

British Certificate of Merit
Krost, Carrie Gullickson

Sir Douglas Haig Mention for Gallant Service on Western Front
Alexander, Bertha M.
Hall, Carrie M.
Marsh, Louise M.
Stimson, Julia C., director of nursing service, AEF

U.S. Army Citation
(*Awarded for bravery and devotion to duty in September 1918 air raid on town where Field Hospital No. 103 was located*)
Harlan, Elizabeth H.
Haviland, Sybella T.
McNamara, Della A.
Randall, Ethel
Roulston, Elizabeth Elliott
Zang, Mary Clara L.

AEF Citation (Silver Star Citation)
Bridge, Ruth H., Field Hospital No. 103
Bunting, I. Gertrude, Camp Hospital No. 4
Frankhauser, Louise, Evacuation Hospital No. 6
Invernizio, Clementina, Evacuation Hospital No. 6
Leckrone, Linnie E., Chateau Thierry
Low, Margaret, Field Hospital No. 103

Gen. John J. Pershing Citation
Alexander, Catherine, Base Hospital No. 55
Allison, Agnes Winifred, Evacuation Hospital No. 4
Andersen, Emmeline, Evacuation Hospital No. 4
Bear, Laura Folsom, Evacuation Hospital No. 4
Bell, Bessie S.
Booth, May M., Evacuation Hospital No. 4
Bunting, I. Gertrude, Camp Hospital No. 4
Christman, Caroline H.

Clark, Margaret
Coyne, Adelaide Irene
Deane, Pluma M., Evacuation Hospital No. 4
Fitzpatric, Margaret M.
Grant, Jessie E., Base Hospital No. 55
Hall, Rosa H., Evacuation Hospital No. 4
Hatch, Inez Pearl
Hollindale, Edith Amy, Evacuation Hospital No. 6
Hosken, Beatrice
Hutton, Katherine A., Evacuation Hospital No. 4
Jones, Blanche
Jorgensen, Sigrid M., Evacuation Hospital No. 4
Kelly, Bree S., chief nurse, Base Hospital No. 65
Kingston, Edna E., Evacuation Hospital No. 4
Lawrence, Henrietta Gordon, Base Hospital No. 55
Leach, Goldie Alberta, Evacuation Hospital No. 4
Lee, Elizabeth C., Evacuation Hospital No. 4
Malloch, Grace L., Base Hospital No. 55
Marshall, Susan, Evacuation Hospital No. 4
McLean, Emily L., Evacuation Hospital No. 4
McQuillan, Rose C., Evacuation Hospital No. 4
Meyer, Minna Theckla, Evacuation Hospital No. 4
Moylan, Mary B., Evacuation Hospital No. 4
Newsom, Mary Palmer, Base Hospital No. 55
Pancoast, Mary E., Evacuation Hospital No. 4
Perkins, Margaret E., Evacuation Hospital No. 4
Perrine, Mae, Evacuation Hospital No. 4
Rathbun, Katherine, Evacuation Hospital No. 4
Robinson, H. Victoria, Evacuation Hospital No. 4
Rottman, Marian E., Evacuation Hospital No. 1
Rutherford, Delia, Evacuation Hospital No. 4
Sands, Tyldesley L., Base Hospital No. 5
Shaw, Maybelle M., Evacuation Hospital No. 4
Thomasson, Ivy L., St. Mihiel offensive
Tierney, Mary Jane, Evacuation Hospital No. 4
Tuthill, Carrie E., Evacuation Hospital No. 4
Ulmer, Florence H., Evacuation Hospital No. 4
Wells, Grace E., Evacuation Hospital No. 4
White, Cassie A., Evacuation Hospital No. 4

Gen. Charles H. Muir Citation
Arnott, Ruth
Beardsley, Ethel Jean
Beckman, Ruth J.
Bowling, Gertrude H.
Brouilliard, Jennie
Conn, Jennie Elizabeth
Conyard, Mary E.
Fiester, Blanche I.
Hueter, Lucy M.
Jones, Annie E.
Kegrice, Mary O.
Macauley, Margaret M.
MacMillan, Grace E.
Sandelius, Elizabeth Dorothy
Swain, Mary L.

Greek Silver Cross of the Order of King George 1
Carr, Alice G. (1923)
Edison, Anna (1923)
Mathews, Stella S. (1923)
Nuno, Christine M. (1923)
Smith, Lily Lyle (1923)
Thompson, Sara R. (1923)

Romanian Order of the Croix Reine Marie
Donald, Jennie B. (member of Red Cross Commission in Romania, 1918)
Meirs, Linda K. (member of Red Cross Commission in Romania, 1918)
Patterson, Florence M.
Rowland, Adeline H.

Russian Silver Cross of St. Anne
(Awarded for service as a member of the Red Cross Commission in Kiev, Russia, 1915)
Bartlett, Kathryn
Cromwell, R. Lee
Echternach, Marion H.
Hansen, Anne
Hard, Gertrude
Hill, Mary E.

Horner, Blanche
Johnson, Cora
Pepper, Margaret
Reinhardt, Hettie
Smith, Anna R.

NAVY NURSE CORPS

Killed
None

Wounded
None

Died
Burmeister, Theresa, January 1919. Great Lakes, IL.
Casterline, Drusilla Marie, January 1919. Mare Island, CA.
Coleman, Maude E., January 1918. Washington, D.C.
Dahlby, Anna Marie. Norfolk, VA.
Good, Victoria R. New York
Grant, Myrtle E., March 1919. Great Lakes, IL.
Hidell, Marie Louise, September 1918. Philadelphia, PA.
Hokanson, Edith B., March 1919. Great Lakes, IL.
Kotte, Ethel, March 1919. Great Lakes, IL.
Lea, Alice, January 1919. Great Lakes, IL.
McClanahan, Ethel, January 1919. Washington D.C.
Martin, Constance, 1918. Chelsea, MA.
Mercer, Jane R. New York
Metcalf, Mildred A. Newport, R.I.
Murphy, Lillian M., Hampton Roads, VA.
Orchard, Helen. Charlestown, S.C.
Peck, Garnett Olive. Great Lakes, IL.
Place, Edna S., September 1918. Philadelphia, PA.
Rockwell, Vera M., 1918. Chelsea, MA.
Schneiberg, Laura, January 1920. Beloit, WI.
Sherzinger, Nellie M., August 1916. Guam.
Story, Amber R. Great Lakes, IL.
Thompson, Alice, October 1918. Scotland.
Treichler, Amy. Charlestown, S.C.
Trimble, Marie E. 1918. Chelsea, MA.

Turner, Marion Pearl. Mare Island, CA.
Young, Mrs. Rose Kirkwood. New York.

Decorated

Navy Cross
Higbee, Lenah S., superintendent, Navy Nurse Corps
(*The following three nurses gave long and devoted service during the war emergency period and died in naval hospitals during the influenza epidemic of 1918. Each was awarded the Navy Cross posthumously.*)
Hidell, Marie Louise, Naval Hospital, Philadelphia, PA
Murphy, Lillian M., Naval Hospital, Hampton Roads, VA
Place, Edna S., Naval Hospital, Philadelphia, PA

Secretary of the Navy, Letter of Commendation
Brooke, Elsie, chief nurse
Elderkin, Mary
Leonhardt, Elizabeth, chief nurse
McClellan, Jeannette
Pringle, Martha E., chief nurse, Naval Hospital, Philadelphia, PA
Van Ingen, Frances, chief nurse, Navy Base Hospital No. 1

French Médaille d'Honneur des Épidémies
Hasson, Esther V., first superintendent, Navy Nurse Corps

Gen. John J. Pershing Citation
Van Ingen, Frances, chief nurse, Navy Base Hospital No. 1

Army Letter of Commendation
Elderkin, Mary
McClellan, Jeannette

DIETITIANS, MEDICAL DEPARTMENT OF THE ARMY

Killed
None

Wounded
None

Died
Keech, Cara Mea (Santa Anna, CA, Oct. 1918)
Peck, Marion H. (Greenspring, OH, Feb. 1919)

Decorated
Hulsizer, Marjorie (Copher). One of the first dietitians to go overseas, she was assigned to the British Army and decorated by King George V and the French government.

ARMY SIGNAL CORPS TELEPHONE OPERATORS

Killed
None

Wounded
None

Died
Bartlett, Cora (Union City, MI, June 1919 in Tours, France)

Decorated
Distinguished Service Medal
Banker, Grace D., chief operator, for her work with First Army
Headquarters in September 1918. Presented in Coblenz, Germany, in July
1919.

Gen. John J. Pershing Citation
(*Awarded for exceptionally meritorious and conspicuous service in the AEF*)
Keyser, Florence
Le Blanc, Marie A.
Le Breton, Louise

(*Awarded for service at First Army Headquarters at Ligny-en-Barrois during the St. Mihiel drive, August 1918, and at Souilly during the Meuse-Argonne campaign, September–November 1918*)
Arland, Berthe
Banker, Grace D.
Belanger, Marie
Beraud, Louise
Flood, Maria

Fresnel, Esther V.
Hill, Helen E.
Hoppock, Adele
Hunt, Berthe M.
Lange, Marie
Peyron, Leonie
Prevot, Suzanne

(Awarded for service as chief operator to the American Commission to Negotiate Peace, Paris, France, 1919)
Egan, Merle

Citation from Gen. Edgar Russel, chief signal officer, AEF
(Awarded for especially meritorious and excellent services rendered in the AEF)
Arland, Berthe
Banker, Grace D.
Belanger, Marie
Beraud, Louise
Dupuis, Cordelia
Flood, Maria
Fresnel, Esther V.
Hill, Helen E.
Hoppock, Adele
Hunt, Berthe M.
Johnson, Maude E.
Lange, Marie
Peyron, Leonie
Prevot, Suzanne
Young, Jennie

RECONSTRUCTION AIDES
Killed
None

Wounded
MacDonald, Harriet. First Unit. Wounded during air raid on hospital in Neuilly, France.

Died in Service
None

Decorated
None

YMCA

Killed
Crandall, Marion G. (Alameda, CA, March 1918). Killed by enemy shell, Ste. Menehould, France.
Martin, Winona Caroline (Rockville Center, NY, March 1918). Killed in air raid in Paris.

Wounded
Brannan, Eleanor (New York City, NY)
Hume, Marion C. (Ottumwa, IA)
Miller, Bernetta A. (New York City, NY)
Resnor, Lucy (Erie, PA)
Sherman, Paula (New York City, NY)
Willmer, Sarah (Chicago, IL)

Died Overseas
Adams, Daisy (Jessup, MD, Jan. 1919)
Branum, Virginia L. (Sewickley, PA, March 1919)
Brubaker, Elizabeth A. (Lancaster, PA, Oct. 1919)
Burrage, Helen M. (Cambridge, MA, Feb. 1919)
Chisholm, Jessie Noyes (Seattle, WA, Aug. 1919)
Ellis, Hariett M. (New York City, NY, Aug. 1918)
Gale, Bessie (Schenectady, NY, Feb. 1919)
Gay, Dorothea (New York City, NY, Nov. 1918)
Hosie, Eugenia (Scranton, PA, March 1919)
Knight, Alice J. (New York City, NY, Feb. 1919)
Leuders, Jean (Philadelphia, PA, Oct. 1918)
Martin, Winona C. (Rockville Center, NY, March 1918)
Ransom, Lorraine (New Rochelle, NY, Feb. 1919)
Robertson, Nellie (Virginia, IL, March 1919)
Rogers, Alice Cunningham (Brooklyn, NY, March 1919)
Rogers, Faith Helen (Superior, WI, Nov. 1918)
Rowley, Blanche A. (Rochester, NY, Feb. 1919)

Russell, Elizabeth L. (Boston, MA, Oct. 1918)
Slocum, Esther (Newark, NJ, May 1919)
Valentine, Gertrude Crissey (Albany, NY, July 1919)
Vrooman, Marjorie R. (Clyde, NY, March 1919)
White, Edith (Petaluma, CA, March 1919)
Zinn, Jeannette (York, PA, Oct. 1918)

Died in U.S.A
Jewett, Elizabeth (Nyack, NY, Jan. 1919)

Decorated
Distinguished Service Cross
Sloan, Emma S. (New Haven, CT)—cited

*Distinguished Service Meda*l
Cushman, Mrs. James S., chairman, War Work Council, YWCA of the United
    States

U.S. Certificate for Exceptionally Meritorious and Conspicuous Service
Janis, Elsie, entertainment worker, AEF
Leonard, Katherine, Camp Stephenson
Miller, Bernetta A., worker with 326th Infantry
Roosevelt, Mrs. Theodore, Jr., worker with AEF
Sweeney, Mary, canteen operator near front lines
Sweeney, Sunshine, canteen operator near front lines

French Croix de Guerre
Arrowsmith, Mary Noel (New York City, NY)
Colby, Leslie Osgood (New York City, NY)
Davis, Cornelia Colt (New York City, NY)
Dwight, Jane R. (New York City, NY)
Ely, Gertrude (Bryn Mawr, PA)
Fleming, Louise Wellford (Dobbs Ferry, NY)
Henthorne, Oril Elsie (New York City, NY)
Herron, Maria Clinton (Cincinnati, OH)
King, Helen Maxwell (Northampton, MA)
Lesley, Olive Mary (Cambridge, MA)
Miller, Bernetta A. (New York City, NY)
Nicoll, Ruby Bacon (New York City, NY)
Smalley, Evelyn (New York City, NY)

Sweeney, Mary E. (Pine Grove, KY)—cited
Sweeney, Sunshine (Pine Grove, KY)—cited

French Army Fourragère
Boyd, Miss (Pittsburgh, PA)
Butler, Hope (Morristown, NJ)
Dunlap, Elizabeth (Yonkers, NY)
Ely, Gertrude (Bryn Mawr, PA)
Landon, Cornelia (New York City, NY)
Morgan, Edith (New York City, NY)

French Médaille de la Reconnaissance Française
Francis, Dorothy (Westfield, NJ)

Order of the British Empire
Chisholm, Jessie Noyes (Seattle, WA)
Davis, May Agnes (Orange, NJ)
Dwight, Jane R. (Great Neck, NY)
Lynch, Gertrude (New York City, NY)

Gen. John J. Pershing Citation
Francis, Dorothy (Westfield, NJ)

General Edwards Citation
Fleming, Louise Wellford (Dobbs Ferry, NY)

Divisional Commander Citation
Dennis, Dorothy (Washington, DC)
Gulick, Frances J. (S. Casco, ME)
Skelding, Marjorie (Zellwood, FL)
Warren, Maude Radford (Ithaca, NY)

Belgian Médaille de la Reine Élisabeth
Hall, Mrs. Gardiner, chief, YMCA women, GHQ
MacGruder, Emma, chief, YMCA women, GHQ
Tenner, Ethel, chief, YMCA women, GHQ

WOMEN PHYSICIANS

Killed
None

Wounded
None

Died Overseas
Thomas, Dr. Henrietta M. (Baltimore, MD, Aug. 1919). Dr. Thomas served as secretary, British Society for Relief of Destitute Aliens in York, England.

Decorated
French Croix de Guerre
Dr. Alice Weld Tallant, director of Smith College Relief Unit and member of American Committee for Devastated France

Médaille de la Reconnaissance Française
(*Awarded to staff of American Women's Hospital No. 1 for service at Luzancy on the Marne; honorary French citizenship was also bestowed upon these recipients*)
Bentley, Dr. Inez
Bonness, Dr. Hazel D.
Cohen, Dr. Frances
Doherty, Dr. Kate A.
Douglas, Helen
Evans, Dr. Mary
Fairbanks, Dr. Charlotte
Fraser, Dr. M. Ethel V.
Hunt, Dr. Barbara
Hurrell, Dr. M. Louise
Kinney, Dr. DeLan
Lehman, Emilie
MacLachlan, Dr. Mary
Manwaring, Dr. I. Jay
Purnell, Dr. Caroline M.
Ward, Dr. Edna

Honorary French citizenship was also conferred upon Anne Morgan and Mrs. A. M. Dike, founders of the American Committee for Devastated France.

Dr. Nellie N. Barsness of Pope County, MN, who served as opthalmologist at the gas hospital in Cempuis, France, was decorated by the French minister of war for her "work under hazardous conditions" (decoration unknown, but probably the Médaille de la Reconnaissance Française).

AMERICAN RED CROSS

Killed

Landon, Ruth (New York City, NY, March 1918). Killed by shell fired from famous German "Paris Gun," St. Gervais Church, Paris, France.

Wounded

None

Died Overseas (Enlisted Women)

Appel, Mary Ellen (Allentown, PA, in France, April 1920)

Ayers, Edith (at sea, May 1917)

Barnett, Edith (New York City, NY, in Siberia, Aug. 1919)

Butler, Maud Mae (Ogden, UT, in France, Jan. 1919)

Cromwell, Dorothea K. (New York City, NY, at sea, Jan. 1919)

Cromwell, Gladys (New York City, NY, at sea, Jan. 1919)

Cutler, Ruth (St. Paul, MN, in France, Dec. 1918)

Drisko, Alice Stevens (Seattle, WA, in France, Feb. 1919)

Durant, Elizabeth (Lily) May (Paris, France, in France, Feb. 1920)

Field, Pauline (La Jolla, CA, in France, May 1919)

Gibson, Adeline P. (Philadelphia, PA, Jan. 1919)

Haarman, Sophia (Gladstone, SC, in Rome, Jan. 1919)

Hamlin, Dorothy (New York City, NY, in France, Jan. 1919)

Heath, Winifred (Brooklyn, NY, at sea, Oct. 1918)

Hershey, Grace W. (Abilene, KA, at sea, Oct. 1918)

Holden, Ruth (Attleboro, MA, in Petrograd, Russia, April 1917)

Kennebeck, Kathleen C. (Carroll, IA, at sea, Oct. 1918)

MacGregor, Ruth (Wilmington, DE, at sea, Oct. 1918)

McCauley, Edna (New York City, NY, in Rome, Jan. 1919)

McDonald, Lottie Brainerd (Needham, MA, in China, Sept. 1920)

McWilliam, Elizabeth (Summerville, NJ, at sea, Oct. 1918)

Moore, Mary Agnes (Hollywood, CA, in France, Feb. 1919)

Scatchard, Fannie Ethel (Oneonta, NY, in France, Feb. 1919)

Shaw, Erma L. (Washington, DC, at sea, Oct. 1918)

Stevens, Mary Catherine (Landsdowne, PA, in France, May 1919)

Tyler, Elizabeth Stearns (Amherst, MA, in Sedan, France, Feb. 1919)
Venn, Emma E. (Natchez, MS, in France, Oct. 1918)
White, Marion H. (Philadelphia, PA, in France, Oct. 1918)

Died in U.S.A. (Enlisted Women)
Hendricks, Jane Minor (Washington, DC, Nov. 1918)
Hermansen, Clara (Omaha, NE, Dec. 1918)
McKechnie, Marsha D. (Canandaigua, NY, Dec. 1918)
Morey, Mabel R. (Elmira, NY, Nov. 1918)
Smith, Ruby (Council Bluffs, IA, Oct. 1918)

Died Overseas (Red Cross Nurses)
Delano, Jane A., director, Department of Nursing, ARC (Townsend, NY, in Savenay, France, April 1919).
McBride, Nettie Grace (Mansfield, OH, in Tumen, Siberia, Dec. 1918)
Seymour, Nina Louise (Middleborough, MA, in France, Oct. 1918)
Winchester, Edith May. (Lawndale, PA, in Armenia, May 1919). Miss Winchester was a member of the Armenian and Syrian Relief Commission.

Decorated
Distinguished Service Medal
Andress, Mary Vail, for her work at Toul, France
Cleveland, Maude, for her work at Brest, France
Delano, Jane A., director, Department of Nursing, ARC
Stimson, Julia C., chief nurse AEF, American Red Cross in France

U.S. Certificate for Exceptionally Meritorious and Conspicuous Services
Austin, Mrs. C. K.
Cleveland, Maude
Hunt, Georgia P.
Spaulding, Gertrude
Vanderbilt, Mrs. William K., chief, Red Cross Canteen Dept.
Walker, Hazel A.

Belgian Médaille de la Reine Élisabeth
Seamans, Mary F., chief, Red Cross GHQ

SALVATION ARMY

Killed
None

Wounded
Platt, Bertha. Wounded twice.

Died in Service
None

Decorated
Distinguished Service Medal
Booth, Evangeline Cory, commander of the Salvation Army in the
United States.

French Croix de Guerre
Burdick, Minnie Saunders

Gen. John J. Pershing Citation
Burdick, Minnie Saunders

U.S. Certificate for Exceptionally Meritorious and Conspicuous Services
Morton, Mae Isabella, for service in battle area, France
Rapson, Triselda (Della), for service in battle area, France
Van Norden, Cora, for service with Seventy-seventh Division

CIVILIAN WOMEN IN WAR SERVICE

Killed
None

Wounded
None

Died in Service
Crittenden, Lucy Ann (Bakersfield, CA, Nov. 1918). U.S. Intelligence Dept.
Holden, Ruth (Attleboro, MA, in Russia, April 1917). Nursing Unit, United
    Suffrage Societies of England.

Tileston, Amelia Peabody (Brookline, MA, in Belgrade, Serbia, Feb. 1920). Independent American Red Cross.

Warder, Winifred Fairfax (Cairo, IL, Oct. 1918). Women's Overseas Hospitals, American Women's Suffrage Association.

Zollars, Anna (Canton, OH, Oct. 1919, Paris). American Committee for Devastated France.

Decorated
Distinguished Service Medal
Patterson, Hannah J., Women's Committee, Council of National Defense

Shaw, Dr. Anna Howard, chairman, Women's Committee, Council of National Defense

U.S. Certificate for Exceptionally Meritorious and Conspicuous Service
Bousquet, Isabelle, for work in hospitals in Paris

Despecher, Clara, secretary to chief of staff, AEF

Gunther, Elsie L., Quartermaster Corps, Tours, France

Herve, Eugenie, Base Section No. 1, St. Nazaire, France

McCormick, Ruby, Air Service, Paris

Richards, Ruth, Air Service, Paris

Richardson, Florence, Quartermasater Corps with Salvage Service

Schunck, M. A., Office of the Chief Quartermaster

Singleton, Ann Celestine, confidential secretary, commander-in-chief

Spencer, Mildred, Quartermaster Corps

Steed, Leonara M., Office of the Chief Quartermaster, Salvage Service

Tracy, Mary Austin, personnel division, AGO, GHQ

French Légion d'Honneur
(Awarded in recognition of services to France)

Cofer, Luisita L. (New York City, NY), founder, Fatherless Children of France society

Cushman, Emma D. (NY), for her work with French prisoners of war in Turkey

De Roaldes, Annie Miller (New Orleans, LA), president of Le Secours Louisianais à la France

Dike, Mrs. A. Murray (New York City, NY), co-founder, American Fund for French Wounded and the American Committee for Devastated France

Duryea, Nina L.

Gassette, Grace

Griggs, Emily F. (New York City, NY), director, Union Franco-American

Harjes, Mrs. H. Herman (Philadelphia, PA), worked in hospitals and canteens, 1914–1919

Holt, Winifred (New York City, NY), president, Comité Franco-American Pour les Aveugles de la Guerre

Lathrop, Mrs. Benjamin Girault (London, England), president in France, American Fund for French Wounded

McIntyre, Anna (New York City, NY), served with the American Red Cross, worked with French prisoners of war in Turkey

Morgan, Anne (New York City, NY), organized the American Fund for French Wounded (which provided medical supplies to the French military) and its offshoot, the American Committee for Devastated France

Morgenthau, Mrs. Henry

Morhard, Jeanne Emma (Cincinnati, OH), for long, faithful, services in cause of France

Norton, Mrs. Henry

Sage, Cornelia Bentley (Buffalo, NY), for services to French art, especially during the war

Skinner, Belle (Holyoke, MA), for reconstruction of village of Hattonchatel, Meuse, France

Smith, Mrs. Joseph L.

Spencer, Carita (New York City, NY), chairman, Food for France Fund

Tuck, Julia S. (Paris, France), for benevolent work in France before and during the war

Tyler, Elisina (Paris, France), vice president of French Tubercular Children's Fund, and of American Hostels for Refugees, and of Children of Flanders Relief Committee

Tyson, Mrs. Russell (Chicago, IL), for her work with American Fund for French Wounded

Vanderbilt, Mrs. W. K., for her work with the Red Cross in France

Wharton, Edith (author, New York City, NY), for extensive relief work in France during the war

Whitney, Belle A.

French Médaille de la Reconnaissance Française

Chew, Ada Knowlton, worked with French nursing service, Paris, and American Ambulance Hospital, Neuilly, 1916–1919

Morgan, Anne, and Dike, Mrs. A. Murray (New York City, NY), founded the American Fund for French Wounded and Committee for Devastated France

De Roaldes, Annie Miller (New Orleans, LA)

Morhard, Jeanne Emma (Cincinnati, OH)
Spencer, Carita (New York City, NY)
Tyler, Elisina (Paris, France)
Tyson, Mrs. Russell (Chicago, IL)

French Médaille d'Honneur des Épidémies
Tyson, Mrs. Russell (Chicago, IL)

French Croix de Guerre, With Palm
Harjes, Mrs. H. Herman (Philadelphia, PA)

Belgian Médaille de la Reine Élisabeth
MacGruder, Emma, chief, YMCA women, GHQ
Seamans, Mary F., chief, Red Cross, GHQ
Spencer, Carita (New York City, NY)
Tenner, Ethel, chief, YMCA women, GHQ
Tuck, Mrs. Edward (Paris, France)
Tyler, Elisina (Paris, France)

Gen. John J. Pershing awards the Distinguished Service Medal to Julia C. Stimson, chief of the Army Nurse Corps, AEF. (Courtesy of the Medical Archives, New York Hospital–Cornell Medical Center)

Friends visit the grave of Esther Slocum of Newark, NJ, one of twenty-three YMCA workers who died overseas. She was interred in Cascade Cemetery, Nice, France, after her death in May 1919. (Courtesy of YMCA of the USA Archives, University of Minnesota, St. Paul, MN)

Two Army Signal Corps telephone operators, Suzanne Prevot, left front, and Marie LeBlanc, right front, received Gen. John J. Pershing Citations at a special formation at American Forces Headquarters, Coblenz, Germany, in June 1919. In the background, left, is Grace Banker, who was awarded the Distinguished Service Medal at the same ceremony. (Signal Corps photo no. 111–SC–162104)

YMCA volunteers Miss Mary Arrowsmith and Miss Gertrude Ely performed myriad services for the troops of the U.S. First Division. Here they prepare to show a movie, one of the lesser duties, at their canteen in Froissy, France, in May 1918. Both were awarded the French Croix de Guerre. (YMCA of the USA Archives)

Index

Abainville, 221
Adams, Merlee, 19
Agamemnon, 228
Aisne, 160, 162, 163
Aix-les-Bains, 135–36, 146
Alaska, 5
Alert, 14
Allerey, 56–57
Allied Peace Conference, 90
All in a Day's Work, 33
American Battle Monuments
    Commission, 75
American Commission to Negotiate
    Peace, 91
American Committee for Devasted
    France, 44, 137, 157, 160, 170, 171,
    174, 176, 274
American Expeditionary Forces (AEF),
    43, 82
American Fund for French Wounded, 44,
    131, 157, 158, 174
American Legion: women's posts, 13;
    first woman member, 36, 41; and
    reconstruction aides, 118
American Medical Association, 172–73
American Medical Women's
    Association, 157, 172
American Occupational Therapy
    Association, 103
American Physical Therapy Association,
    104
American Red Cross, xi, 179–208; and
    wartime hospitals, 44, 170, 181; Na-
    tional Committee on Red Cross
    Nursing Service, 45; nurses, 45, 181,
    198, 200, 203; base hospitals, 45, 49;
    black nurses, 59–60, 75; mercy ship,
    66, 180, 181–82, 200; entertainment,

92; and reconstruction aides, 104,
113; and women physicians (AWH),
158, 162; founding of, 179–80; relief
supplies, 180; wartime organization
of, 181, 198; Junior Red Cross, 181;
Children's Bureau, 183–87, 195;
canteens, 187–92, 201; lines of communication (LOC), 187; searchers,
192–94; Home Communication Service, 191–92; and portrait masks,
195–97, 206–8; and flu epidemic,
197; and prisoners, 197; decorations
received, 201, 276, 277; motor corps,
202; casualties and deaths, 275–76.
See also Delano, Jane
American Women's Hospitals (AWH),
    158–64, 172, 175, 178
American Women's War Relief Fund,
    44–45, 182
Anderson, Merle Egan, 84–85, 91, 92–
    93, 100, 270
Anderson, Meta, 114
Andress, Mary Vail, 201, 276
Angers, 114, 145
Ansauville, 235
Applegate, Evea, 128
Aquitania, 84
Argonne. *See* Meuse-Argonne campaign
Arland, Berthe, 89, 269, 270
Arlington, VA, 36, 62, 205
Armistice, 61, 90, 91, 115, 187
Army Medical Specialist Corps, 118
Army of Occupation, 143, 146
Army, U.S.: and women's participation,
    x; Medical Department, x, 52, 59,
    72, 101–2, 105, 157, 164, 242, 268;
    First Army, 51, 53, 77, 88, 91; and
    black nurses, 59–60, 75; civilian